# TEMPEST-TOST

## THE REFUGEE EXPERIENCE THROUGH ONE COMMUNITY'S PRISM

## ROBERT DODGE

WILDBLUE
PRESS

WildBluePress.com

THE TEMPEST-TOST published by:
WILDBLUE PRESS
P.O. Box 102440
Denver, Colorado 80250

WILDBLUE PRESS is registered at the U.S. Patent and Trademark Offices.

ISBN 978-1-947290-33-4 Trade Paperback
ISBN 978-1-947290-32-7 eBook

Interior Formatting/Book Cover Design by Elijah Toten
www.totencreative.com

# TEMPEST-TOST

## THE REFUGEE EXPERIENCE THROUGH ONE COMMUNITY'S PRISM

*For the very special twins, Jane
Dodge and Judy Anderson*

# ACKNOWLEDGEMENTS

I would like to thank all those who participated in interviews for making this a realistic presentation of the people it was it was intended to portray. Special thanks to Joe Wismann-Horther for providing contacts to different refugee communities and helping me meet the people necessary to know in the Denver community. Drucie Bathin was especially helpful in arranging meetings with the various ethnic groups from Burma, and Carol Cotter deserves thanks for providing an interview location and graciously hosting those events. I very much appreciate Brigid McAuliffe allowing me to include photographs from her *Picture Me Here* project. I also would like to thank Asbi Mizer for his assistance in locating refugees who were willing to be interviewed for this project. Blake Ellis provided insightful advice on writing style that is much appreciated, and Jane Dodge offered advice on presentation that was welcomed and a helpful alteration that the author would not have otherwise considered. My gratitude to WildBlue Press for taking this project and bringing it to the public.

# TABLE OF CONTENTS

# PREFACE

This is a book on refugees, a subject that elicits considerable reaction and divided, often impassioned opinion. It is based on the personal stories and experiences of refugees, including the conditions they fled and their transition to life in the U.S.

It is an educational book with background material based on evidence that comes from scholarly literature, including peer reviewed journals and academic publications offered in support of ideas presented, as well as sources cited for numbers mentioned and statistics discussed which can be verified. To prevent this material from impeding the telling of the many personal stories and interrupting the narrative, all the notes come at the end of the book. This adds a number of pages for a limited audience. The reader will only be distracted by small numbers which are endnotes so that those so inclined can seek to find where data was located or in some cases discover additional information on a topic being discussed. While the author's interviews and research led him to reach conclusions, the book is based on the evidence cited.

# CHAPTER ONE: INTRODUCTION

"The ordeals refugees survive and the aspirations they hold resonate with us as Americans. This country was built by people who fled oppression and war, leapt at opportunity, and worked day and night to remake themselves in this new land. The refugees who arrive in the United States today continue this tradition, bringing fresh dreams and energy and renewing the qualities that help forge our national identity and make our country strong."[1] This was how Barack Obama described refugees in 2014 as the United States welcomed 70,000 new residents who were fleeing oppression and war. A year later Donald Trump was on the scene and he said, "So we have a president that wants to take hundreds of thousands of people and move them into our country."[2] He ominously warned that refugees, "…could be a better, bigger more horrible version than the legendary Trojan horse ever was."[3]

A heated national debate has emerged over refugees coming to the U.S. in recent years. There are those who present refugees as a threat to security in America, while others view welcoming refugees as the tradition that made the country strong and diverse. This book looks at refugees who have settled in Colorado, focusing on the Denver metropolitan area.

Colorado is a swing state that presents a microcosm of America and the broader refugee experience. The intent is to elevate the discussion by helping the reader realize what people endured before becoming refugees and how they have managed since arriving in America. To consider the role refugees have played and should play in America, it is of value to hear their stories and understand their struggles, what they contribute, and what problems they face that could represent problems to the communities in which they are settled.

A point sometimes ignored in the current discussion is that the original English settlers in New England were refugees. While many have fled war and abuse throughout history, the word "refugee" entered the language during the religious wars in Europe following the Protestant Reformation. That Reformation came to England with Henry VIII who broke with the Catholic Church and declared himself the head of the Church of England.

Some felt the new English church remained too similar to Catholicism and hoped to bring it closer to Calvinism and purify it, earning themselves the name Puritans. Those Puritans who were willing to remain within the Anglican Church and work to change it were the Nonconformists. A second group of Puritans chose to remove itself completely from the Church of England, and these were the Separatist. This group was especially persecuted. Pilgrim leader and *Mayflower* passenger William Bradford reported that during the reign of Queen Elizabeth many Separatists were imprisoned and murdered, and survivors petitioned the Queen, "that they may not be 'murdered' by 'hunger and cold, and stifled in loathsome dungeons.'"[4] When James I came to the throne following the death of Elizabeth, the situation grew worse, and Separatist groups became refugees. A group left England in 1608 and secured a settlement in Holland. In 1620, a Separatist group led by Bradford became refugees from England and boarded the *Mayflower*, reaching North America after over two months at sea, and they created the colony of Plymouth. There exists a myth that they came for religious freedom, but they came to practice their own religion and established an intolerant theocracy.[5]

This second permanent British colony in America was founded by refugees from religious persecution and physical abuse who were seeking a better life and set the model for the colony,[6] which would become a recurring pattern throughout U.S. history.

Since Plymouth there has been a home in America for those fleeing danger and persecution. It wasn't until after World War II when 250,000 refugees came to the U.S. that the country passed its first law specifically allowing for the admission of displaced people. This was followed by the Cold War and laws were passed to allow the admission of those fleeing Communist countries. Those escaping countries behind the Iron Curtain were joined by refugees from China, North Korea and many Cubans. The fall of Saigon in 1975 led to the challenge of resettling hundreds of thousands of refugees from Vietnam. Congress responded by passing the *Refugee Act of 1980*. In passing the Act, Congress standardized the definition and government supported services available for refugees.

The *Refugee Act* specified five categories of persecution a person might suffer from that would qualify them for refugee status: race, religion, nationality, membership in a particular social group, and political opinion.[7] Proof of being a victim of one of these would be a requirement when applying for admission to the U.S. Also included was considerable specific direction to states accepting refugees regarding assistance and monitoring, as well as obligations for refugees to follow. From 1975 when the Vietnamese resettlement began through mid-2015, the U.S. resettled over three million refugees in its borders from over 70 nations.[8]

While that has been substantial, it is not in keeping with the recent increase in displacement of people from their homes.[9] Civil wars and famine have resulted in unprecedented numbers of refugees in recent years and as 2016 began 65.3 million people were displaced from their homes. New refugees are added at a rate of 24 per minute and their numbers approach one percent of the earth's population.[10] A limit of 50,000 refugees per year was set in the original Act, subject to change "as the President determines, before the beginning of the fiscal year...is justified by humanitarian concerns or is otherwise in the national interest."[11]

Humanitarian concern has seen the number of refugees admitted vary considerably over the years. In 1980 when the Act was passed, an all-time high of over 207,000 were taken into the country.[12] This included the Vietnamese "boat people" and others escaping from communist Southeast Asia. The numbers soon were lowered, but when the Soviet Union collapsed in 1989, there were again well over 100,000 refugees entering the U.S. annually for several years, with a large influx of Russians and others from Eastern European counties that had been part of the Soviet Block. This was followed by a brief spike in 1999 following the genocide in Kosovo.[13]

Following 9/11 and the *Patriot Act*, admission of refugees dropped to an all-time low of 27,000 in 2002. President Bush called for 70,000 for 2007, but Congress reduced that number to 50,000.[14] In 2008 refugee status was granted to thousands of Burmese and Bhutanese, and within years Burma annually ranked first or second as the country of origin for refugees, while Bhutan ranged from third to fifth.[15] The civil war in Syria resulting in millions of refugees who flooded Europe. German Chancellor Angela Merkel opened the doors and welcomed them.

Named *Time* magazine's Person of the Year for 2015, Merkel said, "If we now have to start apologizing for showing a friendly face in response to emergency situations, then that's not my country."[16] President Obama increased the refugee number to be admitted and added 10,000 Syrian refugees in his 2015 proposal. The governors of 24 states responded by saying their states would not accept any. Obama admitted 85,000 refugees in his final year of office and, for the first time in history, Muslims admitted outnumbered Christians (46% to 44%).[17] There was a drumbeat of alarm over the admission of Syrians and Muslims from other countries and often the entire program of refugee admissions became related to the issues associated with these concerns.

One of the states that has been willing to accept refugees since the program was formalized is Colorado. When many state governors had said they would not allow any Syrian refugees within their borders, Governor Hickenlooper of Colorado accepted them and called for the state to "provide a place where the world's most vulnerable can rebuild their lives."[18] Since the *Refugee Act* in 1980 through 2015 the state of Colorado processed 50,207 refugees for resettlement[19] and the state receives approximately 2,500 refugees per year from countries worldwide.[20] The largest number has come from Vietnam, where nearly 110,000 have resettled. The "first generation" refugees, whose incoming numbers began to decline in the 1980s, were down to double digits in the 90s. By 2010 there were no new Vietnamese arrivals [21]and many in Colorado are largely adapted to U.S. life. The second largest group has been the 6,000 from the Soviet Union/Russian Republic, most arriving in the 1990s. This dropped off in the new millennium and was down to single digit arrivals following 2010.[22]

While many came to Colorado from Somalia at the beginning of the twenty-first century, the large influx of refugees in recent years has come from Burma and Bhutan with thousands of each arriving in the years since 2007.[23] The vast majority of these newcomers have been settling in the Denver-Aurora metropolitan area.

Denver, called "The Mile-High City," is connected to Aurora with a combined population of a million people. They are located on the front range of the Rocky Mountains and have mainly sunny days and a dry climate. The mountainous terrain near Denver and Aurora make the location not quite so dramatic a change for one group that has been placed there for resettlement from a much more mountainous region, the Bhutanese.

In the current controversy, there are claims that refugees represent a general threat, stemming from several incidents of terrorism. These have not involved refugees. The threat posed by refugees is not borne out by evidence, only suggestions of possibilities, as the right-wing leaning CATO Institute pointed out in a recent study noted: "the chance of an American being murdered in a terrorist attack caused by a refugee is 1 in 3.64 *billion* per year."[24]

# CHAPTER TWO: GEORGETTE, CONGO

Georgette is living a relatively unnoticed life as a refugee in Denver, Colorado after fleeing conditions that defy sympathy. First meeting Georgette, and seeing her welcoming smile as she greets visitors to the office, one would not think of what she had endured to be where she was. Her original home, the Democratic Republic of the Congo, was known as Zaire in her youth. She was made a refugee in her home country in 1997 after the first of two overlapping civil wars broke out the previous year. Thinking things were better she returned to her home in time to see the second civil war erupt in 1998. She was soon again a refugee in her own country and eventually in the early 2000s managed to escape the Congo and head to South Africa. *Human Rights Watch (HRW)* described the Congo at that time as enduring the deadliest wars in the world.[1] More specifically, *HRW* reported in 2006 that in the previous eight years 3.5 million had died, and every day more than 1,200 civilians were losing their lives in the country.[2] After years as a refugee in a second country, chance would land Georgette far away in the puzzling new culture of a third home, Denver.

Circumstances dictated the path of Georgette's life. She was born into emerging, interrelating conflicts, including a challenge to the corrupt 31-year rule of the Congo by Mobutu, who would benefit from the Congo's vast wealth in mineral deposits and the presence of warlords. As is frequently the case in refugee stories, underlying causes of the clashes date back to the Age of Imperialism when boundaries were imposed upon areas that did not relate to tribal or ethnic realities or one group received preference over others.[3] An outgrowth of that was the tragic conflict between the Hutus and the Tutsis that engulfed Zaire and its neighbors.

Hutus' name means "cultivators," and they based their lives on growing crops.[4] They first settled in the area surrounding the east side of the Congo between 500-1000 B.C.[5] About 400 years ago a nomadic people from Ethiopia, the Tutsi, also known as Watusi, began to settle in what was the Kingdom of Rwanda. Eventually, the Tutsis intermingled with the Hutus and adopted their language, beliefs and customs. The Tutsis were cattle herders, and that generally made them economically superior to the farming Hutus. In many areas, this economic advantage led to social and political superiority and they became rulers of the Hutus. A Pygmy group, the Twa, settled among them. While Hutu, Tutsi and Twa groups existed before Europeans arrived they were not exclusive categories.

Europeans arrived and divided the continent into colonies and the Kingdom of Rwanda became part of German East Africa. The racist scholarship of Europe that was prevalent in the late Nineteenth Century was brought to Africa. They transformed the groups of their colonies in the east Congo area into ethnic identities that polarized and politicized with devastating results.[6] Prior to European colonization the tribes were based largely on social status and considered part of a single social structure. It was possible for a Hutu to do well and become a Tutsi and vice versa, and all 18 clans in the Kingdom of Rwanda shared military service, compulsory labor and a common religion.[7]

Following World War I Germany lost its colonies and the Kingdom of Rwanda became a Belgian mandate bordering the Congo named Ruanda-Urundi. The hostilities that colonial powers created were repressed by colonial rule and independence came in 1962 when Ruanda-Urundi split into two new countries, Rwanda and Burundi. Ethnic problems soon came to the surface, including a 1972 genocide of Hutus in Burundi. There were other major communal massacres such as the 1993 mass slaughter of Tutsis in Burundi.[8]

Rwandan Hutus gained political dominance over the Tutsis after independence as they were 90% of the population.[9] Exiled Tutsis formed the Rwandan Patriotic Army (RPA) in Uganda and attempted unsuccessfully to invade Rwanda in 1990. Zaire's Mobutu sent his country's forces to aid the Hutu government of Rwanda. On April 6, 1994, the presidents of both Rwanda and Burundi were killed, when the plane they were in was shot down by a surface-to-air missile fired by what were presumed to be Hutu extremists.

This sparked the murder of 800,000 Tutsis and moderate Hutus by Hutu extremists throughout Rwanda during the next 100 days in the Rwandan genocide.[10] The Tutsi RPA conquered Kigali, the capital of Rwanda, and ousted the Hutu government. Fearing Tutsi revenge an estimated 1.2 million Hutus fled Rwanda into eastern Zaire, including 40,000 of the militia responsible for the genocide.[11] Mobutu agreed to host Hutu refugees in camps in Zaire including organized militia groups that were using the camps to launch attacks against Rwanda. Rwanda first entered Zaire to attack the refugee camps for its own security, and revenge against the Hutu militants responsible for the genocide, but as other countries were drawn into the fighting, their focus changed to the overthrow of Mobutu's government.

These were the circumstances when Georgette was first forced to flee her home. She was from a comparatively wealthy family in Kinshasa, the Congo's capital and largest city, where her father was a business executive. The uprising had begun against the country's president Mobutu and rebels threatened the capital in a very bloody conflict. Georgette was just fourteen at the time when she saw war enter her life. She recalled, "Wake up in the morning, you can see people, they are dying, start killing almost everybody."[12]

Soon they were off. "One of my dad's friends, he come to the house one night. They been shooting everywhere. They tell us like 'Run the city where we was living, everybody for cover.'"

Run they did. "We left our beautiful house," she said. That would mark the beginning of an exile that had no happy ending for the family. The struggle that gripped the Congo had roots in tribal rivalries that also haunted its nine immediate neighbors, seven of which were endemically or acutely unstable,[13] and five that would actively contribute to the downfall of Mobuto's regime.[14]

Her family left the city and they hoped to escape from the country by walking toward eastern Zaire, a daunting challenge. "We left everything, walking, just try to survive. Congo was too big." The Congo is the eleventh largest country on earth, and the home Georgette's family left in Kinshasa was in the far west. She and her family hoped to leave Zaire by walking to the African Great Lakes region, nearly a thousand miles to the east through hot, humid equatorial jungle. The African Great Lakes, sometimes referred to as the Grand Lakes, are a string of large lakes including Lake Victoria, Lake Tanganyika, Lake Malawi, Lake Albert and others in and around the East African Rift Valley, located in Zaire, Uganda, Burundi and Rwanda.[15]

What made it uniquely difficult was that Georgette's mother had just given birth to a baby boy three days before they set out and was still bleeding and hemorrhaging from the recent birth. Obviously, the newborn child had to be carried and this duty fell to the weakened mother. The family struggled on even though, "We were so tired. On foot, no water." Georgette's concerns at the time were not personal, as she noted, "I was not feeling bad for myself, but for my mom, with the baby in her hand, no water, no nothing."

This was the conflict that Georgette's family was passing through: there were four government armies, two former government armies and over a dozen rebel groups and ethnic militias involved in violent confrontation in the Congo.[16] Amazingly, they eventually managed to reach the east of Zaire. Georgette described the trek, "We tried to go like Rwanda, there was no way. We tried to go Uganda, but you see, people was being killed in the streets, you cannot believe."

They waited in the Great Lakes, hoping things would settle down. The carnage of war surrounded them. "You can smell people, we are in the Grand Lakes. Grand Lakes, can see the bodies stand up in the lakes, like trash, because they been killed. Blood everywhere, smelling."

Mobutu had been suffering from prostate cancer since early in the civil war and his condition grew worse. Tutsi rebels were led by Laurent Kabila, whose forces soon controlled much of northern and eastern Zaire. Tens of thousands of Hutus that had conducted the Rwanda genocide came to the fight to save Mobutu. This was offset in early 1997 as the Angolan Army entered the war on the side of the rebels and the European mercenaries, who had been supporting Mobutu, withdrew from the fighting since they hadn't been paid.[17] Nelson Mandela and others attempted to intervene to negotiate a settlement between Mobutu and the Hutus, and the widely-supported Kabila's rebel forces who advanced on the capital, Kinshasa. There were rumors that the U.S. became involved in the ouster of Mobutu to insure a billion- dollar contract for an American firm that would gain control of mineral wealth in Zaire, though these claims lack convincing substantiation.[18]

In May, 1997 rebel forces moved through Kinshasa and Mobutu fled for his life. His escape didn't buy him much time, as he died of cancer in Morocco four months later.

For Georgette, this might have seemed like welcome news since at least they were no longer in the middle of a war zone. "After months everything become calm, the rebels took the city, they been going into the capital," as she recalled. The people who had been in power when they were forced to flee were no longer in charge, but it was uncertain who was. They were cautious and didn't rush. "Six month later my dad said we can just now go back to Kinshasa. Our plan was we went through Rwanda, Burundi, Tanzania. It took us three months to come back to Congo."

The return did not mean resuming the style of existence they had once had. Life for Georgette was not about to improve. Laurent Kabila proclaimed himself president and the country was renamed the Democratic Republic of the Congo, but old problems of corruption and ethnic rivalries did not vanish. They were soon to explode in great violence. The troubles began immediately for Georgette's family as she explains, "It was difficult for us to live there because my dad had been arrested for when we was trying to cross the border." With her dad removed, the glue that had held them together dissolved.

In August of 1998, just over a year after Kabila had come to power, rebels backed by Uganda and Rwanda advanced in the east of the Democratic Republic of the Congo, supported by troops from Angola. Zimbabwe, Chad, Sudan and Namibia. They sent in troops that sided with the Kabila regime in the rapidly expanding second civil war. For Georgette, the situation had again become intolerable. "My mom had, like seven kids, and we couldn't survive in my own country. We couldn't survive in Kinshasa because we didn't have house." They left during the war, but not together this time. "You became a refugee in the same country." A ceasefire was signed in 1999, but the fighting continued. On July 16, 2001, Kabila was assassinated and his son, Joseph, would be named head of state in October 2002. Corruption never declined from the Mobutu years.[19]

The outside world took little notice of all this since Africa rarely received media attention. That neglect is a continuing part of the story of the Sub-Saharan continent.[20] It really was the worst of times.

To make the experience of people like Georgette and others understandable, Vava Tampa wrote a comparative study, "Why the World is Ignoring Congo War." He stated, "The wars in that country have claimed nearly the same number of lives as having a 9/11 every single day for 360 days, the genocide that struck Rwanda in 1994, the ethnic cleansing that overwhelmed Bosnia in the mid-1990s, the genocide that took place in Darfur, the number of people killed in the great tsunami that struck Asia in 2004, and the number of people who died in Hiroshima and Nagasaki -- all combined and then doubled."[21]

Georgette fled in the midst of this carnage and a new refugee chapter was soon underway in her life. She headed to South Africa when she was 16 years old, and this time she was on her own. She would not see her mother again until after she had become a U.S. resident. There were many refugees displaced by the continuing war and Georgette followed them. In her words: "Myself, being a teenager, because transportation was so difficult, I just follow people in front of me that would be running."

Whilst being a refugee in her own country had been extremely challenging and dangerous she had been with family which provided some support. Life in South Africa as a refugee, being a young woman and on her own, would be a different experience. Georgette recalls, "That was difficult. I can tell you. I know what it is to be sad, hungry, happy sad, everything; I had my experience. I've been sitting maybe five days, no food, drinking just water." Whether the emotional damage she suffered in South Africa was worse than the danger she faced in the Congo is unclear but it is unfortunate that anyone should spend her life growing up surviving and coping with such conditions.

She was out of the horror of killing, but she was a young woman alone in a strange land. She was in a refugee camp which was where she began going through processing in the United Nations refugee program. She was allowed to leave camp and, "So like all teenagers, a young lady, I tried to survive myself. I looked for a job in a restaurant because I was speaking French." Her family in Zaire had provided her with a good education, and French was the common language to learn when she was young for those who attended schools, though she would eventually speak five languages. She was hired by a restaurant. "It was not bad." Her salary was only about ten dollars a month but she was happy to work there, "Because the job make me feel a little bit like home."

She was lonely and poor, and desperation set in. "Sometimes walk in street, sometimes sleep in street." It was soon more than sleeping on the street, it was, "I was drinking alcohol. Sometimes you have to stay and drink alcohol all night and sleep outside and wake up in morning, because you don't have nowhere to go." Drinking and staying out all night sleeping on the streets was not an indication life was going well for Georgette as a refugee in South Africa.

She spent four years in the refugee camp, but provisions were scarce and her job didn't add much to move her beyond subsistence. She observed, "A lot of the young refugees, girls, they been abused, by the person that have money. You don't have a choice. 'You want to stay here, well, I'll give you where to sleep, I'll take care of you.' Yeah. They will do anything they want to do with you." It was the voice of experience speaking. Some might think of it as a win-win situation since both parties in the arrangement benefit, but it is purely exploitation of the most vulnerable who are too desperate and have no protection from sexual predators who abuse them. In Georgette's case, it led to her pregnancy. "I became a mom. I was 22," she said.

She soon found that her situation had been processed by the UN and learned that she was eligible for the third and final choice for refugees, resettlement. The first option is repatriation, the second, integration in the country where they have taken refuge, and the final option is resettlement in a third country. It might be expected that after living with the slaughter in the Congo, then exploitation in South Africa, Georgette would have been overjoyed to hear that she was heading for the U.S.A. That was not the case. Her reaction was, "With the assistance they say, we have a program, we can take this single person to the United States. Why America? Why you not send to France or to Belgium where I am speaking my French? They told me you going to America. I say 'Oh.' I knew it wasn't easy to come to America."

She was aware it would be a challenge as a young black woman from Africa and, as she added, "I knew it was difficult, because I came with my first child. She was only three months." Georgette was a single mom. She arrived thinking, "There was nothing for me. Nothing's changed. I tell myself, I'm alive. I can die tomorrow, like every other person who is close to me, a corpse. I saw people die every day."

It was eight years ago when Georgette became a refugee for the third and hopefully final time when she came to America. She says "Now I'm good" and Colorado is "feeling like home." She has a steady job as a receptionist and looks after her daughter, who is "a big girl now. She's eight years." Georgette has strived hard and adjusted, but with a mix of acceptance and some regret. "I am not as alive again. No missing food, but so difficult. So difficult in the United States."

She doesn't think she will completely become a typical Coloradan. For her, after eight years, it is still survival, not pleasure. "I never thinking I'm going to go ski, go watching Bronco's game. I think, you know, like working. How can I go to school, how can I help my mom?" In all the confusion of the Congo wars, her mom ended up imprisoned in France, and Georgette made a trip to visit her. This first reunion since the separation of Georgette leaving Kinshasa has left a strained relationship she hopes to avoid with her own daughter.

Life has been a continuing serious struggle for Georgette. She would have liked to have become a nurse but never had the opportunity to receive the training. She has yet to tell her daughter her story and there will be a time for that. She explains: "I think that she is not ready. She need more time to see the trauma. I don't want to tell her my past right now."

Georgette doesn't pity herself, but she sees her story as the standard refugee story. They vary on interest in returning to their counties of origin, but a common thread among the original arrivals is preservation of their cultures and traditions in this new world. In her words: "The refugees, we are missing something inside. Something's missing." In Africa, "We don't have a lot of opportunity but we have love and happiness. It's something I'm missing. You are far away from your family, far away from your culture, far away from your beautiful food, your culture that has singing and dancing. It's something we're missing now."

Considering the daily death and exploitation Georgette encountered, and the poverty and devastation of her life in Africa, perhaps it is a reflection on U.S. culture, that even though there is wealth, food, opportunity, she can say what is missing is love and happiness.

# CHAPTER THREE: FROM COLONIALISM TO REFUGEES

Georgette's story illustrates the problem that is at the root of many refugee stories. Often the conditions in the world that refugees are fleeing were created by Europeans during their domination of much of the globe. Trade had existed across the Eurasian landmass since ancient times, while the Americas were isolated. In the fifteenth century, the small continent of Europe was the most technologically advanced and great wealth was possible if a water route to the goods of the East could be found that bypassed the long, hazardous voyage by land. Spain and Portugal were the early leaders in these ventures. In the 1494 Treaty of Tordesillas, the world was audaciously divided between the two of them by the Papal Line of Demarcation. Spanish conquistadores, having removed the Moors from Spain, headed to America for gold, glory and God. The Aztec and Inca Empires were defeated and gold flowed to Spain, while Catholicism and Spanish became enduring legacies. Portugal claimed only Brazil in America but had the water route to Asia around Africa, and set up trading posts and colonies. These early encounters would have devastating results for the American people as the Europeans brought smallpox and other diseases that would ravage the populations. Africans would also be affected, as the transatlantic slave trade was introduced to provide free labor for exploiting American resources. These profitable sixteenth century ventures were followed in the seventeenth century in both America and Asia by the French, English and Dutch. The colonies of this era were maritime, based on naval supremacy, and mercantile, focused on harvesting raw materials for the mother country and creating markets for finished goods.

A much more extensive Europeanization of the world came in the late 1800s with the Age of Imperialism. This followed the rise of nation states and nationalism combined with industrialization and capitalism. Since Napoleon, the dominant country had been Britain which was also the leading industrial power and the world's financial center, and it had a widespread colonial empire, including India. When Germany emerged as a new country Britain had a rival.

This initiated a contest to expand empires throughout the Middle East, Africa, and Asia until the entire world was largely dominated by Europe. The small island of Britain acquired the largest empire in world history gaining control of a quarter of the earth's land and governing a quarter of its population.[1] Many Europeans struggled to compete as Russia expanded across the landmass of Eurasia and was by far the largest country in area. The scramble for claiming Africa and Asia had several competitors with the British, French, and Germans being the largest players. Late outside entrants were the United States and Japan, but the major struggle was Western European.

There were nationalist motives for this and economically, the raw materials needed for new industries were available only in underdeveloped areas. It was a racist time when white Europeans' attitudes about claiming territory found support in Social Darwinism, which contended that whites had evolved farther and were the proper rulers of inferior people. There were many devoted Christians who felt it was their duty to convert the heathens of the less developed world. Some also felt the superior whites had a duty to bring advances of Western culture to the lesser races. This was the civilizing mission that Rudyard Kipling wrote of in his 1899 poem, "The White Man's Burden":

*Take up the White Man's burden, Send forth the best ye breed*

*Go bind your sons to exile, To serve your captives'*
*need;*
*To wait in heavy harness, On fluttered folk and wild –*
*Your new-caught, sullen peoples, Half-devil and*
*half-child.*[2]

The major change that accompanied the new imperialism was that countries claiming territory were supported by companies that didn't plan to just trade but expected to make large investments in infrastructure such as railroads, mines, warehouses, steamships to gain access to the resources they were seeking. To be sure this was achieved, they wanted complete political and territorial domination. This was really sparked by the Berlin Conference of 1884-85 and its final act, Article 35, that required "effective control" of territories claimed.[3] Unlike earlier colonialism where countries could stake claim to territories and rule them from abroad, actual occupation of the land would be required for a nation's claim to be considered legitimate. The people in the areas they claimed were going to be their subjects and in some cases reduced to their slaves. Little attention was paid to existing social and political structures. While some colonies like India gained advanced infrastructures as Europeans profited and controlled power, others were harshly exploited.

Africa, especially the Sub-Saharan, was where the frantic scramble for grabbing territory began with the least restraint. The "Dark Continent" was made up of tribes, ethnicities, chiefdoms, kingdoms, warlords, where village life and nomadic wandering was the most common lifestyle, and people's loyalties were overlapping. Boundaries were indistinct and related to the changing tribal rivalries or other conflicts. The European concept of the nation state was not an African concept, but was suddenly imposed upon it, as it would be on Asian colonies that contained mixed identities. South Africa had been settled in an earlier land grab and Europe's method and aggressiveness is illustrated in Georgette's home, the Congo. This is where the rush to partition Sub-Saharan Africa began. The case is illustrative of African exploitation and the worst of imperialism.

The African explorer Henry Stanley ventured deep through unknown Africa. He saw the Congo River basin and was convinced it had economic potential. Stanley eventually convinced King Leopold II of Belgium to sponsor an expedition up the Congo and when he returned he had over 500 legal documents tribal chiefs had marked with an X in exchange for trinkets. The chiefs couldn't read the documents and contracts were a meaningless concept to them, but what they had unknowingly agreed to was to give all their territory to Leopold and promised to provide workers for his projects. In 1884, the Congress of Berlin recognized Leopold as the head of the Congo Free State, the world's only private colony.[4]

Leopold claimed this was a humanitarian venture, that he was protecting the "natives" from Arab slave traders and bringing them Christianity. He borrowed money from the Belgian government to finance his enterprise and began by demanding that the Congo produce 2,000,000 pounds of ivory per year for export,[5] but change came when inflatable rubber tires became marketable for bicycles and later automobiles. The great demand for rubber, which was available in the Congo jungle, led Leopold to send his army to the colony, where they went to villages and forced men to join work gangs for the concession companies that would provide for the insatiable demand. Women and children were taken as hostages to force the men to collect rubber. There was resistance, and soldiers were sent out with a known number of bullets that were only to be used on the local population. They were ordered to bring back a severed hand of each person they killed to justify their use of ammunition. But soldiers would also cut off the hands of the living in order to use the ammunition for hunting.[6] Individuals who didn't show up for the forced work recruitments were shot, while those who failed to meet their rubber quotas were flogged, and villages that did not meet assigned quotas were burned.[7] Mutilation was a standard practice, as one district commissioner wrote, "To gather rubber...one must cut off hands, noses and ears."[8] This forced labor system became known as "red rubber" as the rubber was tapped from trees that grew in the blood of the many who died under Leopold's forced labor.[9]

Belgian atrocities in the Congo were being reported in the British press as early as 1885 and in twenty years there was international public outrage. The scandal forced Belgium to take control of Leopold's private colony in 1909[10] and it became the Belgian Congo. Noted authors were inspired to speak out, including Arthur Conan Doyle's, *The Crime of the Congo*[11] and Mark Twain's satire, *King Leopold Soliloquy: A Defense of his Congo Rule.*[12] The writer who most famously told the story was Joseph Conrad, who had spent time there. In his *Heart of Darkness*,[13] the man who had exploited the Congo died, whispering his final words, "The horror! The horror!"[14]

The horror it was remains shocking, in that it has been ranked among the greatest mass murders in all history. The figure has been set by some at six million,[15] though *Encyclopedia Britannica* and the BBC put the number at ten million people who lost their lives as a result of Leopold's Congo policies.[16] This also set the standard for Congo rule and exploitation that remained through Georgette's experience.

An especially lasting legacy of the European acquisition of territory in Africa, the Middle East, and Asia, would be the arbitrary lines drawn as boundaries such as the Congo's. The original rule set out by the Congress of Berlin was actual occupation by the country claiming ownership, which really ignited a race for claiming land. World War I, or the Great War as it was then known, was partly a result of the conflicts that resulted from claims being made and the alliance system that developed for European powers to feel secure against each other as competition increased. Following the War, German colonies were divided up as mandates and given to the victors. In all cases, borders were drawn in Europe along lines that had little relation to the people living in the areas, their tribes, ethnicities, beliefs, and who they identified with in larger groups. In the Middle East, a striking and most revealing example of this is the Sykes-Picot agreement. Sykes was a British aristocratic diplomat and Picot was the same, except French. While they had been rivals for empire, they became allies in 1914 when World War I broke out. One of their enemies was the massive Ottoman Empire that had become Germany's ally and controlled territory in the Middle East, Arabia, and southern-central Europe.

In 1916, in the middle of the war, these two men held a private meeting and discussed what should become of the Ottoman Empire after the war, once the Central Powers (as the German-led alliance was known) had been defeated. Eventually they took out a map of the Middle East and with a pencil and a ruler, drew a straight line with some curves at the ends. They hadn't been assigned this duty by their governments, but they both signed the map and it eventually became official.

They had divided the Empire between Britain and France with a straight line but both were knowledgeable about the area and they had regions in mind for various factions living there. Arabs were helping fight against the Central Powers in exchange for a promise of statehood but were ignored in these plans. Lebanon was to be a haven for Christians and Druze, Palestine would house a large Jewish community, between the two the Bekaa Valley would be left to Shia Muslims, while Syria would be for the Sunnis as they were the largest demographic. Palestine would be under British influence while Syria and Lebanon would be controlled by the French.[17]

Up to the present different sects have lived separately because the Sykes-Picot agreement did not correspond to tribal, ethnic, or sectarian distinctions on the ground,[18] a fact spelled out in an article entitled "The Map that Ruined the Middle East." [19] This pointed out that the Kurdish population was divided between four states, Turkey, Iran, Iraq, and Syria. Shiite Arabs were split among Iraq, Kuwait, Bahrain, and the eastern provinces of Saudi Arabia, while the Shiite Arab sect, the Alawites, now reside along the northern Lebanese, Syrian, and southwestern Turkish coasts. Sunni Arabs, the dominant population of the Middle East, were split into many states. The little-known and closely united Druze were spread between what is now Israel, Lebanon, and Syria. Lebanon was intended as a Christian stronghold but included large Sunni and Shiite populations, and also Alawites and Druze. Circassians, Assyrians, Yazidis, and Chaldeans were isolated in pockets that were spread throughout the area. As the twenty-first century began, minority ethnic groups ruled in Iraq, Lebanon, Syria, and Bahrain.

Some find the influence of this little-known map that was drawn out in pencil without instructions to be negotiated, to have had monumental importance reaching to the present day. Scholarly articles see it as the underlying cause of the Arab Spring, the tragedy in Syria, the rise of ISIS.[20] While this may be a stretch, there is little doubt that the imperialist powers were haphazard in creating boundaries in the Middle East, and as a result, historic local regional hostilities were locked in borders that assured when nations emerged from the borders imposed, internal hostilities were probable. This has bred situations that create refugees, and recently the largest number by far have come from this region.

The boundaries in Africa are unusually arbitrary because of their imperial origin, and again refugees have resulted from the resulting strife. Treaties between European powers and with local chiefs often resulted in the use of straight lines or geographical features, such as rivers, to unite previously separate local, populations. 44% of Africa's borders are straight lines and a 1985 study found that 177 cultural or ethnic groups were partitioned by the borders drawn, representing 43% of the population.[21] The evidence indicates a "relationship between boundary arbitrariness and political instability, civil wars and secession attempts,"[22] but there does not appear to be a simple solution to redrawing boundaries that would eliminate the problem now that they are well established. This imposed identity from colonialism remained as the Cold War came, then when leaders emerged and sought independence for their countries. Similar stories exist in Asia where in some places hostile ethnic groups were forced together and problems were inevitable. Liberation came from colonial rulers, but groups that were naturally hostile to each other were bound in struggles for power within borders that would lead to civil strife and refugees fleeing borders worldwide.

In America during the later 1800s, there was a belief similar to the Europeans' white supremacy, called Manifest Destiny. It was the belief the country was fated to rule the continent from the Atlantic to the Pacific. The Indians were the victims, and when this was achieved, the country became a late joiner in the imperialist scramble. In 1898, while going to war to save the oppressed Cubans from harsh Spanish rule, the U.S. attacked the Philippines half a world away, and claimed Hawaii. After taking the Philippines, Kipling's advice was followed. President McKinley stated, "There was nothing left for us to do but to take them all, and to educate the Filipinos, and to uplift and civilize and Christianize them."[23]

By this time, America had become the place to go to escape persecution and oppression due to personal beliefs and wars to dislodge minorities. One group that had suffered mass murders and rapes was Jews living in Russia, where these attacks were given the name pogroms. The *New York Times* reported on a pogrom leading to the Jewish refugees coming to the United States in "The Russian Refugees: Hebrews in Brooklyn Taking Measures for Their Relief."[24]

The article told of "the condition of the Jewish refugees, and the sufferings endured in the endeavor to escape even with life from the fury of the mob, who wreaked upon an unoffending race of fellow-subjects the blind vengeance generated by oppression under the rule of the Czar." It added, "Within the next three or four months, from all the society could learn, at least 8,000, and probably not less than 10,000, Jewish refugees would be landed upon our shores in comparative destitution; some of them in a state bordering on starvation; many sick, weary, discouraged, and hopeless – strangers in a strange country."[25]

Four years after this story appeared was the centenary of the U.S. proclaiming autonomy from England. To mark the occasion France presented a gift to the United States, a 111-foot-tall statue,[26] entitled "Liberty Enlightening the World." While Philadelphia and Cleveland were considered as possible locations for the impressive structure,[27] Liberty was placed on what came to be called Liberty Island in New York Harbor.

The commemoration of the statue was in 1886 and its designer, Frédéric Auguste Bartholdi, had originally intended the statue to be a monument to abolitionism and the end of slavery in America.[28] Six years later nearby Ellis Island was opened as the main entry point for immigrants to American handling 5,000 to 10,000 daily.[29] From that time until it closed in 1954 three-quarters of all the nation's newcomers entered the country through its portals.[30] The proximity of the statue to Ellis Island made it an unintended symbol, enshrining what became the common belief that the statue represented the hope for freedom and opportunity offered by immigration to America.

This relation of the Statue of Liberty to immigration and refugees was solidified when a $270 million fund-raising drive[31] was required to build a base for the statue to sit on in the harbor. As part of the fundraiser there was a poetry auction. Among those who contributed works for the auction was Emma Lazarus, a Jewish poet who had volunteered in the Hebrew Emigrant Aid Society and visited Wards Island, to help new Jewish refugees from pogroms.

With this background of seeing America accept Jewish refugees, Lazarus wrote the poem in 1883 that she would contribute to the fundraising effort for the base of the Statue of Liberty.[32] Her entry was a sonnet, "The New Colossus." Its last lines would become a part of history. The entire poem submitted by Lazarus for the fundraising was:

*THE NEW COLOSSUS*
*Not like the brazen giant of Greek fame,*
*With conquering limbs astride from land to land;*
*Here at our sea-washed, sunset gates shall stand*
*A mighty woman with a torch, whose flame*
*Is the imprisoned lightning, and her name*
*Mother of Exiles. From her beacon-hand*
*Glows world-wide welcome; her mild eyes command*
*The air-bridged harbor that twin cities frame.*
*"Keep, ancient lands, your storied pomp!" cries she*
*With silent lips. "Give me your tired, your poor,*
*Your huddled masses yearning to breathe free,*
*The wretched refuse of your teeming shore.*
*Send these, the homeless, tempest-tost to me,*
*I lift my lamp beside the golden door!"* [33]

So, the giant woman by Ellis Island was the "Mother of Exiles" who offered a "world- wide welcome." Liberty would not commemorate freedom from the British that drove American colonists to fight the Revolutionary War. Liberty would stand for the freedom to come to the United States and begin a new life without threat of religious or ethnic persecution. America as a melting pot was immortalized and set apart from the "ancient lands" and "storied pomp" of the Europe that had been home to the original Colossus. Since the Pilgrims fled persecution in Europe, America had been seen as the land of opportunity for those who sought freedom and opportunity and now there was a symbol, the Statue of Liberty, to embody that belief.

The sonnet was not originally a part of the Statue of Liberty. It appeared in both The *New York World* and the *New York Times* following the auction,[34] but it was soon forgotten and Lazarus died at the age of 38,[35] shortly after "The New Colossus" was published. Her recognition as a poetess faded, but seventeen years later friends of hers initiated an effort to restore her reputation. That effort resulted in the words of the sonnet being inscribed on a plaque on the inner wall of the statue's pedestal.[36] With the rise of fascism in Europe during the 1930s refugees began to stream in to the U.S., among them was Albert Einstein who was "regarded as the symbol and leader of the entire group of refugee scholars."[37] Soon to follow were two future Secretaries of State, Henry Kissinger and Madeline Albright. By this time, America began to take pride in being a nation of immigrants, and the poem was moved to a prominent position nearer the statue's entrance.[38] Irving Berlin set the most famous lines to music as the finale of his 1949 Broadway musical, *Miss Liberty*.

It has been an uneven path for refugees and other immigrants since the inspirational words were written. As far as refugees "yearning to breathe free," Robert Suro noted in the *Washington Post* that "Economic imperatives, much more than political aspirations, have always driven immigration to the United States. Planters, merchants, servants and slaves vastly outnumbered Pilgrims and Puritans."[39] He is likely correct in terms of numbers, but that does not diminish the great importance of the U.S. and of the Statue of Liberty as a symbol for the many refugees who have fled and continue to flee the ravages of war and oppression, and see a hope for their future and that of their children if they can reach the U.S. For them, the U.S. is still the Mother of Exiles as Emma Lazarus set out so eloquently.

A national debate now divides the U.S. on immigrants and refugees, with voices of fear extolling homeland security at the expense of compassion. Donald Trump, when he began his presidential campaign, became the spokesman for fear of refugees as a danger to U.S. safety, a theme he has continued into his presidency. Among his comments during the campaign about refugees: "Lock your doors," since refugees were being settled where he was campaigning.[40] During his first week in office, President Trump issued an executive order that would reduce the total number of refugees to less than half its previous number.[41] He soon followed with another that would restrict access for many refugees, leading to large protests and many lawsuits. What sounded like campaign rhetoric had become policy and stuck fear into the refugee community in America.

This fear-mongering does a disservice to the many refugees who have found their way to Denver, Colorado, far from America's coasts. In this microcosm of American society, one finds many who still share Emma Lazarus' dreams engraved on the plaque on the Statue of Liberty and are the focus of this work, which introduces real refugees and their stories. These people are the tempest-tost who like Georgette have fled unconscionable suffering and have found hope in the United States. Says a Somalian cab driver who was a refugee placed in the Denver metropolitan area, "For us, U.S.A. stand for 'You Start Again.' This is good life; I have opportunity here. My children can be safe and they can have a better life."[42] As Setu Nepal, who spent over two decades in a refugee camp before being placed in Denver put it, "Thank you to the US government for taking the people who lived in the refugee camp for so long and giving us a chance. We will try to do our best and contribute. Thank you to Denver."[43]

# CHAPTER FOUR: MOHAMMED, SYRIA

The refugee crisis that is currently best known is the one that involves what has been taking place in Syria. This brings on the most heated political rhetoric and arouses fear in some and sympathy in others. Syria gained its independence from France in 1946 and for most of the time since then it has been a Baathist country with the modern Baathists identifying themselves as socialists. This small country has coastline on the eastern Mediterranean Sea and long borders with Iraq, Jordan, and Turkey, and shorter ones with Lebanon and Israel. It is primarily an Arab, Muslim nation but 10% of its population is Christian.[1] In the 1967 Six Days War, Syria lost the Golan Heights to Israel. The leader of the country is the autocratic Bashar al-Assad who came to power in 2000 on the death of his father. In 2007 Israel launched an aerial attack on Syria's nuclear facilities that were under construction. The U.S. had applied sanctions on Syria for providing aid to terrorist groups, including Hezbollah, and allowing them passage into Iraq.

Four years of drought beginning in 2006 caused at least 800,000 farmers to lose their livelihood, and many fled to cities in search of nonexistent jobs. The government was no help. Tens of thousands of angry, impoverished former farmers were crowded into Syria's cities when the pro-democracy protests of the Arab Spring that had been going on in Egypt and Tunisia spread to Syria. Protests erupted in March 2011 in the southern city of Deraa. The incident that initiated all that followed was the arrest and torture of some teenagers who painted revolutionary slogans on a school wall. When demonstrators took to the streets in protest, security forces opened fire on them and some were killed, sparking nationwide protests and the demand for President Assad's resignation. Kidnapping, torture, and killing of demonstrators followed and, rather than suppressing things, the protestors hardened their stance. The country soon degenerated into civil war with outside forces drawn in. With the emergence of the Islamic State (ISIS or ISIL) in 2013, and its rapid expansion in Iraq and Syria, Syria's civil war had many participants, including the U.S., Iran, the Kurds, Russia, Turkey, branches of al Qaeda and Islamist groups, while France and Britain launched air strikes and Gulf states played minor roles.

The results so far have been a half million killed,[2] over five million have fled the country,[3] and 6.5 million have been forced from their homes and are internally displaced.[4] The greatest refugee tragedy now facing the world was created and the politicization of the conflict has left millions of innocent victims. Mohammed is one of them who finally escaped and made his way to Denver.

Mohammed is from Deraa, where the original protest began, but he was away at the time. He had graduated from college, was married, and had young children. His degree was in engineering and he was beginning a career, working in Gulf countries since the start of 2011. For about a month he lost contact with his family because there were no communications available to Deraa, no internet. "I just tried to keep up on what was happening there by what I heard on Facebook and following the news," he said.[5] This was not enough and, although he had work he was supposed to do, he decided to return home. He learned the protest had started out peacefully, as simple nonviolent demonstrations against the regime, with nothing aggressive or no weapons. Once started, things escalated, and by the time he arrived there were mass protests and bombardment by the government. His family decided to move to a different area in the city where it might be safer and Mohammed started a new job.

His living conditions were good because he was a successful young man and, in Syria, that meant being able to afford a house and a car. He had a little park around his home. His new job required him to travel around the city to visit various locations continuously. In the tense world that is Syria that would have catastrophic consequences. He had at one time been in Syrian security but after being observed driving around the city and making frequent stops, he was arrested.

From the moment Mohammed was seized, as was as was common for those detained, he disappeared. He knew nothing about the outside world while those on the outside knew nothing about him. He was first taken to an underground prison and tortured for a month. He recalls that following his arrest, "During the whole time, I was held in total darkness, with no sun, no light, just blackness. I couldn't see anything." They then burned him with cigarettes, beat him regularly, hung him from the ceiling in a torture method known as "shabeh" where they suspended him by manacled wrists while he was beaten. There was nothing he could tell them because he hadn't done anything. He later learned that they were accusing him of using his phone to take pictures and videos of demonstrations when he drove around and made his stops. He was interrogated frequently along with the beatings but he had nothing to admit.

After a month he was moved and things got worse. He was transferred to Damascus, to a facility known as the Palestine Branch, or Branch 235. This has nothing to do with Palestine and is widely recognized as one of Syria's most feared torture prisons. Mohammed survived four and a half months in this torture center where he said, "Every day it's a new story. Every day a new young man dies under this torture." Torture methods reported by survivors included such things as having their fingernails pulled out then being forced to eat them, electric shocks to the genitals from car batteries and electric prongs delivering shocks to teeth, beating soles of bare feet with wooden batons, stapling fingers, chest, ears, and squeezing fingers with pliers. In some cases they just defecated where they stood as they were allowed no movement and were in overcrowded cells, there were the regular beatings with chains, and eyes gouged out, some were left to suffocate, others starved. A military police officer who worked the nearby and very similar Saydnaya prison defected. He brought out a trove of photographs of mutilated bodies of inmates like those Mohammed saw die which Amnesty International made public. The photos included 127 victims from Branch 235 where Mohammed was held. The horrific conditions Mohammed endured are now on display at the United States Holocaust Memorial Museum in Washington, D.C. When Syria's ruler Bashar al-Assad was confronted with the images, which had been authenticated by the FBI, he described them as "fake news."[6]

Mohammed recalled his time there, "And every day maybe somebody, they hit him on the head and he has concussion, maybe is bleeding in the brain. Nobody can take care of him so he dies." He said that most of the people were sick but there was no doctor to help them, nothing they could do. They just continued to be tortured. And when someone was beaten in the head and had a concussion or was bleeding in the brain from being hit by a pipe or chain or something, they might give that person an ibuprofen.

"So, every day I saw all these people dying and I used to be waiting for my turn… I'm going to die tomorrow or the day after." At this point when he was describing his time of torture and the constant presence of death, tears were streaming down Mohammed's cheeks. Our interview stopped for a bit as he started to cry and needed some time to wipe his face and compose himself.

He was willing to continue and spoke of a friend from Hama, a dentist, who was also incarcerated. His friend was married and had a daughter he was hoping to see. Hama and Mohammed had befriended each other in their shared misery until one day, Hama was taken away. That was an everyday occurrence. Mohammed said, "Every day I saw a different person, different people. They say, come on, we want to investigate with you and suddenly they disappear. We don't know about them, they disappear. Whether they are released, or killed, no one know." But in this case, they informed him to increase his distress. They had killed his friend. Amnesty found evidence that 13,000 had been killed in just one of Syria's prisons since 2011 and taken off by truckloads to be buried in mass graves.[7]

This wasn't just a frightful period for him; his family had no idea what had happened to him since he was first arrested. His wife assumed he was in some kind of trouble and that if he was, she and their kids could be as well, so she started moving from neighborhood to neighborhood to keep safe. In time she didn't know if he was dead or alive. For both of them by this time one thing was the same: "Everywhere you are in Syria you can hear this bombardment. You don't know where it is but you can still hear it any time."

His wife finally took their children and crossed the border into Jordan. She had relatives there and thought she would feel safer. She was contradicting Arab culture by traveling without her husband, whom she should follow, but she had no idea if she had a husband any longer as months had now passed and she had never heard a word. He had also never heard a word about his wife and family and had managed to survive. He was transferred to another prison in Damascus. This prison housed soldiers who had turned against the regime as well as civilians. People here were subject to charges and he was brought to the prison court on charges of terrorism. He was accused of using his mobile phone to take many videos of the anti-government protests and sending them to Al Jazeera, which was the widely-watched news network in the region. He hadn't, and they had no evidence, and their torture techniques hadn't broken him.

Mohammed was moved again, this time to a civilian prison in the suburbs of Damascus. There they had another court, a civilian court. He waited two more weeks. Then after all this torture, all this time, they said, "You can go. You are innocent." After spending nearly seven months in prison he was released.

A great ordeal had come to an end but his wife had given up and left the country. Mohammed contacted his sister who was in Damascus and learned what had become of his wife and children. He learned they were in Jordan, so he just followed people heading that way and walked like everyone else. On the way he saw three graves, one adult and two children's. He said, "The feeling that I had when I saw these graves is that maybe one of my family members is here." The border crossing was closed by Jordan, so he was uncertain of what to do. They had no sort of shelter but the Jordanian Army gave them some food and provided blankets. They could attempt to construct tents and shelter themselves from the desert weather which is very hot and sunny during the day, but cold at night. After a week, he and the others moved on to Nassib, where fighting between the Syrian Arab Army and the Kingdom of Syria continued over control of access to the country. Again he failed to get across the border but there was another crossing at Daraa, a two day walk through bombardment.

He continued, along with many women, children, and elderly people, making a very dangerous walk and thought, "…this is the only way we're going to survive." The danger came from the regime and its bombings. They were the real terrorists in Syria in Mohammed's view. He says of terrorism, "It means the Assad regime. This is the terrorist. Not the Syrian people." He stayed at the crossing point and the officials there were aware his family was at Azraq, in what he called the Blue Camp. They checked, and he was soon reunited with his wife, but only briefly. He was allowed to join the 50,000 Syrian refugees in a camp of simple blue and white shacks surrounded by endless empty space, and had no electricity. The camp had a supermarket that was over a mile away, with a monopoly that drove up prices even though many refugees came with little or nothing.[8] Mohammed moved in there while his wife and kids, who had previously lived in the camp, had moved to Jordan to stay with her relatives.

He was told that the camp wanted him to ask his wife to return so his family would be reunited. They asked him to bring his family back, and he said he would have to go visit his wife where she lived in Jordan. Mohammed was required to sign an agreement that said, "I swear if I go, I'm going to come back to the camp."

Then he left and spent a month with his wife and children. Following that, he returned to the Blue Camp. He says that for the person in charge, whom he refers to as "the general," this was a bit of a shock. Mohammed says the man asked him "Why did you come back?" and he replied, "I told you that if I'm going to go visit, I'm going to come back." This apparently made a favorable impression, and the general liked him for keeping his word: "It's up to general there and he let me go in. I was lucky. There's a lot of hard cases there and the behavior of the refugees." This was a United Nations operation under the umbrella of the Jordanian government, so it was possible to register for resettlement, and Mohammed did. They "register all of these families and they say, who knows, maybe you can go or not. No promises for them, it's just write the name and that's it."

After qualifying for resettlement, he left the camp and lived in Jordan with his wife and children for almost two years. He was starting a new life when his folder for resettlement was chosen by lottery in 2014. Then he had to go through the vetting process and all the other requirements.

It was August of 2016 when he was resettled in Denver, a man of about 30 who had recovered from showing signs of what he had endured. His resettlement has had some bumpy spots right from the beginning.

Mohammed's family was placed in a small, old apartment on Colfax Avenue with a wet ceiling and a carpet that had a foul odor. He has a son with allergies and asthma who was sick but the agency that had made the arrangements for his resettlement had signed a year's lease. He decided to break the lease anyway and find another apartment. Fortunately, there were local people who were willing to help make all the arrangements. He now has a very pleasant apartment in a nice location.

Another difficulty he has had in his short time here is with work. Like many well-educated refugees, he took a job well below his qualifications, working for a company that assembles chairs. He soon had a dispute over prayer time that ended that job. He said they, "Let me pray every day during prayer time, at break time. Not Friday prayer, very important, cannot leave." Friday prayers, called Jum'ah for Sunni men-- which constitute the vast majority of Muslims -- is considered obligatory. For Mohammed, after all he endured, he feels he has "a more spiritual relationship with Allah," and that meeting his religious needs comes first. "Friday prayers it's not acceptable to leave this company and come back." Because there was no way he could continue at his work and be allowed time tor Friday prayers, he left the company. He believes it is his religious right in a country where we have religious freedom. "We need to understand the cultures of these families," he says.

Nobody has accused him or said anything to him about terrorism, which is encouraging. He is still adjusting and his life will always be haunted by being an innocent victim of a regime that is willing to turn on its own people in a situation where no easy answer is available. He is warm and welcoming, as is his wife, and while he was approaching his ninth month in the U.S. at the time he shared his story, he had come a long way in making a very dramatic adjustment from tortured prisoner to Denver resident.

# CHAPTER FIVE: TURMOIL IN BURMA

The largest number of recent refugees to settle in Colorado have come from the relatively small country of Burma, with about 4,000 arriving between 2007 and 2014.[1] Burma is a country in Southeast Asia nestled between giants China to the north and India on the west. Its rhombus shape has a peninsula hanging down from the bottom that runs along the Bay of Bengal, giving it an extensive border with Thailand. A succession of kingdoms, conquests, and empires dating back to ancient times ruled in the area that is now called Myanmar by its government, but still commonly referred to as Burma.[2] Buddhism came early, arriving first among the Pyū people of the southern region, though there is considerable disagreement on when that took place.[3] What is certain is that by the time King Anawyatha founded the first Burmese empire in 1044, Burma was predominantly Buddhist,[4] though the area descended into warfare between various tribes, small kingdoms, and there were periods of dynastic rule.

When the nineteenth century began, Burma's many ethnic groups were held together under the rule of the Konbaung Dynasty. Britain soon began its intrusion into the area as it was expanding its colony of India.[5] This conquest was completed in 1886 and Burma was annexed.[6] It became a province of India, which it remained until 1937.[7] Upon annexation, Britain reconstructed the new expansion of its Empire by dividing it into two sections. The central part was Ministerial Burma, including the majority Buddhist Burmans who were administered by foreign outsiders.

Surrounding this were the Tribal Areas, the ethnic minorities in the hills that British and American missionaries attempted to convert to Christianity. The imperial policies instituted by the British from the beginning of their control of Burma laid the groundwork for Burma's future and contemporary problems, in what became a very divided country. Throughout its history, prior to British occupation, Burma had been organized along religious and patron-client lines.[8] The British categorized people according to ethnic groups, then distinguished between indigenous and colonizers, introducing Western notions of race, territoriality and border, that had not previously determined opportunity and living conditions.[9]

There are more than 135 different ethnic groups in Burma with separate languages and cultures.[10] The Burmans, the largest group, who are Buddhist and make up 68% of the population, gained control of the military and the government. Their native language is Burmese, the country's official language.[11] The largest of the others, including the Karen, Kachin, Chin, Mon, and Shan, held significant territory but not large populations. Only the Shan and the Karen had populations in excess of a million by 1980.[12]

World War II came and the Burmese first attempted to exploit it to gain independence from India, though different ethnicities originally fought on opposite sides. The most prominent Burmese nationalist, Aung San, had long been involved in resistance to British rule, and in 1942 the Japanese assisted him in forming the Japanese Independence Army. It joined with Japan in invading Burma, on promises of independence from Britain following the war.[13] Once he saw the harsh treatment of Burmese officers by Japanese officers and that the Japanese were losing the war, Aung San broke with them in 1945 and sided with the Allies.[14] Following Japan's surrender, Aung San created a political army and became what was effectively the prime minister of Burma.

Clement Atlee had replaced Winston Churchill as prime minister of Britain and negotiations began for Burmese independence. Aung San and six of his colleagues were assassinated on July 19, 1947.[15] His daughter would famously become prime minister many years later.

When British rule came to an end in 1948, the border people, including the Karen, Kachin, Chin, Mon, and Shan, agreed to join the Burmese federation, on the condition that they would have local autonomy and the right to withdraw in ten years if they chose. Local autonomy was not respected and the Burmese army imposed forced labor, torture, and sexual abuse. The army waged war on the border people who sought to resist. The dominant Burmans considered border tribal people "uncivilized." After ten years, none of the border people were allowed to leave the federation of independent Burma.[16] While a number of the ethnic groups are primarily Buddhist, including the Shan, Mon and Pa-O, some have significant proportions of Christians, including the Karen, Kachin, Chin, and there are also are the Muslim Rohingya as well as animists.[17]

Civil war broke out in 1949 between the Karen National Union that had control over land in the on the border of Thailand and the Burmese government. This conflict has yet to be resolved and is the longest ongoing civil war in the world.[18]

U Nu was elected in 1960 on the basis of his Buddhism and support of making that the state religion, causing more internal problems.[19] General Ne Win led the *coup d'état* of 1962 as a result of the increased politicization of ethnic groups in Burma.[20] This marked the end of civilian rule in Burma. The general soon founded the Burma Socialist Progamme Party, and proclaimed a new national ideology, "The Burmese Way to Socialism," under a government that would be ruled by a military junta.[21] Other political parties and unions were banned and protests suppressed, then the new government proceeded to write a constitution.

The country was transformed into an authoritarian military socialist state under a 1974 constitution.[22]

The "Burmese Way to Socialism" led to an economic crisis in Burma, and by the late 1980s Burma was on the list of Least Developed Countries, a status it retains to the present.[23] In July 1988, after 23 years as dictator, Ne Win decided to resign and the regime transferred power to General Lwin. This led to a general strike by students and power was briefly transferred to Dr. Muang, who ended martial law and freed political prisoners, but the protests spread to more cities and towns and beyond students to professionals and monks. The military cracked down, killing thousands of protesters, and General Saw seized power in September and formed SLORC, the "State Law and Order Restoration Council." Direct military rule was in place and would be until slight modification in March 2011.[24] Presidents Clinton, Bush, and Obama would all issue economic sanctions against Burma for "large-scale repression of democratic opposition."[25]

These demonstrations and crackdown led to the rise of numerous opposition parties, the foremost being the National League for Democracy, or NLD, under the leadership of Aung San Suu Kyi. She had said, "Democracy is the only ideology which is consistent with freedom. It is an ideology that promotes and strengthens peace. It is therefore the only ideology we should aim for."[26]

Though she had been under house arrest since July 1989, she was the General-Secretary for the NLD and decided to stand as a candidate in the 1990 elections. These were the first elections in Burma in 30 years to allow more than one party. In all, 93 parties competed for seats in the Pyithu Hluttaw, the Burmese parliament, and nearly 73% of 21 million eligible voters turned out to cast their ballots.[27] The NLD won 392 seats and the next highest number any party won was 23,[28] meaning government leadership should pass to the party's head, Aung San Suu Kyi. Though there was talk of a transfer of power from SLORC to the NLD, the junta refused to be involved in discussions on the grounds that it was a military, not a political government. The results of the election were ignored, and Aung San Suu Kyi was back under house arrest. She was awarded the 1991 Nobel Peace Prize, where the committee called her "an outstanding example of the power of the powerless."

A big event that led to refugees fleeing Burma and many ending up in Colorado came in 2007. With half the population at or below the poverty line, 30% of children malnourished, primary school dropout rates approaching 50%, widespread malaria and tuberculosis,[29] in August the government announced a large increase on gas and oil prices and also increased bus fares. The bus fare increase especially affected the poor who had been forced out of cities to shanty towns, and could not afford the new rates to get to work in urban areas. There was considerable economic frustration that young people and, notably, young monks were unafraid to express. By September these frustrations with economic and political conditions set off massive demonstrations where leading figures were often Buddhist monks, whose robes gave the name of the events, the Saffron Revolution.

There were thousands of monks marching down the streets of Rangoon calling for democratic change as they pledged to "wipe the military dictatorship from the land of Burma."[30] Increasing numbers of civilians joined their cause as days passed, but it was a short time before the army cracked down hard. Within days the shooting and beating of protestors ended their hopes for change and many thousands of monks were imprisoned, while many fled the country.

While the number of refugees spiked, little changed as a result of the challenge to the government. The *New York Times* wrote a year after the event: "Last week was the anniversary. During it, a bomb explosion in downtown Yangon wounded four; web sites run by dissenters and exiles were attacked and shut down; and about 100 monks filed silently through the streets of a western fishing town to commemorate the crackdown. But this seems hardly dramatic enough to undo the disillusionment that set in after the defeat of the Saffron Revolution. In some ways, it only underscores it."[31]

The year following the big protest, Burma was hit by a devastating cyclone that drove many more out. On the evening of May 2, 2008 Cyclone Nargis struck the Irrawaddy Delta in the Bay of Bengal with winds of 150 miles per hour. A nearly 12-foot wall of water killed 10,000 in one town alone as the giant storm struck the densely-populated area of Burma. Overall, Nargis left nearly 140,000 people dead,[32] and 3,200,000 homeless[33] in Burma. To put this in perspective, Katrina, the massive hurricane that struck New Orleans in 2005 left 1,836 dead and 60,000 homeless,[34] numbers that wouldn't register noticeably if they were added to or subtracted to the Nargis casualty list.

Though Nargis was the third deadliest storm on record, much of the damage was self- inflicted as the military rulers refused to allow foreign aid workers into the country and rejected most outside assistance. It was part of the government paranoia that relief workers' real purpose would be to overthrow the ruling military junta.[35] This was another reason for some on the fringes to leave to find an opportunity to survive.

The recent news from Burma that has brought more refugees is the country's continuing rejection of its Rohingya Muslims, many of whom live in the north of the western state, Rakhine. This group has been described as being among the world's most persecuted people.[36] While nearly 90% of Burma's population is Buddhist, the Muslim Rohingya are frequently singled out for persecution. They can trace Burmese ancestry back to the eighth century,[37] while others say twelfth century.[38]

A large number came in the nineteenth century when Burma was under British rule. Under the country's 1982 Citizenship Act, they are not recognized as one of the country's national races. They are denied citizenship, forbidden to marry without official permission and forced to do manual labor on government projects. Estimates put their number at between near a million and a million and a half, while several hundred thousand have fled. The problem has existed at least since World War II when the country was still a province of India, and the Rohingya fought on the opposite side to the rest of the country. They sided with the British, hoping for a Muslim state following the war. Most of Burma sided with Japan in hopes of liberation from Britain, until the final year of the war when they changed side and fought for the Allies.[39] Military campaigns in 1978 and 1991 forced more than 450,000 Rohingya out of the country with systematic arson and murders.[40] There was communal violence in 2012 that left many dead in the Rakhine State and over 100,000 displaced.

Many, including President Thein Sein, refer to them as Bengalis, and think that since they are intruders from Bangladesh, they are subject to deportation.[41] This resulted in a stark choice for the Rohingya in the fall of 2014, when the government announced to them, prove your family has lived here for more than 60 years (since independence) and qualify for second-class citizenship, or be placed in camps and face deportation.[42] This led to a flood of refugees fleeing the country, many with tragic results.

Attempts to escape have resulted in overcrowded boats at sea with no country willing to grant safe landing and hundreds dying when the boats capsized. A recent report from the BBC declared that a UN official had described the policy of the Burmese government's dealings with the Rohingya as "ethnic cleansing."[43] While both ethnic cleansing and genocide are being used to describe the treatment of the Rohingya, President Obama and Secretary of State John Kerry were very vocal in their support of the group. They were rebuffed to a surprising degree by Aung San Suu Kyi. Burma's most famous citizen now holds the title of State Counsellor, as the constitution prevents her from being president because her children are British. But her overwhelming victory in the country's 2015 election made her de facto head of the government. Her position on the Rohingya is to follow official military government policy. She avoids journalists and press conferences and when forced, says she believes the military is operating according to the "rule of law" in its Rakhine operations against the Rohingya.[44]

The government contends Rakhine are setting fire to their own homes, which is why so many images of fires are detected by various rights organizations and no visitors are allowed into the Rakhine state. Aung San Suu Kyi also said she would refuse to use the name Rohingya to refer to the people, a position the government takes, and the U.S. ambassador was advised to not use their name since the country does not recognize their existence.

Obama pointedly used the word in speeches in 2012, 2014, and 2015. In December 2016, a group of 11 Nobel Laureates as well as other philanthropists and activists wrote to the UN to express frustration with Aung San Suu Kyi and her failure to take action to help the Rohingya.[45]

# CHAPTER SIX: DRUCIE, BURMA, KAREN

Drucie Bathing is well known amongst the Burmese in the Denver community. She was born in Burma in 1965 and is ethnic Karen. From the beginning, hers was an unusual story. The Karen were at war with the government of Burma since independence from India as they hoped for an independent state. She says ethnic cleansing had been going on by Burmese in the government since the British left, but "They die in the jungle, nobody knows."[1] Drucie's life revolved around that conflict. Her father was a very prominent leader in the Karen resistance and they were Christians, like many other Karen. The group had sided with Britain throughout World War II, which put them at odds with the Burmese government until the final stages of the war. Drucie's connections with her father and the Karen resistance made her life in Burma constantly challenged by the heavy-handed state.

Drucie's father, Pado Ba Thin Sein, joined the Karen National Union (the KNU), when it was founded and went underground in 1949. The KNU was the leading Karen force in military and economic resistance, fighting against the Burmese government from independence until into the first decade of the new millennium. Drucie's father eventually served as the KNU's Secretary General from 1983 to 1999, and was Chairman from 2000 until he died in May of 2008.[2]

She says her grandfather and father's generations were educated and could speak English well. Her grandfather spoke in English when he was with her father and his five brothers because they were educated during British rule. She was raised by her mother in a teak house in a village most of the time, while her father remained hidden in the jungle. Drucie was an eager learner, but the situation made it difficult as she notes, "I was very nosy. I wanted to know things. The government didn't like that, never wanted you to know anything. You're supposed to be so dumb. They want to kill some people in front of you and maybe don't want you to know, or if you know you don't talk about it."

Drucie tells of the conditions surrounding her birth. Her mother was put under village arrest - they didn't allow her to go outside of the village. She would sneak out and meet Drucie's dad secretly in the jungle. The government knew she was doing this and would interrogate her, but learned little. They made her sign her name on a statement that said "I will never leave the village again." She was cautious though, so she would still sneak out. But when she came back, she would be pregnant. And then she would sneak out again and once again be pregnant upon return. Drucie says, "They know back then that they did not cheat, so they know she'd been sneaking out. My mother give birth in the dirt, in the field. Because she was hiding, she gave birth like that. Was lucky I was born in a village."

Drucie didn't actually meet her father until she was five. She recalls, "First time I met my dad, I remember the attack. I was very little. They came in attacking and I was hiding in a bunker." He spent his time in the jungle with the resistance hiding from the Burmese army. His wife lived on the border of Thailand and Burma. She later wrote a poem dramatically describing the day.

*Suddenly the horrified voice of my youngest aunt,*
*DaBoe, who lived across the street yelled*
*"The Burmese soldiers are coming!*
*They are at the edge of the rice field."*
*"Run to the bunker," my mother ordered.*
*The sounds of guns were bloodcurdling,*
*Their shells were falling like Monsoon rains.*
*We heard the crossing boots that passed by,*
*We listened and we waited,*

*We waited until there was silence.*
*We were safe for the time being*[3].

Drucie's aunt died in this attack and one of her uncles died in the area. They left the village in the1970s. From then on, they were moving three or four times per year, building new houses in each location, and seeing her father occasionally. "You don't have a stable place. You always move." This made her early education a challenge but she managed by attending what she describes as "backpacking school." This was the education method for young Karen children who were fleeing the Burmese government. Drucie explained that she went to school regularly, but "You study in the jungle, even when you are in the hiding place." The teaching was done by students who had completed the tenth grade, which meant high school. Students and teachers had to be ready to run at any time in case they were discovered. If attacked, "You run in the woods and you stay, teaching in the woods." This was a jungle production line, where "After you graduate from school you start teaching another student, and they graduate from grade ten." Like the backpacking schools, the Karen had backpacking clinics, where doctors and nurses would meet patients in the jungle to treat them without government awareness of their activities.

One day Drucie's mother told her children that they were moving to another village, as they did so often, and she was put in a cart. The next thing she remembered was being in someone's hut in a village and then walking down a road, with one eye closed. Drucie was walking through the jungle, holding her uncle's hand for guidance. She didn't bother to open her eyes because it was so dark and the night passed. The next morning she woke up by a riverside and was very sad and confused. Her first thought was, "What is this place? We had already move out from the village and we move like that so many times. But you know, I never cried."

Drucie, her siblings and mother continued until they reached a small bamboo hut where her father was waiting and the family was reunited. A new phase of her life was about to begin. Though the time would not be long, her father would have considerable influence over her. The family headed deep into the jungle and established a camp for the resistance. She learned from him that "You have to be happy with what you have and then look to those who are poorer than you who have less and see what you can do." It was a lesson that stuck into adulthood.

They were called away to a more established jungle location that housed the rebel headquarters. Drucie was 12 by that time, and for the first time she attended a regular school. Stability did not come with her father's new position at headquarters. When the army came close, they would tear things down and move to another remote location; Drucie recalls, "Our boys, the high school students, have to carry the gun to school to defend the school."[4] Learning to face fear was a part of the life young Drucie coped with during this time. There were tigers in the jungle that roared at night as well as internal worries and difficulties in the camp.

A special challenge and a new type of fear presented itself when her mother's medical complications, a result of living a life hiding in the jungle, away from professional medical care, left her deranged and hysterical for a time.

Drucie's mother had another baby, but this one died in her womb. The retained fetus eventually became physically septic and released toxins in her. She was hallucinating from it, a considerable stress on Drucie. Her mother demanded that she burn all of their clothes in her ravings. Drucie obliged.

Drucie was developing the character necessary for the role she would take on early. Struggle and suffering would be a part of it. Drucie says of the Burmese, "They don't really feel the pain because they didn't go through what we went through. You only feel it when someone cut you, when you know the pain."

She was a naturally curious person and few career options were available for women. Being a teacher or nurse seemed to be her choices, and she chose to become a teacher. She rose through the ranks of the Karen Women's Organization and married the son of another resistance leader when she was 20. They had two children, a boy, Len, and a girl, Mu. They were a successful young family in a poor country so they could afford babysitters, cooks, and drivers. Still, Drucie lived in fear. She was fatalistic from the time she moved to the resistance camp, saying, "If you want to be a leader in Burma, you have to consider yourself a dead person, because then you will be willing to fight."

She had grown into a woman in a resistance camp where tribes tried to hold off the autocratic rule of the military junta in power. According to her children, things changed in April 1995 when Burmese soldiers seized the jungle community where they were located, torched houses and shot the villagers. Drucie's daughter, Mu, said, "When you start hearing gunshots, the human instinct is to just run," and her son, Len, added that the only things their mother had time to grab were a Bible, some crackers and a bottle of water.[5]

This village had been their resistance headquarters and Drucie says the government continued to take over Karen land, piece by piece, and drive them to the border. Staying hidden was a challenge, as she described, "I was in the wood, the jungle, for months, no food. Every Sunday we would worship under a tree. Nothing to eat and I went into jungle and picked leaves." They were near starving and sick with diarrhea, but they carried on and Drucie built two refugee camps along the way while she was training at the border.

The incident in the village they refer to happened during the time there was a challenge to the dominance of the Karen movement by Drucie's father's KNU. The government-allied Democratic Karen Buddhist Army (DKBA), which protested the Christian domination of the KNU, successfully attacked its headquarters in 1994.[6]

The war had really come to her and she spent much time burying those who were shot or killed in some other way. "I bury so many people my whole life." She had taken on a leadership role and was directly involved with the Karen opposition forces, and buried soldiers and villagers who had been killed. She tried to give them all dignified burials, and prepared their appearance for its final resting, what she calls "open their faces." Of the many, she said, "There is a face that I'll never forget. He was a very handsome teenager, probably. I thought, Oh my God. Who is the mother?" It was just part of how she lived her life.

She had become resilient, or perhaps somewhat indifferent from all she had witnessed and experienced. Her comments are, "Was I really sad? Not really. Did I know how to cry? No." She also took her kids with her when she buried all these people in Burma and they were very young as they watched her "open" all the faces, as she prepared mutilated bodies quickly for burial with as much dignity as could be provided.

Years later when she began writing poetry she would relive these years in verse:

*Day in and out the invader dictator comes to conquer her land*
*He burns the children in midday sun and slaughters the father and son*
*She hops as fast as a calf with her head band white scarf*
*He seizes her on the shoulder, and drags her down on the ground*

Drucie husband was abusive and the marriage didn't last. She divorced him, then moved in with her sister and raised her children in a refugee camp on the Thai side of the Burma-Thailand border. She was becoming hardened by life. In her words, "For me, you cut me you don't get the blood."

Once she was in the camp troubles continued. Her sister received a call from someone who was asking for

Drucie, and threatened to kidnap her child. Her sister was concerned that Drucie had brought trouble with her. The refugee camp wasn't safe because the Burmese would cross the border and attack it.

She left the camp, took her children and moved to Mae Sot in western Thailand. She hoped to prevent her children from going through the kind of life she had led, but didn't know if she could protect them. She was a single mother and the Burmese government was actively hunting her. There were Karen leaders who wanted her to stay and keep up the fight, but her father, whose approval mattered most, agreed she should leave. He knew of an American who could help her. She says that there are many Burmese like her who don't want to leave, and to this day, she keeps going back and forth. Though she would like to return the government is not changing. Her view is, "The outsiders may think it's changed, but for us it has not. Aung San Suu Kyi is getting old and I think she try, but she can't control. She's Buddhist and it does matter." Drucie says the Buddhist dominated government has been killing Christians for years,[8] and warns, "After killing Rohingya, what is the next step? You have to watch. Wait and see."

She was interviewed by a Vietnam Vet as part of the resettlement program and she had to show that she was in danger. She had plenty of evidence she turned over. She had photos, including some in her camera, that she had taken from under a Burmese tank of soldiers destroying villages, killing villagers. She had hoped to use the photos to expose the Burmese military, but neither her camera nor her photos or the film in the camera with more pictures were ever returned to her. She also revealed how her life had been endangered several times. She was asked about her father, about the first president of Burma, whom the interviewer was especially interested in because of having attended the same college or something similar. The result was that Drucie was approved to come to the U.S., and it sounded like expedited placement, since it was to happen in about three-and-a-half months. It was also determined that her life was in danger in her present surroundings, and she was to be placed farther south in the large city of Bangkok for safety purposes.

Drucie and her children were put in an apartment in Bangkok, where they remained from 1997 into1999. She was certain she was being watched by Burma's government all of that time. People would often come to their door, and she believes they "thought she was a Karen spy." She was also convinced that her "life was in danger" to a degree that was somewhere between fear and paranoia. She now has some apprehension over how she treated her children during this time. For the entire period of two-and-a-half years she went to Thai school on Saturdays and church on Sundays, but the children were never allowed to leave the apartment. After their early life of witnessing burials then confining them to years without interaction with peers, she is concerned about what she put them through.

In 1999 Drucie and her children flew from Thailand to be resettled and Drucie cried. For the first time. She recalls, "I cried only one time, when I came to the U.S." She realized she could no longer live in denial, and that she was truly exiled. "You know, because when you live in denial, you hold the hope that you always live in Burma, you think you live in Burma. Even when you live on Thai side you sneak back and forth." Once she was on the airplane and was exiled, she accepted it. She hasn't been happy about it. As she says, "I listen to the news, 'refugee, refugee,' who wants to be a refugee? Nobody. Don't you want to be in a place where you don't want to eat cheese? They speaking different from you, they look different from you."

Coming to the U.S. was not some dream come true. She was leaving her home and about to become a real stranger. They arrived in their new home, East Lyme, Connecticut. But Drucie jumped right in and started her new life. She began with English and GED classes and took low-paying work at a Motel 6, Burlington Coat Factory, and had a job at a daycare center. As her English and education improved, she was ready to try college and attended Eastern Connecticut State University, where she majored in history and took up writing poetry. In 2008, she had her college degree and was working part time with a refugee resettlement agency. She had another unsuccessful relationship that resulted in another child, and soon after came the death of the one critical man in her life, her father. Her decision that it was time to move on coincided with Colorado's decision to hire someone to communicate with the major influx of refugees it was receiving from Burma.[9]

Drucie is described by Melanie Asmar as "petite, with sweeping bangs and straight black hair that she pulls back. She laughs easily and warms up quickly."[10] She fit the Denver area scene well, and formed the Colorado Rangers Organization with the purpose of bringing the tribes together, including the Muslim Rohingya. The same ethnic divisions that exist in Burma were transported to the U.S. when refugees came, and can be seen when there are concentrations, such as in Colorado. She tells them, "This is America, not Burma. If you cannot talk to each other, how can you talk to the white people, the African- American, the Hispanic?" She says she finds younger people who have spent more of their lives in the U.S. are considerably easier to convince that intermixing among Burmese is the way to be when living in America.

Drucie has concerns for her community since Donald Trump was elected, "I wonder about this president." She studied history and learned about the Ku Klux Klan, remembers crying in the classroom when she studied the Holocaust, and about the Native Americans. She says that people asked her, "What's wrong with you?" She recalls learning about how the Americans put the Japanese in internment camps and her friends said, "You don't need to worry about that, Drucie. That isn't going to happen again." Drucie added, "And if I came here earlier,

I don't think I can sit down. I think I have to stand up; I think thank God to the African-Americans, I can sit down." She says she sees those attitudes coming back, that she sees them posted online. In her words, "I think a lot of Americans; they don't know their history because they don't focus on their history. I think I understand, with so many of the immigrants that come in here, they think we don't want anyone coming here."

For Drucie, the anti-refugee talk is personal. She was stateless before she came to the U.S. "I was not born in Burma; I was not given identity. This is my first country. If you kick me back, I don't know anybody, so I worry."

# CHAPTER SEVEN: GRANDMA ESTER, BURMA

Ester was a midwife in her village in Burma. She was happy delivering babies and had two of her own. She lived in the Karen State and her son was involved in the resistance. When the Burmese crackdown came, the army tried to arrest her son but he was away at the front line. They then attempted to capture his wife, but she escaped. That left Ester with their children, her three grandchildren, so she took care of them and brought them to school.

The army didn't give up easily. Since Ester's son and wife were away, they ended up arresting her and the oldest of her grandchildren. She was in prison for eight months with her granddaughter. Ester says, "They put me in jail, because they wanted to make sure my son would come back to come for me, but my son didn't come."[1] The army arrested Ester as bait to attempt to capture her son. They were also convinced that she could provide information about her son that she did not possess.

After being arrested Ester wasn't allowed to eat. She first went three days without food as the army hoped word of her detention would get to her son. Then they let her write a letter they would take to the villagers where she lived to say that they could bring her food. The villagers began sneaking her some food soon after but even the letter had a qualification. To take the letter to a relative of hers in the village, she was told she needed to pay them 100 kyat, (Burmese money).

Burma's weather can be very hot, and after Ester had been locked up for a bit she wanted to take a bath. She asked the guards, but she says they did not dare grant her permission. Ester was not easily deterred. She said to them, "If you will not, or do not dare to give me permission, can you go talk to somebody who is in charge of the cell? Can you tell them that the grandmother wants to talk to you?" She was in a strong position compared to some, as Burman tradition values respect for elders, along with respect for parents, respect for teachers, and respect for those in authority.[2]

Her assertiveness was successful and someone came in to tell her that she and the rest of the women would be allowed to take a bath. She recalls there were more than ten other women and this was rural Burma, where taking a bath meant washing yourself in a stream or river. Ester describes it as, "They let us go like animals, like cows go together in a group, and we go to take a bath. And we came back and we ask, where do we hang our clothes? (They had bathed in their clothes to wash them as well). And they told us to just put it on the ground, on the grass. So, we just put it on the ground to let it dry. And after six o'clock they let us out so we could get our dry clothes." A small victory.

Many days later Ester asked them, "Why did you lock me up like this? I was not your enemy. Why don't you go find your own enemy and kill them? I was not your enemy." The Karen resistance cause was her son's cause, not hers. Her role in life was a different one, and she thought she was being punished for something that had nothing to do with her. Again, she was not willing to hold back on expressing her feelings. Ester said, "Why did you do this to me? I was a mother, I gave birth to my children. You, too, are a parent. Make sure you do not give birth to children, because when you give birth, because when your children grow older, then they follow their mission. So now because of my kid, I have to suffer like this." That brought laughs from everybody.

Following that, the intelligence officers, the soldiers and guards were all coming to visit her, and they called her "mother." She remembers, "They tell me, 'Mother, you live a good life, you pray, you don't curse'." Her response was that the reason they told her she didn't curse was because she had said to them, 'You, too, you have your wife and she gives birth. So, when your wife gives birth, you expect something good, Then, you end up in jail because you have a child'. Again, she made them laugh. They soon told her that they would be releasing her. She asked what she had done wrong that she should have to be in jail for eight months, but received no reply.

Her oldest granddaughter, who had been in her care and arrested with her, had been released after seven months in jail. One of Ester's relatives was a leader for the village, and since the girl's parents were gone and Ester was in jail they let her granddaughter stay there.

The army plan to capture Ester's son by taking her prisoner had clearly failed by this point, and she was returned to her village. She lived there quietly from 2001 to 2003. Then there was an incident carried out by the rebel forces and they came after her again. This time, it would be a more serious effort but she was still unaware of her son's whereabouts or activities. Ester was once again in trouble for being his mother.

There was a bomb explosion in a Burmese station and army suspected her son was involved. Ester was arrested again but not taken to the same jail as before. This time she was shipped far away to a more specialized facility in the west. She didn't see ordinary soldiers, only intelligence officers and their families. Things seemed to begin in threes. Again, she was not allowed food for three days. There were three intelligence soldiers who came in to interrogate her. Each one came in each day for three days. They apparently were unsuccessful, so after the initial three days they came again. Each of them would ask her the same questions with different phrasing or words.

They also were using enhanced interrogation techniques on Grandma Ester. They covered her face with a blindfold and covered her head with a black plastic hood.[3] She describes more: "They kick me, they're making the noise like they're getting ready to shoot me. I hear the sound of the clickety-clack, clickety-clack, and I'm asking, what did you do to me?" They tried to intimidate her and trick her with noise of guns near her head and strange machines. They would also take her hands and make her walk very fast, saying "let's go, 'let's go," even though she could not move faster. She was despondent to the point, "I told them, don't do this to me. If you think I make a mistake or something, just kill me." She witnessed as well as experienced the harsh treatment, commenting, "I saw them torture a lot of people. Those officers, they would kick them and they would hit them. They cover people with the plastic bag and they have them dive in the water."

Things didn't get better. When she was interrogated, officers would order the elderly woman to "stand here" and answer questions concerning things she knew nothing about, because she had no way of knowing. When she told them she didn't know and that she had never seen the resistance forces personally, they called her a liar. Ester did tell them, "The only thing I know is the people who carry the guns, they are the soldiers. I told them I don't know the Karen rank. I don't know the Karen leader. All I know is from the top to the bottom, everybody eat the same food, wear the same clothes. They don't have power. They don't have specific brigades like you. All I know, the Karen soldiers, they will set up the hut underneath a tree, then after a few months they will go another place. And they move around a lot like that."

The interrogators then informed her that they had been keeping written records of what she said, to see if she would contradict herself. Ester's response was, "Why don't you just kill me? I don't want to go through this. If you think I make a mistake, then just kill me."

She made that request repeatedly. She told her interrogators, "If you arrest me, I die. If I live, I live. By arresting me, you don't have more enemy, you don't have less enemy. Then why you arresting me? I tell them, you arrest me; I didn't do anything wrong. You arrest me because of my son. Because of my son, this is the kind of suffering I have to go through. And I told them my daughter-in-law, she is not a bad person. But because of my son, she is afraid of them, and so she run away from the country because she want to escape. I think of how I am suffering because of my children."

One person took note of Ester and surreptitiously took her side and showed some kindness. It was the wife of the leader at the center, the head interrogator. She brought Ester something to eat, and told her that she had wanted to bring her some food because Ester was very old. She had been afraid to because she knew that the leader would not want people bringing food to those being interrogated. She said she knew that Ester didn't do anything wrong so she had decided to bring her something to eat. Ester saw the woman later and asked how much longer she would be detained there. "She said, 'You leave in probably two or three more days. She tell me don't tell anybody about this information. And I know other people will not be free.'"

After spending a month at this location Ester learned the commander's wife was correct. She was released shortly after their brief conversation. They hadn't learned anything from her, as there was nothing she knew that was secret information about the Karen or about her son. Even her final encounter with the guards was a partial change. "And when the soldiers came to my door they would kick it hard, scare you. This time they opened it nicely. They said we will let you free. They put me in the car and they still cover my face."

Though she was released, she wasn't free. Ester was sent to another intelligence facility, where the person in charge greeted her with, "Oh, I thought they killed you already." The intelligence officers hadn't given up. Interrogation and another attempt to capture her son began again. They told her to "rest here and we can talk."

This was less austere and intimidating, a new approach. They offered her water and asked about how she supervised her kids when they were little. She told them that like every mother, she wanted her kids to grow up and to be good. She sent them to school, she sent them to church. By the time they had grown older, her son had become a man with his own family, he decided his own mission. She was told to write a letter to her son to tell him to come home. So, Ester wrote the letter.

When it arrived at the village leader's house, they knew that the Burmese wanted to catch the rebels, so they just hid the letter. After waiting for two weeks and seeing that her son did not return, they came to Ester again to tell her that, and question her on why. Ester says she asked them where they sent the letter and they said they had sent it to her younger sister. (There's some confusion here but perhaps that is the person to whom she addressed it.) Ester said she asked them why they sent it there, and that they should have sent it to somebody who had responsibility like the village leader. Later on, her jailers said that they had not received any news from Ester's son so they wondered what she wanted them to do with her, as they seemed to be giving up on her usefulness. She told them, "What kind of question is that? You captured me. If you kill me, I die, if you let me go, I'm free. What kind of question you asking me like that?"

They told her she was being released and asked where she wanted to be sent. She said she wanted to be returned to her village and they agreed to take her there.

Ester's ordeal with prisons had finally come to an end but it was uncertain. It was a joyful homecoming, as she relates, "I was back in the village on Sunday so all the people were there, 'Oh Grandma come home, Grandma come home!' Everybody was happy." For the three days following her return to the village, intelligence officers would make daily visits to her house. They came in the day; they came in the night. That was too much for Ester. Her decision was made. "I was so disappointed. I knew if anything happened I would be arrested. I secretly sent out everything from my house. I left. I move here, I moved there, always changing locations." Once she had her things shipped out, she crossed the border and left Burma. Ester became a refugee in 2005 and ended in a refugee camp in Thailand, beginning the process that would bring "Grandma" to Denver. This is now home to this gentle, elderly woman.

# CHAPTER EIGHT: RHETORIC

There has long been confusion and fear of the "outsiders" who weren't what some considered true Americans, meaning white, Anglo-Saxon Protestants. Catholics have become acceptable, but nativism has been on the rise as "America first equals patriotism" appeals to many who have felt they were suffering from globalization. Resources and investment have been devoted beyond the country's borders while jobs have migrated to areas where labor costs are lower. Many newcomers have entered the country and there are suspicions and fear of the potential dangers they pose.

This was used for political advantage by Donald Trump, who famously tweeted of Mexicans early in his presidential campaign, "They're bringing drugs. They're bringing crime. They're rapists. And some, I assume, are good people."[1] At a New Hampshire campaign rally, he said that he would deport the Syrian refugees currently in the U.S. if he became president, telling supporters, "If I win, they're going back."[2] He followed that with a more basic appeal to the lowest common denominator with "Donald J. Trump is calling for a total and complete shutdown of Muslims entering the United States."[3] As the campaign went on, he appeared to step back a bit from a total Muslim ban to advocating a ban on allowing immigrants or refugees from countries with ties to terrorism. His son and advisor, Donald Trump Jr., attracted attention when he posted a message on Twitter that compared Syrian refugees to a bowl of Skittles sprinkled with a few that "would kill you."[4]

At the end of his first week in office, President Trump issued Executive Order 13769,[5] banning Syrian refugees from entry into the U.S. and included a list of seven Muslim countries for which entry was suspended for 90 days. This was met by massive protests and rallies and condemnation from Republicans as well as Democrats, along with immediate court challenges which soon ended it. That was a temporary ending. On March 6th, the president issued a second ban in which Iraq was eliminated from the list of countries,[6] but it soon met the same fate in court as the first and was suspended. The Supreme Court gave the ban partial approval but a final decision comes in in the fall. The effect on the refugee community has been chilling, as the bans were accompanied by calls for massive deportations and few felt comfortable, though many community meetings and rallies were held to offer reassurance.

Some of the language sounded surprising, as though fringe talk from extremists was being voiced in inappropriate places. The talk was nothing new. Warnings of the dangers of letting in foreigners has been common practice throughout the nation's history. "The boast that our country is the asylum for the oppressed in other parts of the world is very philanthropic and sentimental, but I fear that we shall before long derive little comfort from being made the almshouse and place of refuge for the poor of other countries," said the Mayor of New York City in the 1830s.[7] Eighty years later when Woodrow Wilson had begun his first term as president, he said, "Some Americans need hyphens in their names because only half of them came over."[8] Ten years later the Speaker of the House spoke about immigration and said, "I am not here as having one vote in the national legislature to shut the door in the face of any one of the Caucasian race that are willing to come, whether they be educated or uneducated"[9] These statements would be likely to appeal to some voters today. The Supreme Court also spoke to a current issue with clarity that refugees might find frightening. In 1912, noted jurist Oliver Wendell Holmes, Jr. wrote, "It is thoroughly established that Congress has power to order the deportation of aliens whose presence in the country it deems hurtful...nor is the deportation a punishment; it is simply a refusal by the government to harbor persons whom it does not want."[10]

This Court ruling has special meaning following President Trump's determination to "secure the border" by hiring 15,000 new immigration enforcement agents and border patrol officers to get tough on illegal immigrants. Increased raids followed that announcement, again bringing fear to refugees and other immigrants, many of whom are citizens, out of the lack of specifics and certainty of what will follow.

There are several general fears about immigrants and refugees that a segment of the population shares but evidence doesn't suggest there is reason for these views, any more than there had been for the views of previous newcomers to America's shores. In Grover Cleveland's words, "It is said that the quality of recent immigration is undesirable. The time is quite within recent memory when the same thing was said of immigrants who, with their descendants, are now numbered among our best citizens."[11]

The common arguments against accepting refugees and also other immigrants are that they represent a threat to the nation, that terrorists are sneaking in (this commonly refers to Muslims, but many are not very discriminating, and apply this to "others," those who look and speak differently). The appointment of Steve Bannon as the president's chief strategist and, for a time, a member of the National Security Council, has heightened this concern, which has been found to be without merit.[12] There is also a worry that refugees don't work and depend on welfare, or the U.S. tax payer, for support. Anxiety about refugees committing crime is sometimes a concern. Another idea is that they work for low wages and are stealing jobs from U.S. workers. During the presidential campaign, Donald Trump said that he would put an end to "low-skilled immigration that continues to reduce jobs and wages for American workers."[13] He also made that argument to minority voters at a rally that refugees and people living in the U.S. illegally "take jobs from hardworking African-Americans and Hispanic citizens."[14]

The website for Donald Trump continued to state, "Donald J. Trump is calling for a total and complete shutdown of Muslims entering the United States until our country's representatives can figure out what is going on," until May 8, 2017. It was deleted following a reporter questioning White House Press Secretary Sean Spicer about why it remained there at a press conference. That press conference was on the day the case of the president's second travel ban began in a federal appeals court in Virginia.[15]

One concern that gets conflated with undocumented workers is the threat of refugees as dangerous criminals. Donald Trump campaigned on the threat of immigrant crime and, after being elected, he created an office in the Department of Homeland Security called VOICE, for Victims of Immigration Crime Engagement, to publicize crime committed by immigrants, and the safety threats created by sanctuary cities. He singled out immigrants as criminals despite studies regularly showing that refugees and immigrants are less likely to commit crimes than native born Americans.[16] The House of Representatives passed two laws aimed at illegal immigrants in late June, 2017. One was "Kate's Law," named for Kathryn Steinle, who was shot and killed by a repeat felon and undocumented immigrant from Mexico who had been deported several times. The other was the "No Sanctuary for Criminals Act" that would increase penalties on undocumented immigrants who attempted to reenter the country illegally after being deported and cut government funds that sanctuary cities receive. Fox News, a traditional supporter of President Trump, reported, "In reality, illegal immigrants have lower incarceration rates and live in places with lower crime rates than native-born Americans."[17]

The president's economic arguments about refugees and other immigrants taking American jobs were addressed by the U.S. Chamber of Commerce, which shares his concern with high employment, and they were all found to be without merit.[18] Academic research supports this, finding immigration and refugees have little or no negative effects on overall wages and employment and wages of native-born workers in the longer term, and a positive impact from comes from skilled immigrants. First generation immigrants, including refugees, annually cost the government about $57 billion, but in the second generation they are contributing $30 billion. The third-generation families' yearly addition to the government's budget is about $223 billion,[19] so they become a considerable benefit.

As for protecting the country from terrorist attacks, as has been reported on many sites, there has not been a single death in America caused by an act of terrorism committed by a refugee since the Refugee Act of 1980 was passed.[20]

The economic impact of the rhetoric is real. According to recent news stories, 40% of colleges and universities reported a decline in applications from foreign students in March 2017 when acceptances were being sent out. *Time* cited a survey that found the factors international students listed for declined interest in studying in the US were presidential administration (69%), travel restrictions (55%) - personal safety in enrollment from overseas will have an economic impact. An official from the group that organized the survey said, "There's an overall perception that the climate in the U.S. is less welcoming for international students."[21]

A report in *Inside Higher Ed* listed the following as the major concerns foreign students had about coming to the U.S.: a) perception of a rise in student visa denials at U.S. embassies and consulates in China, India and Nepal; b) perception that the climate in the U.S. is now less welcoming to individuals from other countries; c) concerns that benefits and restrictions around visas could change, especially around the ability to travel, re-entry after travel and employment opportunities; and d) concerns that the executive order travel ban might expand to include additional countries.[22]

While these reports were not about refugees, they indicate the effect that anti-refugee/anti-immigrant oratory has had, and the fears inspired by executive orders for travel bans. While this may appeal to a segment of society, it has been frightening to those who had seen America as the beacon of hope and freedom. The rhetoric matters, and it is frightening away some the U.S. would like to attract, as well as intimidating others who already arrived legally and are seeking to be productive and beneficial members of society.

# CHAPTER NINE, HLIANG MOE, BURMA, BAMAR

Hliang Moe Than is Bamar, or ethnic Burmese, who are also referred to as Burman. This is the group that makes up about two-thirds of the population and controls the military and the government. This makes his story as a refugee a bit unusual. While there have been many refugees coming in from Burma, they have mainly been from the ethnic groups who have fled the powerful Burmese who were in control.

His is the story of one who objected to the policies of the government and suffered for expressing his opinions in a country where such behavior is very much discouraged. In 2007, the country ranked last in the world for its allowance of its citizen's freedom of expression and it has consistently held a low spot for decades.[1]

Hliang Moe was teaching engineering and technology students in the capital city of Rangoon in 1988 when an uprising broke out against the socialist government. There were early protests in the spring to demand an end to one-party rule that were dealt with harshly and the government closed the universities. Students and pro-democracy supporters planned a nationwide demonstration for August 8, 1988, auspiciously named "8888." General Ne Win had taken power saying his "Burmese Way to Socialism" would lead the country to become one of the fast-developing Asian Tigers, but it was among the world's poorest counties.

On August 10, the state-run radio announced that 1,451 "looters and disturbance-makers" had been arrested, and 12 days later 100,000 protested in Mandalay. Four days after that Aung San Suu Kyi, who was in Rangoon on a visit from Oxford to see her sick mother, first entered the political arena. She gave a speech before 500,000 people at the Shwedagon Pagoda and urged the crowd to use non-violent means. She became the symbol for the struggle for democracy in Burma.[2]

Hliang Moe was one of those involved in the protest at this time. He recalls, "I was an advocate for the democracy and human rights when I was inside Burma."[3] On September 18 there was a military coup, and the State Law and Order Restoration Council (SLORC) was established. The new government announced that it had taken power "in order to bring a timely halt to the deteriorating conditions on all sides of the country." Over 1,000 students, monks and school children were killed in the first week they took power and by the end of the month the number had reached 3,000.[4]

Hliang Moe's fate wasn't as bad as some, but he was arrested and spent six months in prison for being a participant. After he was released he became more involved in politics and became an activist against the regime. Soon he was in more serious trouble: "They arrest me on December 10, 1991."

At that time, Aung San Suu Kyi was awarded the Nobel Peace Prize, and Hliang Moe supported the prize winner against the military government, but it was costly: "They arrest me, and sentenced me to 15 years in prison. We were demonstrating, just peacefully demonstrating. And I have to stay in the prison for a long time." That is a very long time to be sentenced to a Burmese prison when his crime was protesting peacefully.

He describes being incarcerated by the military junta, "Prison is like hell. Every day is really, really bad and really hard for me. To pass one day is like to climb a very steep, high mountain." Hliang Moe thinks that spending what would end up being ten years in prison in Burma turned him into a tougher person, because he went through so much degradation and suffering. He sees it as a sort of

Nietzsche "That which does not kill us makes us stronger" positive in his life. In his words, "I think my prisoner life when I was in Burma make me more mature. I can stand so many kinds of pressure, and stressful condition. So, my personal life got, I had so many kind of personal problems before that I could say, 'no matter, so what,' because my prison life made me stronger. It was like a very good exercise for me. Because, when I had to face hard situation here, I think, already I faced prison inside Burma. I can take it."

Hliang Moe was released after ten years in prison, but hadn't given up on his beliefs. He was "involved in the politics very secretly, because the situation is really dangerous." Then came 2007 and the Saffron Revolution. This was the really big protest against the regime and trouble soon found Hliang Moe.

"At that time, I was a leader. They also tried to arrest me again. The police and military intelligence, they followed me everywhere. In my house, at my friends' houses, at my relatives' houses, everywhere." This proved to be too much for Hliang Moe and he decided to leave the country rather than risk returning to prison.

In October 2007, he became a refugee and fled to Thailand. He stayed in a small town near the Burmese border where he lived in Mae Sot township and unlike most refugees, didn't go to the refugee camp. At that time, his situation was apparently considered unusually perilous and he was granted resettlement status very quickly. He said, "I have to stay in Thailand for five, six months. Came to the U.S. in March 2008." How he was processed so quickly while some spent decades waiting for an assignment is uncertain, though it has been reported that the Department of State does fast-track individual cases, and might have considered him in imminent danger. However, there was no publicly available written policy or procedure that described such a procedure when he was resettled from Thailand after leaving Burma.[5]

He was not given a choice in location and was taken, then flown to a destination and dropped off. He was in Buffalo, New York and it was 2008. He arrived as the economic crisis hit and "the economic situation, it was very bad in the United States." He was also totally confused, "I don't even know how to buy at the vending machine. Everything. I have to learn a lot." The Catholic Authorities had accepted him as their client and he said they had very good programs, but they didn't suit him. He mentioned, "They have some refugee school that is really low level. Children, they don't know A to Z, they start teaching. It was not for me." While he had been in prison, he spent much of his time learning English and read the full dictionary from beginning to end. So, once he arrived he was better off than many, "except my pronunciation, my accent is not so good."

Hliang Moe spent two-and-a-half years in Buffalo and finally decided it wasn't the place for him. He chose to move to Denver, where he stayed within his own community. He points out that the roles are reversed, now that he is a resettled refugee, coming from where the Burmese were the majority and dominant, stating, "I am Burmese, we are a minority. Ethnic groups are the majority here." He is active with the Burmese community in Colorado, which he said now numbers around 3,000 people, though state records put the number closer to 4,000.[6] Hliang Moe noted that the refugees from Burma remain within ethnic groups when they relocate here, and that Aurora is a big hub. Aurora is a major city in the Denver metropolitan area.

His move to Denver was a successful one and he thinks that many Burmese refugees feel likewise. Cold weather is a new experience and a challenge for many refugees who resettle from tropical regions like Burma. Hliang Moe noted that and said, "Here, it is a little bit cold. We have to adjust by ourselves to the weather. But most of our people really like it here, in Denver. We have good opportunities for the job and we have good opportunities for the second generation." This point is a reoccurring one, that the sacrifices and hardships refugees endure are often for their children to have opportunities that they never had. He brought up the number of refugee children attending the Denver public schools or Aurora public schools that might go on to the colleges or universities. "We are hoping for our second generation, not first"

He also is an advocate for Burmese refugees who lack education and skills, and manage to contribute and do what they can. As he says, "They don't need to speak, they don't need to write, they just need to work with the machine, something like that. It is very hard for them but they are very hard workers."

Hliang Moe's reception in the Denver area has been fairly good, he thinks. Like many refugees and immigrants, he became a driver for Uber, while many drive for Lyft. This brought the observation that, "When I was driving Uber, some of my passengers would ask me, 'Why do you come here?' something like that. I would honestly answer, 'I came here as a refugee.' Most of the people say okay. They even gave me tips when they know I came here as a refugee. So in my opinion, I think in Denver it's okay, but I don't know all over the United States."

His story began nearly 30 years ago when Hliang Moe was teaching engineering and technology.

This points up another problem that is common for well-educated refugees and immigrants when they come to America: although they may have graduated from universities or received credentials for specialized training in the countries of their birth, those credentials are often not accepted once they resettle in the U.S. Many end up in jobs below the level of status and educational qualifications that they had held in the country they were forced to abandon.

In Hliang Moe's case, it wasn't just driving for Uber. He said, "Here they did not accept my degree from Burma. I work at Denver Public School as an assistant teacher, not a real teacher for five years, because they don't accept my degree." He gave up on that after five years and worked for the Postal Service as a carrier associate, which he described as also a rather demanding job.

Hliang Moe suggests the West does not understand the internal situation with Burma and the ethnic groups, particularly the Rohingya, though as a Buddhist, he still lays the blame on British imperialism. "For the Civil War of Burma, we got some bad heritage from the British colony. They ruled the country with a divided rule." He contends that the army's power derives from that, and while civilian groups became weaker and weaker, the military grew stronger and stronger. "Because of the war, you know, the generals have more power than the ordinary people. So that's why we want to make peace among the ethnic groups."

While the treatment of the Rohingya has shocked the western world[7] and Aung San Suu Kyi coming under criticism for her failure to act on their behalf, Hliang Moe views the situation differently. He believes Aung San Suu Kyi doesn't have true power and has to negotiate with the army. He says that outsiders don't understand Burma and that the media can say whatever it wants because they have no responsibilities. That brings him back to the Rohingya, which he sees as a western media-hyped story. His view is, "The Rohingya, problem, we are thinking about the Rohingya, problem. It is not at the very first, or in the middle. It might be at the very last." For Hliang Moe the problem with Burma is the need to reunite the country and change from a military regime to a country with democracy and human rights.

While the ethnic groups may not view this the same way, his struggle really remains with the military junta that rules the country.

For now, Hliang Moe works to keep Burmese heritage alive in Denver and encourage young people to continue their education while being involved with Buddhism in the area. He has a son whom he wants to receive his education in the U.S., but he says he is "dreaming every day" of returning to Burma.

He has modified that to "back and forth," since the country has made so little progress on the road to the ideals for which he spent ten years in jail.

# CHAPTER TEN: WHO IS AN AMERICAN?

It has been an uneven path for refugees and other immigrants since the inspirational words about "Give me your tired, your poor..." were written. Refugees frequently comment on how happy it makes them to become U.S. citizens, proud to be Americans. The current arguments about the dangers of welcoming refugees and immigrants to the U. S. have been heard many times over the years.

The path for new arrivals has been an uneven one since the inspirational words were written and the debate over who deserves to be called a U.S. citizen has existed since the nation was founded. The original 13 colonies were British and dominated by white male Protestants from England and other Northern European countries. They were Americans.

Inequality was enshrined in the founding of the Republic. While most can recall Thomas Jefferson's profound statement of equality that opens the *Declaration of Independence*, "We hold these truths to be self-evident, that all men are created equal," less attention is given to his enumeration of complaints against King George III, which included: "He has excited domestic insurrections amongst us, and has endeavored to bring on the inhabitants of our frontiers, the merciless Indian Savages."[1] Jefferson, who owned over 180 slaves when he declared all were created equal and later increased that number to 267[2], also assumed that the country's original inhabitants were not among the "all." The *Constitution* included its famous three-fifths clause which not only rejected African-Americans as citizens but reduced them to less than complete humans. It states: "Representatives and direct Taxes shall be apportioned among the several States which may be included within this Union, according to their respective Numbers, which shall be determined by adding to the whole Number of free Persons, including those bound to Service for a Term of Years, and excluding Indians not taxed, three fifths of all other Persons."[3]

In the original Thirteen Colonies, nearly a fifth (19.3%) were slaves and when the new country first passed a naturalization law in 1790, that stated applicants were only eligible if they were "free white persons."[4]

Citizenship is defined nowhere in the Constitution and the only discussion in the original concerns "natural citizen" as a requirement to be President of the United States.[5] Civic guarantees and responsibilities were left primarily up to states until the Fourteenth Amendment was ratified after the Civil War, guaranteeing all citizens basic rights.

There was little immigration to the United States during the first half century of the nation's existence,[6] and if regulated at all, it was by states, rather than the federal government, until many years later. Anti-immigrant talk was entering the national conversation in the 1830s when numbers increased, taking many of its forms that have remarkable parallels to today's talk. Telegraph inventor Samuel Morse wrote a series of articles for the *New York Observer* and an 1835 book *Imminent Dangers to the Free Institutions of the United States Through Foreign Immigration, and the Present State of the Naturalization Laws.*[7] In Morse's writings one can hear similarities with Donald Trump's December 7, 2015 call to ban all Muslims from entering the U.S.[8] Morse contended there was a papal plot to overpopulate the US with Catholics who would take over the country, undermine liberty and impose rule by Rome. He argued that Protestants should overcome their religious differences and unite against Catholics, Catholic schools and weak immigration laws, and cooperate together against Catholic office holders. It was a threat to the nation and Morse said, "We must first stop this leak in the ship through which the muddy waters from without threaten to sink us."[9]

Two years later Maria Monk wrote a book that sold hundreds of thousands of copies and stoked fears of the dangers of Catholicism, though it was entirely false. She claimed she was a former nun who learned of the evils of Catholicism when she entered a convent. Her book asserted that in the convent nuns were forced to submit to sex with priests, after which the babies that resulted were strangled and taken to the convent basement and buried. She escaped when she became pregnant and hoped to save her child, and was rescued by a kindly Protestant minister.[10]

Scare tactics about a "foreign" religion changing America began when overseas changes brought a large influx of refugees and immigrant to the U.S. shores. Economic crisis and political unrest that culminated in the revolutions of 1848 throughout the German states sent 1.4 million Germans to the U.S. between 1841 and 1860.[11] A big inflow of refugees came from Ireland. Acre after acre of the Irish countryside was covered with black rot from 1845 to 1849 as a fungus destroyed the potatoes that were the staple of the Irish diet. Soon the Great Rot caused the Great Famine and the desperation was such that the dead were sometimes found by roadsides with grass in their mouths, as the lack of food had reduced them to eating weeds. In villages, the poor grew weak from hunger whilst cholera and typhus spread, eliminating entire populations. In a country of eight million, more than 1.5 million died, while many emigrated, with nearly 1.7 million Irish fleeing to take refuge in the U.S. between 1841 and 1860.[12]

This flood of immigrants and refugees, many of whom were Catholics, heightened the political consequences that sound familiar today. Fear of outsiders and their strange religion, with its leadership in Rome, led to political action. For the first time in history, the U.S. had a third political party. It began as a secret society with secret passwords, handshakes, promises to never betray the order, and an initiation rite called "Seeing Sam" (for Uncle Sam). The group was made up of pureblooded Anglo-Saxon Protestants and when asked about who they were by nonmembers, their response was "I know nothing." In 1853, they transformed into a political party called the American Party but came to be called the Know Nothings. The new party advocated an elimination of all Catholics from public office, a 21-year naturalization period for immigrants, deportation of foreign beggars and criminals, mandatory Bible reading in public schools, and an America that enshrined as its highest values, Protestantism, self-reliance and a work-ethic.[13] On this basis by the late 1850s Know Nothing candidates had been elected as eight governors, 100 congressmen, and held the controlling share of half-dozen state legislatures, plus thousands of local political offices.[14]

During the late 1850s, the Dred Scott decision and John Brown abolitionist raid made it clear that slavery overwhelmed all other issues including immigration. This would also bring an end to the Know Nothings in the 1860s. Members of the party in the South and North splintered over slavery. The nativist position they supported would reappear frequently in the years that followed.

In 1875, the Supreme Court also declared regulation of immigration was a federal responsibility and some legislation began to be passed. This coincided with concern in California about the many Chinese who had come during the gold rush leading to what was called the "yellow terror." H.N. Clement expressed this fear in the California State Senate, warning, "The Chinese are upon us. How can we get rid of them? The Chinese are coming. How can we stop them? We have a great right to say to the half-civilized subject from Asia, You shall not come at all."[15] Arguments against the presence of a growing Chinese population in America were that they were permanently alien, threatening, and inferior on the basis of their race, culture, labor, and aberrant gender relations. These proved persuasive and on May 6, 1882, Congress passed The Chinese Exclusion Act[16] and introduced a "gatekeeping" ideology into law to restrict who could come to America based on race and class, ideas that echo to the present. The law was upheld by the Supreme Court later in the decade in *Chan Chae Ping v. United States.*[17]

1880 is the date used for the beginning of the "new immigration" which was spurred by rapid urbanization and industrialization. Earlier immigrants and refugees had come mainly from Northern and Western Europe and with the exception of the Irish they had been predominantly Protestant. In the years from 1880 to 1920, the U. S. took in over 20 million immigrants and most of the new arrivals came from Eastern Europe or Central of the South, and were mainly Jews fleeing religious persecution or Catholics. The maximum came in 1907 when 1.3 million entered the country legally.[18] 1907 was also the year when another "yellow terror" further restricted Asian immigration by the "Gentleman's Agreement" with Japan.

What would prove to be the greatest challenge to both immigrants and refugees would be an idea born in Europe that was adopted by the United States during the Progressive Era. The Progressive Era was the time between 1890 and 1920 when reformers looked for solutions to problems caused by industrialization and urbanization by promoting social welfare, controlling big business. This was the time of breaking up monopolies, pure food laws, concern for humane treatment of the mentally ill, women's suffrage and more, and with a scientific, efficient approach to government and business. While considerable lasting good was accomplished, there is one aspect that was popular with progressives that had disastrous effects on immigrants and refugees. Pulitzer-prize winning historian David Kennedy gave the progressives a pass on being blamed for problems in later eras, writing, "The progressive era, in sum, was an era of transition, and that transitional character is one of its most significant aspects. We cannot look to it for the source of all aspects of our modern life nor can we make the progressives the heroes or the scapegoats for the triumphs or failings, as the case may be, of the rest of the century. Progressivism, after all, is past, and must be so treated."[19]

Kennedy's analysis does not stand in the case of the embrace of eugenics by progressives and its lasting effects. Eugenics was born in England in the late nineteenth century after the rediscovery of Mendel's work on dominant and recessive traits in the heredity of beans and Charles Darwin's cousin, Sir Francis Galton, invented the word. To Galton it was the science of improving human heredity by encouraging the breeding of the best human specimens and discouraging the breeding of others. To accomplish this, they designated racial categories and ranked them in a hierarchy assuming ethnic groups or races had specific social and biological qualities. This would be the "scientific" method of promoting the breeding of a superior gene pool. The taxonomies or ranking systems varied, but in all the Teutonic people of Northern Europe ranked as elite with Anglo-Saxons as the top, though in the U.S., American Whites were seen as a special breed of Anglo-Saxons and the apex of the entire complex racial-ethnic structure.

"Degenerate races" such as the Jews and the many people of color in Latin America and Asia were below Slavs and Mediterranean Europeans, while Blacks were at the bottom. In England the idea gained a following especially among the elite, including Winston Churchill, then soon spread to America, where it seemed in tune with Progressive thought. Advocates included among others President Theodore Roosevelt, who said after the Spanish American War the U.S. should annex the "half-caste…wild pagans" of the Philippines because if the country failed to do so, "some stronger and more manful race" would. Roosevelt also warned against intermarriage out of fear of "race suicide" if "inferior" races were to interbreed with Whites.[20] Woodrow Wilson was a Ku Klux Klan admirer and shared these racial preferences. His successor, Calvin Coolidge said in 1921, "Americans must be kept American. Biological laws show… that Nordics deteriorate when mixed with other races."[21]

Eugenics had academic credibility and courses on it were taught at Stanford, Harvard, Yale and Princeton. By 1928 there were 376 American colleges offering eugenics classes.[22] Eugenics believers were headed for victory when the United States Immigration Commission, known as the Dillingham Commission, completed its four years of work and released a 41-volume report. Under eugenicist Dr. Henry Laughlin's advice and beginning with the premise in J. Deniker's *The Races of Man* that there were five basic races: Caucasian, Ethiopian, Mongolian, Malay, and American,[23] the committee included a *Dictionary of Races or People* that identified 600 branches and 45 distinct racial categories of immigrants in the U.S.[24]

The way was paved for passage of the Immigration Act of 1924, the Johnson-Reed Act.[25] This established the quota system for immigration based on the 1890 census, to a degree. Immigrants from Northern and Western Europe remained welcome, while the "new immigrants," primarily from Eastern, Central and Southern Europe, and largely Catholic and included Eastern European Jews, were severely restricted. Although up to 350,000 would be accepted annually, the number from Black Africa was limited to 200,[26] while all immigration from Asia was completely eliminated.[27]

This was the biggest racist setback for entering the U.S. and would be a major setback for diversity in citizenship and hopes many immigrants or refugees might have. As the *Journal of American History* stated, "The law constructed a white American race, in which persons of European descent shared a common whiteness that made them distinct from those deemed to be not white."[28]

Interestingly, this whitening of the American population drew praise from now Attorney General Jeff Sessions in a 2015 interview with Trump advisor until August 2017, Stephen Bannon. On Breitbart radio, Sessions said, "The numbers reached about this high in 1924, the president and congress changed the policy, and it slowed down immigration significantly...and created really the solid middle class of America."[29]

The U.S. Holocaust Museum speaks less favorably on the rigidity of the quotas. In late 1938, 125,000 applicants lined up for the 27,000 visas available to the U.S. and by June 1939, shortly before the beginning of World War II, the number had increased to over 300,000, but most were unsuccessful. That month a ship with 900 Jewish refugees from Germany reached Florida, but was forced back to Europe where many died in the Holocaust. Near the end of 1941, when reports of mass killings of Jews were filtering into the U.S., stricter limitations were placed on Jewish immigrants for "national security reasons." Immediately following the War there were hundreds of thousands of displaced people in camps but the quota restrictions remained in place.[30] This remained true for years even though the eugenics they were based on became a rejected idea following a full understanding of the Holocaust and where the idea had led.

The situation changed in the post-War world emerged as the Cold War emerged. Congress passed the first refugee legislation in 1948, following the admission of more than 250,000 Europeans who had been exiled because of the War, though the quota system was not revised. Additional laws provided for admission of people fleeing Communism, the large numbers coming from China, Hungary, Korea, Poland, Yugoslavia, and Cuba.

The mood was changing by 1960 when Eleanor Roosevelt did a campaign ad for John Kennedy that she began by saying, "Our country is the oldest democracy in the world, but it is less than two-hundred years old. It is a country with ample room for growth. It is a land which needs today just as much as ever before to live by the prayer written about the Statue of Liberty." She then recited the famous lines that begin "Give me your tired your poor...," which she followed with, "Our nation enjoys its strength and its vitality because we are a melting pot...If we are to be the spokesmen for the free world we must begin at home by assuring all our peoples regardless of religion, race, or national origin, equal opportunity under law and under God."[31] She then endorsed Kennedy as standing for this.

President Kennedy did not live to see it, but rights for newcomers to America finally changed with President Lyndon Johnson's Great Society. Johnson signed the Immigration and Nationality Act of 1965, eliminating the quota system. The Statue of Liberty had become such a symbol for immigration by this time that he did the signing using it as a backdrop. This Act eliminated race and national origin as selection criteria for new Americans, a change in immigration laws that had been specifically race conscious since the Coolie Act of 1862.

While more varied refugees and immigrants entered, it was not until the fall of Saigon in 1975 and the huge influx of refugees from Vietnam that Congress faced the crisis of how to deal with the situation. The *Refugee Act* of 1983[32] established standardized federally-supported resettlement services for all refugees the United States admitted to its shores. This remains the law that governs the admission of refugees into the U.S. to the present. Since that time, refugees coming to America's shores can become citizens, Americans, though threats to that status have many alarmed.

# CHAPTER ELEVEN: NURULAMIN, BURMA, ROHINGYA

Nurulamin is a Rohingya from Burma. In recent times, the Rohingya of Burma have been described as among the world's most persecuted people. They are a stateless people since Burma's Citizenship Act of 1982 does not recognize them as one of the nation's races. To have citizenship, they would have to prove their ancestors had settled in Burma before 1823, a nearly impossible task.[1] The Rohingya are Burmese Muslims with a long history in the land that is Burma and they have faced persecution previously, but it has recently been taken to new levels where some describe the government's assault on these people as constituting ethnic cleansing,[2] or have gone so far as to designate it as genocide.[3]

Contrary to Burmese government assertions, the Rakhine State, which is home to the Muslim Rohingya population, has had a Muslim population from the Eighth or Ninth Century.[4] They have been vastly outnumbered by Burma's Buddhist population throughout most of history and that has been a telling factor in their story. Nurulamin would find this out in a painful lesson. He said, "The reason I suffer very much is, you know majority and minority. Those people that tortured me, they are majority and the government supported them. Even when you are suffering this much you don't have a place to go and report it or talk about it."[5]

While problems are longstanding it appears Buddhists and Muslims lived together in the Rakhine State and this was the case under British rule (1824-1948) when Burma was incorporated into India. Under British rule there had been a great deal of resentment as the British occupied the top social, economic and political positions, while Indians were the midlevel, as were some Chinese, and Buddhist Burmese followed. The 135 ethnic tribal groups had no influence, and many people from regions of India were moved into Burma. This led to anti-colonialist sentiment that would play a role in World War II. A label that would emerge in Burma from this resettlement years later for people like Nurulamin and others is *kalars*. This is a racist term for dark-skinned people of Indian origin or Muslims who are considered untrustworthy and must not hold positions of significance in Burma's government or military.[6]

When World War II began, the Burmese Independence Army, under Aung San, father of Aung San Suu Kyi, sided with the Japanese, while the Muslims stayed loyal to Britain. An estimated half million Indians and Muslims fled when Japan attacked, and Aung San is alleged to have executed a Muslim headman during the war. The British considered charging him with murder but after he changed sides and became the country's popular leader, they decided against it. Many Muslims never forgot the incident.[7]

Aung San soon emerged as the one figure that the country could rally around and became the new nation's first leader. Nurulamin gesticulated dramatically, making a chopping motion, to illustrate what he thought the British had done to the Rohingya people. In creating boundaries as they partitioned India in 1947, they had established East Bengal bordering on the Rakhine State, while the tribe was included in both, he maintained. East Bengal became East Pakistan in the 1950s, and later Bangladesh.

Nurulamin was born in 1961 and in 1962 the army took control of Burma. It was also the year he and his parents opened a bicycle shop in Rangoon. Nurulamin spent some time in Rangoon but he grew up in Rakhine. He was soon required to do forced labor by the army even though he was young. He recalls, "The Burmese soldiers, when they need help they would make us to work for them, do the labor for them. They don't provide us food, they don't provide us transportation to go to the place. I went through it myself. We had to carry heavy stuff, sometime we had to build the road. When you are not able to do the work, the soldier will kick you." He says they were guarded when they were working and in the area where he lived, there were both Buddhists and Muslims, but the Buddhists were not forced to do labor.

Along with that, "So the Buddhists, they would take money from us when we went out to work. Then we report it to the officer. They don't do anything if you are a Muslim."

The army burned his family's house down, a practice that has persisted. As he grew a little older and was well into his teens he began getting into trouble. Once it was for doing something kind. He was in the Rakhine State and because his parents owned a shop, he had some money. There were some people in his neighborhood who were sick and were poor. He had been in a youth group that believed in charity and he tried to help them out by offering them a small amount of assistance. When he did, Burmese soldiers arrested him. To this day, nearly 40 years later, he retains clear evidence of how he was treated for attempting to help people in need. There is a circular scar on his upper back that he says came from being poked by a steel rod. His forehead still has a distinct mark from being hit with a rifle stock. On his leg, there is a scar from where he was cut by a bayonet. Every morning after they arrested him, he says they "made me walk like a cow," which was to crawl, and his knees remain discolored to this day from the scarring that inflicted.

This was in the time of the mass exodus of 1978. An Army campaign to relocate Muslims, communists and Rakhine nationalists was launched with the military operation name "Ye The Ha," and a census operation to check identity papers called "King Dragon."[8] The exodus was inspired by the use of Burma's famous "Four

Cuts" counterinsurgency strategy, cutting off access to food, funds, information and recruitment.[9] There was widespread army brutality, rape, murder, and destruction of mosques involved that resulted in over 200,000 Muslims fleeing in fear. Many returned and Burma's government blamed it on "armed bands of Bengalis" or "wild Muslim extremist" attacking Buddhists.[10]

Nurulamin might have been caught up in this as he remembered, "The little kid do nothing and they will cut the kid head off and they will throw it into the fire. And they will cut the kids' heads off, and throw them in a pile, and they will burn the house. The people do not do that, that's the government. When I see somebody start to suffer I will cry." All these years later, he still struggles with what he witnessed when he was young and what his people suffered as the world ignored them.

This led Nurulamin back to Rangoon to complain about the treatment of Muslims. He thought he could speak to someone about the suffering of Muslims in the Rakhine State. But what he found was that when he complained, the government kept a record of it. He was told that "you wrote a letter about this and you talk about it there." Government officers came to him several times to warn him about speaking out. Things escalated when his parents had their shop taken away by the government.

His advocacy had become dangerous for him and he says, "They tried to arrest me, that's why I escaped." He became a refugee in 1983 and left Burma for Thailand. His problem then became his identity. He had gone through a transition with identification documents. Following independence Burma had given people ID cards and he received one. He said they started taking those from the Muslims in the 1970s and they were given papers. These were temporary registration cards and were replaced with a white temporary I.D, which he said was taken away in 1986. He was out of the country and had no documentation to confirm his identity.

Nurulamin was pointing out what would be a standard problem for the Rohingya and an unresolved one. Things had been getting steadily more challenging, then in 1982 Burma passed its revised Citizenship Law that excluded the Rohingya from its list of 135 national ethnic groups which effectively denied citizenship to the Rohingya. 800,0000 became stateless people.[11]

He managed to be accepted in Thailand and lived there for a little over a month. When he was there he didn't feel safe, commenting, "I was afraid to live in Thailand, because Thailand is also Buddhist country. Although Thailand people are very good people, I'm thinking that back in my country, the Buddhist people are giving me a whole lot of trouble, and maybe these people will be the same." Since he was afraid, he headed south to Malaysia.

In Malaysia, there were no refugee camps, only detention camps. It is primarily an Islamic country, so that was better. He ran into a new problem because he did not have any legal travel documents or valid identity papers, so he had to make do and still had to work. Since he wasn't there legally and didn't have any identity, he was frequently stopped by police and, "Always have to give them money."

When he went to the United Nations to register they had given him a card which he hoped would help serve as identification. It didn't help. "Then when you are arrested, they look at this, and say this is not an ID from our government." He found jobs in a restaurant and in the markets. He claimed that he was most successful working for the Chinese. "I worked for a Chinese company. The Muslims in Malaysia wanted to offer me a job, but they were also afraid to offer a job to Rohingya Muslim because I don't have any identity. When the police arrest me, they can also arrest the owner of the shop. The Chinese always offer money to them and they go to the police, so that's why we getting jobs."

Nurulamin says that after five years away, he made one trip back to Burma. It was in 1988 and the pro-democracy rallies were taking place, and he says that he "went back through the Karen State. I still had my Burma ID. I tried to be careful when I went back myself, I had to be careful what happened to me." The ID he had was out of date but it was a tumultuous time and, according to him, he was there for an important reason. Aung San Suu Kyi had made her return from England while her husband and child remained there. She was reintroducing herself to Burma at a huge prodemocracy rally. There was going to be a meeting for her to introduce herself to the ethnic groups at the General Hospital and Nurulamin was there to represent the Rohingya.

He was not impressed. He says, "When I talked to Aung San Suu Kyi, I look at the face, and I know the face that she shows is not one that really loved the country. She came back for the power. Coming back not as someone who loved the country, but for the power. Her father had been the very first one, and that's why she came back."

His view of her is, "Two paths, one for show and one, she will follow that is what the military wants." Other ethnic minorities have expressed similar thoughts. And certainly, as far as the condition of the Rohingya is concerned, she has disappointed.

Nurulamin remained in Malaysia. He had spoken to the United Nations Commissioner stationed there about resettlement in a third country who "told me that nobody wanted to sponsor me to go to their country, because I was Muslim nobody wanted to take me." That was it for some time. He waited for 20 years. Then, "In 2007 I got heart disease. I told them I cannot work here." During his stay in Malaysia he worked with a company that put 120 kilos of ice and water in boxes, and he had to carry them. He put them on a roller to transfer them to a container. When he was diagnosed with a heart condition, he could no longer lift heavy boxes.

He made a second effort. "I talked to the United Nations High Commissioner. He said, 'I don't have any other ideas to help you.' I said, 'You cannot help me and the Malay government cannot help me and I'm getting old. I cannot do the heavy duty anymore so can you help me apply for the third country, any country?'" He waited for over two more years, then a phone call came from the Commissioner who said "I got arrangement to get you resettled in a third country." He asked Nurulamin if he had a choice about which country he would like to settle in. Nurulamin replied that he didn't care and that he didn't know. He asked the Commissioner to "choose a country, a good country, where I'm going to go. I go to that country if I can get any care for my health. They picked Colorado." He arrived in Denver in May 2012 and finds, "They're taking care of me very well. The doctors really care for me."

He has been a bit reclusive in Denver, he says, in that he doesn't choose to mix with the general Muslim community, "Because our language and our culture is not the same, I really don't have any connection with them. I just associate with my own community." Although he has been welcomed by some Burmese, he says the same ethnic boundaries apply here that existed in Burma, "Oh the group from Burma you're the Burmese, you're the Muslim, you're the Karen and then they don't talk." In the community and at work, he explained, "The people here ask you to do things, they ask you, you do it. After I'd been here over three years, I couldn't find a job." His wife got a job but his English was very weak. After eventually working in a hotel, he started working at lipstick production. That is a good job for hard working people who do not have good English speaking skills, as it just involves assembling containers.

Nurulamin's perspective after what he has experienced is, "My belief about human beings is that you are human beings, you have to forgive one another. If you understand about the message that come from God or from Moses, it is if you can't help people, don't give them problems. If you cannot help that's okay, but don't give them more problems."

He stays with his community and knows those who have followed him to Denver. He is also well aware of what has happened to the many who were less successful than he in managing to escape.

What has been happening has been is tragic and some have managed to make it to Denver. Joe Wismann-Horther, a Colorado authority on refugees observes, "I would say of all our refugee communities they faced the greatest persecution before their arrival here. I would say some of that is still residual in terms of their treatment here as well. By Burmese customs, the degree to which that happens I'm not entirely sure. But I would say, within the Burmese community there is still a tendency to look on them as interlopers who didn't come there legitimately."[12]

In harrowing attempts to migrate to nearby countries like Malaysia and Indonesia, many Rohingya ended up packed on overcrowded boats at sea and found no country willing to grant them safe landing. Hundreds of others have died when such migrant boats capsized. Malaysian authorities discovered mass graves and barbed wire pens at camps abandoned by human traffickers. A similar discovery was made in Thailand. Human traffickers also hold Rohingya captive, and demand ransom from their families.[13]

Outside criticism has been notable but to no avail with much falling on Aung San Suu Kyi, leader of Burma's first democratically elected government since 1962 as head of the National League for Democracy and Nobel Peace Prize Winner. A letter was sent to the UN Security Council by eleven former Nobel Prize Peace Prize winners, criticizing Aung San Suu Kyi and demanding that she take action to crack down on what they described as "ethnic cleansing" of the Rohingya. The Pope strongly criticized Burma's treatment of the Rohingya.[14]

To all this Aung San Suu Kyi responded, "I'm not saying there are no difficulties. But it helps if people recognize the difficulty and are more focused on resolving these difficulties rather than exaggerating them so that everything seems worse than it really is."[15] She objected to the U.S. ambassador to the country using the name Rohingya, maintaining a position long held by the rulers of the country. Buddhists in Burma commonly refer to them as Bengalis, to suggest that they are illegal aliens who have entered from Bangladesh.[16] When Secretary of State Kerry was to visit Burma and the name Rohingya was used in a statement issued by the U.S. Embassy, the building was picketed by hundreds of protesters. Aung San Suu Kyi told Kerry when he arrived, "Emotive terms make it very difficult for us to find a peaceful and sensible resolution to our problems. All that we are asking is that people should be aware of the difficulties we are facing and to give us enough space to solve all our problems."[17]

On February 3, 2017, the UN Office of the High Commission on Human Rights issued a "Flash Report."[18] A committee visited Burma and did hundreds of interviews, collected photos, and studied satellite images to assess the damage inflicted on the Rohingya by government forces in the past year. Their report stands as a stark contradiction to the words of Aung San Suu Kyi that people are "exaggerating." The report found, "Extrajudicial executions or other killings, including by random shooting; enforced disappearance and arbitrary detention...The killing of babies, toddlers, children, women and elderly; opening fire at people fleeing; burning of entire villages... massive and systematic rape and sexual violence...66,000 people fleeing into Bangladesh and 22,000 being internally displaced...very likely commission of crimes against humanity."[19]

While the life Nurulamin leads in Denver might not be ideal, he was very fortunate to have escaped Burma years ago.

# CHAPTER TWELVE: DISTINCTIONS

There has been a considerable amount of discussion about people entering the U.S. from foreign lands in recent times and much of it has added little clarity and considerable confusion and often distortion. Different categories of people enter the United States from other countries for varied reasons, but recently there has been extensive conversation about "securing America's borders" from dangers that are presented as lurking everywhere.

There is news about all categories and in commentary and diatribes, the distinctions sometimes get blurred; however, the legal status, opportunities, and requirements that apply to each vary considerably. What binds them is that they are all the "other," the "non-American," though a substantial number include U.S. citizens. English isn't their first language and their complexions may be a bit darker than the white that many assume is the standard.[1] While some are Christian, many are Buddhists, Hindus, Muslims, and other faiths and belief systems.

People entering the United States are immigrants. Most legal immigrants come in one of six categories: immediate relatives, family-based, employment-based, refugees, asylees, and lottery admissions. The guiding law for this is the Immigration Act of 1990.[2] There have been modifications since this time, but none have been comprehensive. This law was sponsored by Ted Kennedy and signed by President George H.W. Bush. Amongst its provisions, it raised the cap on worldwide immigration to 700,000 initially and 675,000 beginning in 1995, and created preference tracks that placed family relationships highest, with well over half going to hopefully expedite the reunion of immigrant families in the U.S.[3] Family reunion included spouses, unmarried minor children, and parents if the petitioner was over 21. Employment-based, sponsored immigration was divided into categories, with the top category going to "priority workers," such as people with extraordinary abilities or outstanding professors and researchers, executives, managers. This was followed by a category of those holding advanced degrees or special abilities, then "skilled workers" and "other workers," though a small number was allotted to unskilled laborers. Non-employer-sponsored immigrants included ministers, religious workers and entrepreneurs who could invest at least a million dollars in a commercial enterprise. One other provision was "diversity" immigration, which required the Attorney General to look at nations that had been "adversely affected" by the quota system prior to 1965, and for a three-year period, allow 40,000 visas to those states.[4] The Act included Temporary Protected Status (TPS). TPS allowed the Attorney General to designate people of a foreign country as eligible to remain in the U.S. if conditions in that country were seen as a danger to their personal safety. It was granted for a short term but could be extended, and aliens in TPS received work permits and were not subject to deportation, regardless of whether they had legally entered the country. The Act also enhanced the Immigration and Naturalization Service (INS) authority and authorized personnel to execute warrants, make arrests, carry firearms and use force, and permit apprehension for deportation.[5]

Especially controversial have been the immigrants who have not entered the country through the INS. Illegal immigrants, or undocumented immigrants, depending on one's political persuasion, is a neutral term that is sometimes used is unauthorized immigrants. These are foreign citizens who enter the country without an immigrant visa or avoid inspection and cross the border. They can also be people who enter the U.S. as visitors or tourists or on business legally but overstay the time they were legally allowed to remain. If they do not leave and make the U.S. their home but are not citizens, they become resident aliens. In 2014 there were 11.1 million, which is down from the high point of 2007 when there were 12.2 million.[6] There has been a decline in Mexican movement to the U.S. that has been offset by an increase from Asia, Central America and Sub-Saharan Africa, but Mexico remains the primary source with 52% of the illegal entrants.[7] This is the group that is the subject of President Trump's plan to build a wall. It is also the target of the increased immigration enforcement that was seen when on February 21, 2017, by order of the president, the Department of Homeland Security issued orders instructing agents of Customs and Border Protection (CBP) and Immigration and Customs Enforcement (ICE) to quickly identify and capture every undocumented immigrant they encountered. To help enforce this there was a call for the hiring of another 10,000 ICE agents and 5,000 border patrol officers.

One dispute that commands considerable debate surrounds "sanctuary cities." This is a term that has no legal definition but is used to describe locations that protect undocumented immigrants from deportation by limiting cooperation with federal authorities. Some decline to use city or state tax money to enforce federal immigration laws and many prohibit local officials from asking people about their immigration status. One of Donald Trump's campaign promises was to end sanctuary cities and he paraded around grieving victims of violence that he claimed would have been prevented had these cities not existed. He issued an executive order "Enhancing Public Safety in the United States."[8] This set the stage for an announcement that the government would take "all lawful steps to claw-back"[9] federal funding awarded to cities that do not fully comply with federal immigration enforcement.

There are many cities and areas that fall under the generally understood idea of sanctuary locations, and a large number have expressed no willingness to comply with the new order. Many have suggested that both the order on which it is based and the threat of withholding federal funds as a form of extortion, are unconstitutional. While the House has taken action on this, the Senate hasn't followed and should that happen, this appears to be an issue for court adjudication.

Less known is the origin of sanctuary cities. While now a divisive line between conservatives and progressives, it began with the arrival of Central American refugees in the early 1980s and a phenomenon called the Central American Refugee Sanctuary Movement. These refugees were fleeing political violence and social instability. In 1982, the congregation of the Southside United Presbyterian Church in Tucson, Arizona, declared their house of worship a sanctuary. They followed this declaration by calling on other congregations to join them and the number adopting the cause grew to between 20,000 to 30,000 church members in over 100 churches and synagogues, and spread to all areas of the country and into Canada. This faith-based network made several resources available to the undocumented population such as food, shelter, money for bail, legal representation, support for asylum applications, medical aid, resettlement. By 1987 one governor had declared sanctuary as had 22 city councils.[10]

A controversy related to illegal aliens that has received less attention recently, but was a topic during the presidential debates, concerns "anchor babies." This was the name given to children born in the U.S. to illegal immigrants or other non-citizens. They were called "anchors" because the Fourteenth Amendment to the Constitution makes anyone born on U.S. soil an American citizen. The contention was that people came to the U.S. to have a baby that received American citizenship and that baby could provide a means for the rest of the family to stay in the United States or to return to the United States as immigrants after the child reached adulthood. Donald Trump had made an issue of this when he claimed that "I don't think they have American citizenship," in an interview with Bill O'Reilly on Fox News. He said that repealing birthright citizenship "would take too long," but thought it could be challenged in court.[11]

More terminology originated in 2001 with the introduction of the Development, Relief, and Education for Alien Minors, or DREAM Act. In total it was proposed in Congress 24 times over the years, including the 2007 version that was championed by the unusual combination of John McCain, Ted Kennedy, and President George W. Bush.[12] The proposed legislation would have allowed undocumented young adults under the age of 35 to legalize their immigration status if they had entered the United States before they were 16, lived in the United States for at least five years, and had graduated from high school or obtained a GED. Spending time in the military was another path. The DREAM Act would make about two million undocumented young people eligible for legal status, but successive Congresses failed to pass it. These educated young people who had grown up in the U.S. and included many veterans, were known as Dreamers, or DREAMers, and represented a different image than illegal immigrants sneaking across the border.[13] Rather than legal status, they face deportation.

The frustration these young people felt led some to organize and seek change, especially on college campuses, but their efforts were not successful in achieving legal modification, though public opinion was favorable to them. On June 15, 2012, President Obama changed many of their lives when he announced the Deferred Action for Childhood Arrivals, or DACA, that offered two years stay without fear of deportation plus the ability to work legally in the U.S. Although there was considerable debate over Obama doing this by executive action, polls after the announcement the showed the public favored that DREAMers be allowed legal status by a large margin, ranging from 76%-19% to 62%-34% depending on the wording of the question.[14]

A group that gets confused with refugees is the unaccompanied children. In the spring and summer of 2014, tens of thousands of unaccompanied children from Central America were crossing the border into the United States seeking asylum. There were 69,000 who showed up at the U.S.-Mexican border that year, coming all the way across Mexico from El Salvador, Guatemala, and Honduras.[15] In total, 112,840 such children have arrived since 2012 and 67,699 of their cases remain unresolved by U.S. authorities.[16] Children were leaving this area, known as the "Northern Triangle," because it is dominated by criminal gangs that have cooperation of the police. Gangs force children to become members with those as young as six or seven having the choice to join or die. Young boys are often used in the gang's extortion racket, which is the largest business, or to sell or run drugs; while girls run drugs, and are used as "gang girlfriends," who understand their role is to have forced sex with gang members. Girls are also a vehicle by which gangs take revenge against families who refuse or cannot make extortion payments.[17] Most of the children who fled are victims of physical abuse and sexual abuse, molestation, domestic violence,[18] and have witnessed community violence regularly. The three countries rank first, second, and fourth in the world in homicides against women.[19] The children have been aware of the difficulties of the journey, but made the choice that the risks were outweighed by the danger of remaining where they were.

Efforts were made by the U.S. government in three ways to slow down the influx: a multimedia public information campaign began in 2014 called "Danger Awareness" followed in 2015 with "Know the Facts," which included billboards and radio and television ads warning of the risks of the trip and the slim chances of being allowed to stay in the U.S. There was increased U.S. aid to help Mexico secure its southern border to prevent the migrants from beginning the journey. Expediting the removal process of those who had arrived was supposed to be increased to make it clear others would not get asylum. Raids were carried out in January 2016 seeking individuals who had exhausted their asylum claims.[20] These actions were meant to deter Central American minors from attempting the trip to the U.S. but they failed, even though the information was successfully spread to the countries in question. Among the reasons for the lack of success was the processing of those detained. These children had to go through formal removal proceedings, unlike undocumented workers, and after initial processing were released to parents or other relatives, which was one reason many came. They, or some assigned agency, took care of them, while they waited for an appearance before an immigration judge. Most who appeared before immigration judges did so without representation and, in many cases, they failed to appear because their sponsors failed to get them to the location at the appointed time.

Even so, because of immigration court backlogs, unaccompanied minors taken into custody when the influx began were given a waiting period of approximately two years for their court dates to be called.[21] It might be that this slow process helped create a false impression that children who entered would get legal status, since they arrived and stayed for years. It may have been why others continued to attempt the dangerous trip for a time.[22]

The whole treatment of the unaccompanied children raises questions. Sending them back to poverty and danger while many had relatives, often parents, in the U.S. where they could be safe, worries some who have worked with them. A high proportion already suffered from PTSD at their early age. A substantial number were settled in Colorado and Joe Wismann-Horther, the Integration Partnership Coordinator, observed that some people in the Denver community confuse unaccompanied children for refugees. He also had serious questions about how the government handled their arrival. Wismann-Horther found it morally troubling that these children were fleeing persecution, which fits into one of the five criteria to be determined as refugees, but when they crossed the border, there was no agency to determine them as refugees. They were detained by border patrol, then passed over to Office of Refugee Resettlement. He said, "We're not doing the right thing at the border. That's my opinion."[23] Unaccompanied children do not qualify for refugee benefits. Their immediate care comes from a line in the Office of Refugee Resettlement budget as refugees. Unfortunately it comes from the same line item budget. When the big crowd came, that budget was inadequate, and as Wismann-Horther recalled, "It's a horrible thing to position unaccompanied children against refugees for budget dollars."[24]

Another group that is included in immigration categories that receives little attention, except when it is a major defector, is asylee. An asylee is an alien who is either in the United States or attempting to enter and is unable or unwilling to return to his or her home country because of persecution, or a well- founded fear of persecution. The persecution or fear of it can be based on race, religion, nationality, membership in a particular social group, or political opinion. Currently the most famous person seeking asylum is probably Edward Snowden, who is seeking it away from the U.S., but several prominent Chinese dissidents have found asylum in the U.S. in the past decade.[25] After one year in the United States, asylees are admissible for permanent resident status. Although there is no limit on the number of people who may be granted asylum protection in any year, aslyee admissions for permanent residence are limited to 10,000 per fiscal year.

A category of immigration is lottery admissions commonly known as the "green card lottery." This provides 50,000 visas each year for the purpose of diversity and was called for in the Immigration Act of 1990 to make up for countries underrepresented previously by immigration restrictions. Small numbers are available for countries that had sent immigrants in without restriction, while larger numbers are available for those that had been denied by the quota system. Winners are selected by random choice.

Alexander was a green card lottery winner who now lives and works in Denver. His route was indirect. He explains, "I left Russia in 1990. In 1990, Russia had been in big troubles with communist government. Almost starvation. I left because terrible situation in the country. I am Jewish and if something happens, something goes wrong, people go, you know, blame the Jewish people."[26] He says there was trouble in Russia that brought on an anti-Semitic campaign against the Jews. "That's a good Russian tradition. That was time of escape of big Jewish population to Israel." He lived in Israel for eight years, then he won the green card lottery. Although Alexander had emigrated to Israel, it didn't work out well. "I didn't like to live there. Climate not for me, mentality not for me." He says it had been his dream since he was young to go to America. He was not a refugee and had no real option for moving to the U.S. except trying the green card lottery, so he applied. After repeated attempts, he was a winner. "I applied to green card lottery and finally I got lucky. I won the green card." Alexander had graduated from technical college in Russia and was a commercial appliance technician so he came to the U.S. with a marketable skill. When it came to relocating, "We didn't have any friends in America, just in Denver. We've got friends and they helped us. I like Denver."

A big issue facing groups in these categories is deportation. Anyone in the U.S. on a visa or green card risks deportation if convicted of a crime, particularly those labeled as "moral turpitude" or "aggregated felonies." That includes all people in all immigration categories, until they gain citizenship.

These crimes can include, but are not limited to, battery, theft, fraudulent tax return, failure to appear in court, consensual sex between a 17-year-old and a 16-year-old, perjury, tax evasion, carrying a concealed weapon, and child abuse.[27]

The sixth immigration category that also has concerns about deportation recently is refugees.

# CHAPTER THIRTEEN, MIMI, BURMA, KAREN

Her early years were difficult to recall. Though Mimi was sick much of the time she didn't stay home in bed, not because her parents weren't willing to care for her or lacked interest in her welfare, they were hoping to keep her alive. They were hiding from Burmese soldiers. There were regular patrols, "So, you cannot sleep at your house every night. You have to keep running, and then like at three or four a.m. you come back. You sleep in the forest."[1]

This continued for some time, but how long, "We don't know the year, we don't know the month. We kept running month by month, year by year." Eventually they stopped running but more challenges awaited. When she was seven they moved to the border of Burma and Thailand and by that time her family and others could settle down. Mimi also returned to regular school but there were border problems between Thailand and Burma at the time. In Mimi's words, "The Karen people and the Thai, they don't get along."

This was before refugee camps were available in Thailand to those fleeing Burma, and most remained in Burma. Thailand didn't begin accepting refugees from Burma until 1984.[2] Her father was Karen, but she could get into Thailand earlier than most other refugees because her situation was different. Her mother was Thai, so Thailand was willing to accept their family. They could come and go and didn't have any problem with the Thai government. But the Karen people had a problem. The Thai government didn't want to accept Karen people at this border, though it was an ill-defined line in the jungle.

This situation had been going on for years. Burmese crossed the porous jungle border that was unguarded in most places, and Karen people in small border towns have held Thai citizenship, like Mimi's mother, and made their way out of Burma. A 2015 report described the oldest Karen resident in Mae Sot, a Thai town near the Burma border, and she had crossed the short distance from Burma and settled in Thailand in the 1950s.[3] In 1975 Thailand had a huge influx of refugees on its eastern border from Cambodia, Laos and Vietnam as a consequence of the Cold War, and the U N took interest in the refugee situation there. This attention finally turned to the Karen entering in the west. The Karen had been able to settle in a refugee camp in Thailand since their leaders had negotiated permission for refugees to cross the border to come to the camp called Mae La in 1984, located near the village of the same name, eight miles from the border and operated by the Border Consortium, a charitable organization from the United Kingdom. Eight more camps would follow opened by the group to offer some assistance to the large number of refugees.[4] Approximately 10,000 Karen refugees crossed from Burma to Thailand that first year.[5]

With the emergence of the State Law and Order Council, commonly known as SLORC, and the continued civil war waged by the Karen, many were fleeing the country, which was when Mimi's family left. She said, "Karen people they can't live there anymore. They don't have the food. The Burmese soldiers burned their house, burned their rice paddy. So, we also we had to move forward. We crossed into Thailand." At this time it was the Thai government that was providing their shelter. It had limited resources.

In her years in the refugee camp, Mimi received some education and made her way through high school, which led her to getting a job. She, "learned to speak some English in Thailand from school, people who had been in war," but had limited conversational skills. She also learned reading, writing, and after studying English, Burmese, and eight other subjects, she finished high school. Mimi found an opportunity when she met a foreigner who came over from England, or perhaps Australia, who provided capable students a curriculum for teacher training. She spent two years attending teacher training, and when it was complete, received a certification of some sort to be qualified to teach.

Her training didn't get her out of the refugee camp, but it improved the lives of others there. She says that after finishing, "Then I can become the teacher, and I can teach the students. I taught refugees for three years. You don't get salary, you get rice, you get oil, you get fish paste. But it's not enough. You had land. You can plant anything. So, the Thai government, they allow you to plant the vegetables, so that is grateful."

Her family's situation changed, and her teaching job was insufficient to meet her needs. It appeared a change was called for but options are very limited in refugee life. She was from a big family with four brothers and four sisters who she said were, "all together at that time" along with her mother and father. Living in a camp on rations and being restricted on work was the refugees' life, but Mimi says, "It's not OK. You work all day and you do not have money. You cannot go anywhere, you want to buy the new clothes, but you do not have the money."

Year after year passed this way, then things got worse. Mimi's father got cancer. That was it for her teaching career. She explains, "So, he got a cancer and if you go to the big hospital in Chang Mai or Mae Sot, you got to pay a lot of money. You don't have the money. So, I decided no more teacher, and I went to learn about the Nurse Park. Maybe, I can take care of my father. I got the training at the Nurse Park at the Dr. Cynthia Clinic in Mae Sot."

The Dr. Cynthia Clinic is actually the Mae Teo Clinic that was founded by Dr. Cynthia Maung, a Karen refugee who fled Burma following the pro-democracy uprisings of 1988. After medical school, she had worked in a small clinic in the Karen state and when the military seized power and thousands were at the border fleeing the country, she and 14 colleagues decided to go with them. They carried what supplies they could and treated people along the way as they spent a week hiking through jungle. In February 1989, she was offered a dilapidated dirt floor building in Mae Sot, where she could open a practice with her companions to treat malaria, gunshot wounds, and landmine injuries, as well as other problems related to the flow of incoming refugees. Her clinic prospered and remains very successful. Currently it still serves the refugees in the area and sees between 400-500 people daily, and over 2,700 babies are annually delivered in the facility.[6] Mimi spent three years as a nurse in the refugee camp and her father survived.

Again, it was time for something new. She said, "All of my family, they live in the refugee camp. They live in the refugee camp, but I have to support my family. So, I get out of the house, get out of the camp, and then went." Where she went was to Thailand's major city, Bangkok. In Bangkok, she took a job in housekeeping and sent the money she could save to her parents. She was there for three years when her life took a big turn. She met and married a Japanese businessman. They went to Japan where they lived for eight months.

Her husband traveled on business, which led to the next big adjustment. Mimi recalls, "I never, ever think of coming to the United States, but then one day my husband want to do the business and he like America. He like Colorado and he travel a lot so then one day we travel and then we stop, and we settle in Colorado." She had the idea that everybody in America would be very rich. It surprised her when she arrived to see that wasn't the case. People weren't all rich and they had to work very hard. But it was not the same as where she was from as she noted, "You cannot compare with life in the refugee camp, with life in Burma, with life in Thailand. You work, you get it, you can eat, you can buy, you can survive.

Here, whatever you want to eat, you can buy. Over there, you work 12, 15 hours every day, and it's not enough to survive." Mimi, who began as a refugee, ended coming to the U.S. in 2001 as an immigrant wife of a businessman.

After arriving she decided to work and found that she was not being treated fairly. Her experience was in Denver shortly after she first arrived. She got a job at Sushi Den for $4.50 an hour, unaware of minimum wage laws that required $6.00 an hour at the time. Mimi recalls, "I worked very hard, and I had an American friend, a skinny high school boy. They checked and said, 'Mimi, how come, you work very hard and you earn so little?' I thought maybe it because at the time I didn't have my G.E.D." Her young colleague showed her his check and she said, "Evan, how come I work more than you and you make more than me? That's not fair." Evan told her that she had to complain to the manager, but she felt shy as a new arrival at the time, and didn't speak English well and so was reluctant. He said, "You're in America now. We are equal. You have to speak to the manager." So, she complained, and still feared she had done something wrong, but her pay was changed to $6 per hour.

She thinks that happens to refugees and immigrants when some employers think they can get away with it, or that their workers won't complain because they fear legal repercussions. That wasn't all that was negative about her first work experience in the U.S. She observed that "the kids that were at the Sushi Den, they were high school. And I am Asian and don't speak English well so I think they looked down on me. My English has improved, broken, but I'm not shy any more. It's my fifth language."

Early on, Mimi found resettlement in Denver a bit lonely. Though she had chosen to move, she missed her culture, her roots. She says of when they first came, "In that time I don't know anyone, no Karen people. Later I know just only three family. I know one family and mom from the refugee camp when I went school time. So, when I met them I'm so happy."

That was just the beginning, as Burmese refugees were about to be entering the Denver area in very large numbers, and Mimi strove to reconnect. "So, 2006, around that time, maybe 50 or 80 people Karen. Just like that, Burmese people. We met at the church. I try to go to the church once a week so I can meet the Karen and the Burmese people. We talk, I talk, just like that. Don't keep separate. I like to talk and to make friend."

In 2010, following the influx from the Saffron Revolution, she took a position where she could work with new arrivals. Mimi hears them speak of their difficulties and dejection, especially the older arrivals. "They come here, they don't know what to do, they very upset. They very depressed. They don't know how to go to the hospital. They stay at home. They don't know how to go shopping, they don't know anything. And to use the cooking, they don't know. So, they starving, they very upset. Oh, if die, better. They want to die."

She says that many tell her they don't want to live their life in the United States, they want to end their life in the United States. They came from refugee camp to United States with no idea of anything at all and they got more frustrated and more depressed. They already had trauma from what they had encountered and endured years of struggle, but they came to the United States. They wanted to die. "Die is better."

Communication is the major problem for many, a point worth remembering if one encounters a newcomer to our country. Our forefathers did not arrive speaking perfect English, and new refugees don't either, but by the second generation that has changed. Mimi comments on this recurrent theme: "They think refugee camp better because you can ask somebody: Can I get the food? We don't have any food. Do you have any food? We can share. But in Colorado, no food, no speak English. They don't have anything to share, nobody to talk." She added again that many wish their life would end.

In her work, she tries to go to where the Asian community is, where there are Karen people and Burmese people. She likes to wear Karen clothes, or carry a Karen bag so right away when they see her, they will recognize her as someone who would understand them. This was especially true in the early days when the community was very small but now that she reaches out to the expanded community she continues the practice. "When I saw more the Karen people, the Burmese people, the Burmese Muslim people, I feel very grateful. So, I talk to them, and they talk to me, they share to me and they tell me everything, how they suffer, how they feel, how they want to kill themselves. I say please, don't do yourself yet."

As for the family Mimi left in the refugee camp, she has two brothers in the U.S. One brother was working in a nursing home, but now he has a mental health problem, so he just stays home. "He can still help take care of the family, can cook, but he just doesn't want to talk to people, he doesn't want to meet people." Two of her siblings died in Thailand. One was killed at 19 after volunteering for the military. Her mother and older sister live in Canada.

Mimi is going to remain in the U.S. As for returning to Burma someday, she says, "Yes, for a vacation, for the vegetables." That sounds like enough unless there is a significant change.

# CHAPTER FOURTEEN:
# KAHASSAI, ETHIOPIA

Kahassai is a refugee from Ethiopia, a country with a long heritage that he remembers well and with fondness for the culture that developed in a land where human existence dates back the farthest. "Lucy Welcomes You Home," is written above a picture of a walking skeleton in the National Museum in Ethiopia, that houses the 3.2 million-year-old hominoid skeleton nicknamed Lucy. As *National Geographic* reported, "A sense of returning to the root of everything pervades the whole country."[1] With Lucy, and more recent finds of even earlier human skeletons, Ethiopia is frequently viewed as the cradle of humanity since the world's first known humans appeared there.[2] Located on the Horn of Africa in the tropics north of the equator, this is Africa's oldest country and the only one to survive without being colonized. As part of the Land of Punt it carried on trade with Ancient Egypt between 3,500 and 2,000 B. C. and its first civilization arose around 1,500 B.C.[3] Herodotus, the Ancient Greek historian, describes Ethiopia in his writings and the Old Testament of the Bible discusses the Queen of Sheba, a land near Kahassai's home, visiting Jerusalem. Legend contends that the founder of Ethiopian Empire, King Menelik, was the son of the Queen of Sheba and Solomon,[4] and when he returned to Ethiopia, he brought with him the Ark of the Covenant, the case built about 3,000 years ago by the Israelites to house the stone tablets on which the Ten Commandments were written.[5] While this is historically questionable it remains a story so familiar to Ethiopians that Kahassai mentions it when discussing his homeland,

and there have been quests to Ethiopia since the Knights Templar in the Middle Ages up to the present, attempting to locate the sacred Ark.

Christianity came to Ethiopia in the fourth century with the Coptic Christians of the Orthodox Church,[6] and it became the country's major religion. Kahassai is a devout Orthodox Christian. The rise of Islam in the seventh century isolated Ethiopia from European Christianity until Portugal arrived in the 1500s and established trading posts for control over Indian Ocean control. This led to conflict and Ethiopia expelling all foreign missionaries in the 1600s, and contributed to Ethiopian hostility towards foreign Christians and Europeans that isolated the country for the next two centuries, as local rulers contended for power. Emperor Tewodros brought the modern state together in 1855. In the late nineteenth century Africa was partitioned by European countries. When Italy attempted to colonize Ethiopia, they were defeated by Ethiopia at the Battle of Adwa, the first victory of an African nation over a colonial power and the first time since imperial expansion began that a non-white nation had defeated a European power.[7]

Haile Selassie became emperor of Ethiopia in 1930 when Mussolini was in power in Italy - the Italians soon had their revenge. The Italian Army, with tanks and machine guns, attacked Ethiopia's barefooted soldiers armed with spears and bows and arrows in 1935.[8] Italy's hold on the country was brief and Haile Selassie was back in power soon after World War II began when England pushed the Italians out five years later. His long rule continued for decades. In 1962 he annexed Eritrea, and later in that decade Kahassai was born in Tigrai near the border with Eritrea.

When Kahassai was ten the situation was created that would set his life on its course. Haile Selassie was overthrown in a military coup and a government called the Derg took over, followed by infighting that resulted in a Marxist dictatorship. It was a rough situation for the young Kahassai when he was growing up. He says that, "After Haile Selassie all the parents was scared."[9] He kept attending school where he learned some English along with his other subjects but he found another outlet. Kahassai was a soccer player and a good one. By the time he was in his teens, he was playing club soccer, the highest level of the sport. It was the Cold War and the repressive government prohibited public gatherings, hoping to avert uprisings. This meant Kahassai was prevented from getting together with his friends socially even in small groups. "Whatever they say to you, you have to accept it." So that's what he did. The government's practices were soon made known when, within years of taking control, a group opposed to the junta attempted to organize a protest for May Day, 1977, demanding a civilian government. The government responded by killing over 1,000 young people, their bodies left in the streets to be ravaged by hyenas at night.[10]

One day, when Kahassai was still in high school, his father vanished. He had been taken to prison. Kahassai tried to find out what happened, "But who do you ask? When you ask, they put you in prison. You have to keep silent." After waiting a while he heard others talking about all the people taken to jail.

People were asking him what had happened to his father, but "He doesn't know about politics. He was an old man." One night his mother heard a car stop in front of their house. She looked and it was a jeep. It moved on after a bit and she heard what she describe as a "ka-ka-ka" of shots being fired. The next morning a friend picked up Kahassai and they started to bike to soccer training. When they got a short distance from the house Kahassai saw his father dead in the street. He thinks the government was going to kill him in front of their house but he pleaded and they moved on. His mom found out that morning and, "She cried, she cried. Those people outside from the government, they watch you. If you cry, they take you to jail. There's nothing I can do. Me and my mom, I locked the door and we cried inside. Nobody can see us."

Kahassai's father was a victim in the Ethiopian Red Terror. The Red Terror was a campaign of torture and murder to eliminate all rivals to the government that had been initiated by the Derg. The murders began in the mid 1970s but the terror intensified in 1977 when Mengistu Haile Mariam became leader and continued into 1980. Amnesty International put the number of people killed at 150,000 to 200,000, though others put it as high as 500,000. When families were fortunate enough to be allowed to identify the bodies, many were required to pay for the bullets used to kill their relatives before they could claim them.[11] "The government kill a lot of people then. On the street, because what the government did was to make scared with the other people," recalls Kahassai. The Derg's oppression would carry on and between 1977 and the late 1980s, an estimated 1.5 million Ethiopians died, disappeared or were injured.[12]

This situation got mixed up with the civil war and border war that Ethiopia was fighting. Since Eritrea was annexed that former Italian colony had been fighting for independence from Ethiopia. With the Derg's crackdown and harshness, which was focused mainly on young people, guerrilla forces within Ethiopia launched a war against the country's government. "That is why a lot of young kids, they just run to fight the government with the guerrilla fighters. There was a lot of different kind of political organizations at this time," said Kahassai.

It was a difficult decision for him but in 1982 he concluded, "So finally, I will decide to go from that country, the place I'm born, the place I love, and the place I used to play soccer." It was a tall, strong, athletic 18-year-old Kahassai who was about to leave his home. He told his mom, "They kill my dad, it's going to be me next. I can't live here anymore." She responded that it was the right decision and she didn't want to see him end up like his dad.

He then escaped the country and made his way into Eritrea where he joined the guerrilla forces of the People's Liberation Front (PLF), also called the Ethiopian People's Liberation Front (EPLF). He was with the guerrillas for nearly a year but hadn't intended to be. When he first arrived they gave him pamphlets, papers, and sat him down with others to explain their options. He explained, "They ask do you want to fight with us, do you want to run to Sudan, do you want to teach kids, we can pay you, or do you want to stay here, become a trainer. I told them I want to go to Sudan. They say okay, but even us, we can't stay here, because the government force they are very powerful, with the tanks. We have to move constantly, every day, every night."

Kahassai repeated his request daily to go to the Sudan but was told he couldn't. During this time fighting for the guerrillas, he saw many people killed. What stayed with him most painfully was being close enough to witness three Russian MIGS attack a village and drop incendiary bombs like napalm or white phosphorous that caused many civilian deaths. The Soviet Union was closely allied with the Ethiopian government since the overthrow of Haile Selassie.

Kahassai finally tired of getting no response to his request to leave the fighting and go to Sudan. He and several friends decided to escape and make their own way. They found a local farmer and gave him some money to get directions. They then slipped out in the darkness of night. "It was raining and we didn't know where we was going. We been walking all night. The next day we came back to the same place. We did this thing and we kept quiet like we did nothing. We kept quiet." Their escape had been a folly as they had spent the night walking in a circle.

Two weeks later they made a second attempt. This was different. "We just run away. During the day, we just stay somewhere like in a tree. During the night, we have to walk." Walk they did, barefooted, all the way across

Eritrea, worried that the guerrilla soldiers would have followed them for deserting the camp. That was just one concern. They were walking through equatorial jungle and, "There were a lot of hyena when we walk. They follow us. There was a lot of snakes, poisonous snakes. The weather it was 120 degrees." They had almost no food except for some *kolo*, a roasted barley snack, that they brought along, and there was water in the jungle to be found.

They didn't know where they were going so, "There's a lot of different clans, they speak different languages. We don't know how to communicate with them. We communicate by sign, we go 'how to get to Sudan?'. We can't communicate with each other but when we say the word 'Sudan,' they show us by sign."

Overcoming all of this, they finally made it to Sudan, where communication continued to be a problem as neither Kahassai nor his friends spoke Arabic. They soon found that, "There were lot of Ethiopian people there. We tell them our story, how we get there. They were wondering how did you walk seven days with no food, no water. If you decide to do something from the bottom of your heart you can do it, even without food." That determination is Kahassai's story.

The Ethiopian community directed Kahassai and his friends to the office of the People's Liberation Front, the organization behind the guerrilla fighters. When they arrived, the people working there were aware of them and that they had left the guerrilla camp. Kahassai recalls, "They told us, 'Why you guys escaped? If you be patient, we already made a plan to bring you guys here.' That's bullshit, I told them. We been waiting, waiting, waiting for almost a year. They said once you got here we'll help you." Kahassai was skeptical. He located his aunt, who took him in and took care of him. She suggested that he learn Arabic and find a job. Kahassai decided to go to the U.N. office and register for resettlement. There was no refugee camp so this was done by a U.N. representative.

Kahassai and his friends told their story and how they had arrived there. They filled out the many forms involved for background checks and other required paperwork. "Finally, waiting, waiting then 'Oh, congratulations. You guys, you passed.' I was happy. I told my aunt. She was happy." He was going to be off on a new adventure, leaving his home far behind.

Later that year Kahassai boarded the plane and headed for Seattle. A group of 25 left the Sudan, sponsored by the IRC, the International Refugee Committee. They had an agent to greet them at the airport in their new country and arrange housing, provide some money until they could find jobs. Although Kahassai had learned English in school he rarely spoke it, so he attended ESL (English as a Second Language) classes and soon took jobs, working as a dishwasher and in housekeeping. He had many friends in Seattle but his health was poor.

The weather was obviously a big change but he thinks that wasn't the problem. He was a stranger in a strange land. "I sick in my heart. I miss my mom, I miss my home, I miss the place where I was born. Those two years I live in Seattle I didn't feel very well. They sent me to the tropical doctor, there's nothing. They check everything."

A friend who lived in Denver and worked as a manager of a 7-Eleven came to Seattle in late 1984 and Kahassai remembers that he told him, "Oh Kahassai, you don't have nothin', that's why you are sick. Why don't you move with me to Denver?" Kahassai thought he might as well give it a chance and it was the right choice. He had found home. "He brought me here in late 1984 and when I see the mountains, when I see the weather, I like, I love it. Because my hometown, it is surrounded by mountains and when I see mountains it and it reminds me a lot of Tigray. Oh, this is my state."

Things just got better. He loved the state and next he met a woman to make life complete. He explains the circumstances, "After I live here about a year some friends, they invite us to their house. I use to play krar (a five-stringed, bowl-shaped lyre). The girl she told them when he plays, his smile is nice." He was attracted and asked her to a movie, and things soon became serious. She was also from Ethiopia but from a different district, Oromo. "When I see her, I love her, she love me." They were married in 1986 and Kahassai was very happy.

They had two children, first a daughter and then a son. All were leading happy lives in their new country and they managed to relocate some of their family to Denver as things improved little in Ethiopia. Kahassai was reunited with his mother by bringing her and a brother from the Sudan to Denver. His wife's mother is also in Denver along with her brother from the Sudan, who has married and has two children. Kahassai has a good job as a driver for hotels on escort service to the airport.

Tragedy burst this bubble of happiness and success when Kahassai's wife was struck with ovarian cancer. "She was suffering for almost a year. We been suffering with her too." In 2014 she died, leaving him shattered. He says, "Always I used to cry. She's still in my heart. After she die I'm by myself but my kids helping me." Kahassai has a core that is built on religion and belief in determination that allows him to mourn for this as another of the many tragedies he has seen in his life, while not ceasing to look for hope in the future. Of his wife he says, "She was everything to me. She's the kindest person I ever met. And I always say thank you to God that I ever met her." Of her death his observation was, "This was a part of nature. There is nothing you can do. Something like that is for God." He's proud of his children, especially that "they love each other. Love is the key."

Kahassai's son inherited his father's size and athletic ability. "That's what he say all the time.

'Daddy, one day I'll make you proud.' " If he inherited his father's determination he might achieve his goal. As a successful college basketball player, he has his sights set on being the first Ethiopian to play in the National Basketball Association (NBA). Kahassai doesn't doubt him. That is his message after experiencing Ethiopian repression, the murder of his father, fighting with guerrilla forces and witnessing atrocities, walking across a country barefoot through a jungle with nearly no food or water while being followed by hyenas, then losing the love of his life: "We could do it. If you think, you decide from the bottom of your heart that you can do it. You can do it. We did it."

# CHAPTER FIFTEEN: ASBI AND LEELA FROM BHUTAN

Two refugees from Bhutan who ended up moving from the rooftop of the world to the rooftop of America are Asbi Mizer and Leela Timsina. Bhutan, the Land of the Thunder Dragon, is a small landlocked country about the size of Switzerland that sits between the world's two largest countries, China and India. Located in the Himalayas, it has a continuous history as a culture for over two-and-a-half thousand years. Leela and Asbi are included in the 135,000 people of Nepali origin who were forcefully expelled from Bhutan. One hundred eight thousand ended up living in the seven refugee camps in eastern Nepal administered by the United Nations Commission on Human Rights.[1] The first group of refugees had arrived in the U.S. before the end of 2007 with much larger numbers to follow by the spring of 2008. The U. S. was expected at the time to take up to 60,000.[2] In early 2008 absolute monarchy technically ended in Bhutan when a parliament was elected with two parties contesting for seats. Democracy was presented as a "gift from the king" and the two parties competed on their loyalty to the king and which would better implement a vaguely defined "gross happiness index."[3]

Those driven out of Bhutan had been and became long time refugees, existing in subsistence level camps. Resettlement in Colorado for many began after many years of exile and their stories tell of what they endured, the challenges they faced, and the opportunities a new life offered.

Buddhism was introduced from India in the eighth century and the following century small independent kingdoms were established by Tibetan lamas. Descendants of these settlers form the majority of Bhutan's present population. Tibetan Buddhism and religious feudalism followed as the country became a Lamaist theocracy where monks (lamas) were both religious and political leaders. Tibetan monk, Shabdrung Ngawang Namgyal, united the area within its present borders in the 1600s and the small territory has 18 distinct indigenous languages.[4]

This had remained the situation for centuries, interrupted by periods of rule by Tibet and China. In the 1700s there were border clashes with India which began conflict with Britain. As border raids and tensions continued a British army invaded Bhutan and it was quickly defeated, making Bhutan a virtual protectorate. In the late nineteenth century, the British encouraged large-scale immigration of Nepalese into southwestern Bhutan where they were known as the *Lhotshampas* (southerners). This Hindu minority was not assimilated by the Bhutanese. Asbi and Leela would eventually be among this group.

There were competing factions for power in Bhutan since the theocratic powers had taken hold. In 1907 state control by one of the governors, Uygen Wangchuck, gained supremacy over the others and transformed Bhutan into an absolute monarchy. His power remained solely within the borders of the country when three years later, by the Treaty of Punakha, Bhutan became a full protectorate of Britain, with British India controlling its foreign affairs though it remained a kingdom. The majority of Bhutan's Buddhists were members of the Drukpa sect of Tibetan Buddhism. They were used to theocratic rule and accepted the state and religion as synonymous. In Bhutan Buddhism was not a matter of what Buddha preached, but of how the state interpreted it to perpetuate despotic rule. The king was the equal of Buddha so criticism of the king could lead one to be charged with treason of religion.

Rejecting the king's rule was considered sacrilege. The king and Buddhism were interwoven.[5] For the Hindu Nepalese minority, such a close association of church and state threatened serious danger.

Britain recognized Bhutanese autonomy in 1935 and in 1959 Bhutan banned Nepalese immigration, while persecution against its Nepalese minority was widespread. In 1972 Bhutan's Jigme Dorji Wangchuk, known as the *Druk Gyalpo* or King of the Dragon People, died at the age of 45. His 16-year old son, Jigme Singye Wangchuk, assumed the throne with the audacious title of Fearless Thunderbolt and Master of the Cosmic Powers.[6] The new king created Bhutan's first cabinet but did not increase public political participation.

By 1988 there were growing concerns about the increase of the proportion of the population that was Nepalese and the government responded with the policy of *Driglam Namzha*, or national customs and etiquette. This is sometimes known as "Bhutanization". Mass deportations began of Nepalese in Bhutan. The Nepalese population in Bhutan was estimated at 40% in 1990 and was down to 28% within several years.[7]

Leela was in fourth grade when he first recalled feeling organized national persecution. It was February of 1991 when the Royal government of Bhutan banned the use of Nepalese in schools in its program that led to ethnic strife in Bhutan.[8] The ban was imposed in a manner to intimidate as he remembers, "The first thing I witnessed was we were all were called out in front of the school and all Nepalese books were burned in front of me."[9]

The Bhutanization program was directed against the Lhotshampas and eventually rid the country of this group, to such a degree that some who experienced it have described as "ethnic cleansing"[10]. While these policies were particularly directed against the Nepalese ethnic community and its increasing population, limits on freedom of religion also applied to Bhutan's other Hindus and Christians as well.[11]

Everyone in the country was forced to adopt the culture and styles of the indigenous Buddhist population, most of whom lived in the north of the country, and were known collectively as 'Drukpas'. When it began, the Hindu Lhotshampas and others were forced to hide their identity. This involved not being allowed to use their language in school or wear their traditional dress. In public, the Lhotshampas were required to wear the "national dress."

National dress meant females were required to wear a *kira*, a rectangular piece of cloth wrapped around the body and secured at the shoulders by the silver clasps. Males wore a *gho*, a robe-like garment, pulled up at the waist to form a large pouch over the abdomen. Women were expected to abandon Nepalese hairstyles. Large fines were imposed on those who violated the new policy and wore their traditional clothes or spoke Nepali. Students were forced to get identical haircuts, then came religious persecution. Leela described, "We were forced to eat beef and pork in the school, even though we were Hindu and don't touch pork and we don't eat meat."

There was a backlash against Bhutanization and changes instituted by the government with its north Buddhist Drukpa domination. Teknath Rizel initiated a human rights movement in Bhutan as he formed the People's Forum for Human Rights, Bhutan (PFHRB). Another organization that was active in demanding change was the Bhutan People's Party (BPP). Supporters of these movements organized the first peaceful protests in Bhutan's history in the early 1990s. Leela was beginning to understand the oppression his people faced and "realized that there was no human rights." The government responded to this nonviolent expression of dissatisfaction by unleashing a reign of terror against its Nepalese citizens in the south. When 18,000 demonstrated in nine separate places during September and October, 1990 the government feared an open revolt and labeled them "terrorists". [12]

Leela recalls, "They were making application to the king, and instead of hearing the people's voice, they started torture our people recklessly." Asbi says he "witnessed mistreatment."[13] The army moved in to clear out the Nepalese, and atrocities were committed. The stifling of identity would motivate many more Nepalese in Bhutan to become activists.

Raping women as a show of force was a common Bhutanese government terror practice. Both Asbi and Leela were too young to be activists but they recall what called Leela described as "The intensity of torture and random rape scenarios"[14] Asbi said that every night, the army would come to his village and women were lost. He used to hear them cry out, sometimes women's cries and sometimes young girls'. In Leela's words, "They raped our mothers, our sisters and all the girls in the community." This included pregnant women and young girls who were still children in his recollection.

Leela's house was burned down by the government, like those of many other Nepalese, and his father had a narrow escape from threats to his life, while government authorities hung his older brother upside down and forced him to pledge to leave the country. Amnesty International detailed torture and rape carried out by the Bhutanese Royal Army against its Nepalese-speaking population in a 1992 report.[15]

This was all too much so both Asbi's and Leela's families fled Bhutan in 1992 and became refugees. Asbi was 13 at the time and Leela several years younger. Asbi noted that "we were barefooted." Leela says the army closed in on them and was "lining up in our village with bullets and guns, so we thought it is better to be safe." To escape Bhutan they made their way to the Indian border but when Asbi, Leela and the other Lhotshampas reached India, they were denied entry. Says Leela, "The Indian government, they didn't want us to be there, because of their diplomatic relation." In Asbi's words, they were, loaded in a truck "like animals," and police took them to West Bengal. They had left their home and were being transported but these children knew little more. For

Absi, the one stable thing was having his mom there the whole time to hold him. It was a rough journey and he remembers asking his mom, "Where are we going?" She told him through her tears, "We are going, we are going." That was it. Where they were headed was to Nepal. Leela explained, "So, the Indian government, they loaded us in a truck. And brought back to Nepal-Indian border, and they threw us back into Nepal." Nepal would soon ask the UN for assistance as the refugee numbers were so large.[16]

The first refugees from Bhutan had arrived in Nepal in 1991, with another large influx that included Asbi and Leela in 1992. Only a small trickle came in the months and years that followed. Their official population would soon reach 101,300.[17]

Leela was admitted to a Bhutanese refugee camp in Nepal in June 1992. There was something final about arriving there that was especially difficult at first since it made leaving Bhutan real. He noted, "I observed that my parents were gazing toward the north, the location of our country, sobbing with tears due to the cancerous pain on leaving their motherland."[18]

They would both spend nearly two decades and grow into an adult in Nepalese camps, living on hope at a barely subsistence level. Absi explained the 1992 situation: "There were already five camps I think, because Nepal has two districts. One is eastern part of Nepal and one is Jhapa and the other is Morang. I was in Morang district of Nepal. That is Sanischare Refugee Camp." There would soon be seven Bhutanese refugee camps located within an hour's drive of each other.[19]

It wasn't a pleasant place and they were children. Asbi said, "Refugee camp was like a prison." As for living conditions, another Denver refugee from Bhutan who spent 22 years in the Nepali camps said that he and his family, "lived in the refugee camps in crowded bamboo huts that often caught fire."[20] The refugees had escaped danger but lived in squalor. They began on the bank of a river where temperatures were extreme and their shelters were small plastic huts. The United Nations' Higher Commissioner for Refugees (UNHCR) provided for their basic needs, but food was not adequate, medical supplies were insufficient, safe drinking water was in short supply, and facilities were not sanitary in these initial camps. Asbi said that rations consisted of rice, some vegetables, oil, and that to have anything else they had to buy it from the market. Since most had no money that meant they were undernourished and used to get meat perhaps once every three or four months.

The demands of refugee life took a toll. A study done on detained Bhutanese refugees in Nepal three years after Asbi and Leela arrived that found a majority of those interred suffered from some form of mental disorder related to stress or trauma.[21]

Sepu Nepal is a Bhutanese refugee who spent 22 years in camps in Nepal before coming to Denver where he worked providing advice on getting medical services for refugees. He said, "Most of the refugees, they have mental difficulties. Like they have Post Traumatic Stress Disorder. Spending hard, hard life. Then they have mental issues."[22] These comments on refugees from Bhutan and PSTD are supported in academic literature.[23]

Both Asbi and Leela received an education in refugee camp. While Asbi felt that his rights were severely restricted, including freedom of movement and the right to work, he is grateful to a group called Characters Nepal that provided English instruction and was responsible for education in his camps. Asbi had hoped to return to Bhutan but made no attempt. He explained the political situation at the time as, "When the bilateral talks, Bhutan, Nepal, representatives from different countries, when they talked, we could not find any solution."

For Leela, school in camp would lead him to his major life-changing adventure. He was put in grade five when he arrived. After several years and beginning to mature, he understood more about politics. As he did, he learned about his homeland's past. Following his completion of the ninth grade in 1996, Leela became active in a youth movement. "It's a nonviolent organized movement that tried to go to Bhutan and appeal to the King." Since he had been a young boy when they fled, he thought he hadn't done anything wrong there, so he wanted to return to his country. "So, I decided to join that group." Leela was just reaching adolescence by this time and the decision would have more consequences than he could have anticipated. He and his group optimistically planned to leave the refugee camp and make a peaceful march to Thimpu, Bhutan, the country's capital. Once there, they hoped to meet with the King for reconciliation and repatriation.

Not surprisingly their trip didn't go as planned. Leela and his group made their way to the India- Nepal border and when they attempted to cross, they were detained by the Indian Army and Indian police. He recalls, "So I was stopped at the India-Nepal border by the Indian army, Indian police, and I was detained in prison along with another 174 members." They were arrested for violating section 144 of the India Penal Code and put in prison for 15 days. Section 144 was initially drawn up by India´s British colonial rulers after World War I to prohibit public gatherings for Indian independence. Their march received attention in the Asian press.[24]

The Indian government got pressure from local communities and they were transferred to a different prison for another 15 days. This led to greater pressure from outside human rights and civil rights organizations, as well as the local community. The pressure led to their release on the condition that they could not again march on Indian land. "So, we were out and we decided to go and march again, and we were arrested."

This time, in January 1996, Leela received an eight-month sentence as a 14-year-old. He went to prison for his attempt to appeal to the King, then had to return to Nepal and refugee camp. While the quest was a failure, he considers his prison sentence a very pivotal time in his life. He read the biographies of Martin Luther King, Jr., Mahatma Gandhi, Nelson Mandela, and Aung San Suu Kyi: "When I was in prison, that motivated me in my whole life to become a social leader or a community leader." In a way, it was time well spent, even though the attempt to reach Bhutan was a failure, and it would be some time before he could put what he had learned into practice.

Leela was back in the refugee camp and looking for other options. There were many people like him who were seeking ways to escape life in the camps. He began looking at the option of resettlement and approached the UN about the process. It was a long procedure but until it was initiated nothing would happen. In the camp, Leela continued to attend school and eventually finished high school, though not as a member of the class he had begun with because of his venture to India and time in jail.

The refugee camp allowed arrangements for working and studying outside if there was good reason. Ethnic and linguistic similarities permitted some de facto integration. Leela and Asbi both took advantage of the opportunities they could find to prepare for the future. Since education only went to the high school level in the camp, they sought exemption to carry on outside.

Asbi got a scholarship to go to India for his undergraduate degree and following that, did his master's degree in Kathmandu. It took him several years to complete his master's in linguistics and English, but he says, "If you have money you can go and have education," though he could only come and go by reporting to the authorities.

Leela also received higher education, attending Tribhuvan University in Kirtipur, near Kathmandu. He received a bachelor's degree in sociology and began work on a master's. He worked as an assistant teacher at and elementary school, a middle school, and a secondary school and was eventually named assistant principal, then principal of a school. He was masking his identity as refugees were considered illegal workers. While they shared culture and values, "It was a humiliation to live in Nepal in a fear of false identity."[25]

In 2008, the UN began placing Bhutanese refugees in countries willing to host them, and Asbi applied. He had three options. Their first choice was repatriation, to send him back to his home country which was his preferred choice. The second possibility was local integration, that he would resettle in Nepal. The third option was being resettled in another country. Through much of the time they were in Nepal, there had been negotiations between Bhutan and Nepal about the large refugee population. The murder of the King of Nepal and his family in 2001 led to instability in that country, hampering already shaky prospects. A joint ministerial meeting between Nepal and Bhutan reached an agreement that effectively eliminated the possibility of nearly all refugees' possibilities returning to Bhutan.[26] Integration into Nepal was rejected by the Nepalese, and integration into India was rejected for consideration by the refugees. Repatriation to Bhutan was no longer an option.

Absi's decision was clear. "I chose the final option, to be resettled." Leela also applied for resettlement. The U.S. originally agreed to take 60,000 from Bhutan, but the *Himalayan Times* announced in September, 2016, that the 90,000th Bhutanese had departed Nepal for resettlement in the U.S.[27]

Asbi and Leela applied in 2008 but resettlement is a lengthy process. They found that there were many steps to be taken. It began with their interview which was followed by screening. There was a thorough procedure and a long time before the results were final, so the wait was extensive. For Leela it took two years and he was approved in 2010 after 18 years in refugee camp. For Asbi his approval came in 2011 after three years wait and 19 years in camps. When everything was done and they got a flight schedule, the final step was cultural orientation. A number of factors go into the location of resettlement, including community and relatives. These led them both to Denver. Leela recalls making the long trip and landing at Denver International Airport with $15 and 15 kilograms of belongings. What was clearly extreme culture shock was made easier, as waiting to greet him when he arrived was his case manager and his brother's best friend. These were people who spoke his language, and it made him "feel very welcome at that situation when I see people from my same community and mainstream people there to welcome me."

Asbi arrived a year later, landing at 8:30 P.M., but it was still light, since it was in June. For him it was a family reunion. Along with his case worker, there were two of his family members who had arrived before he had, "I felt so welcomed!" A furnished two-bedroom apartment had already been prepared for him and his two sisters who accompanied him.

After arriving in Colorado, they went through cultural orientation once again. Asbi said at that time, "USA means You Start Again." One way both Asbi and Leela started again was by enrolling for ESL classes at Emily Griffith, the premier school for refugees and immigrants in Denver, to improve their English. Leela's first attempt to get to Emily Griffith was a positive introduction to the Denver public. He took a bus and all he knew was that his stop was Weldon Street. He was riding, and recalls, "I heard the bus driver was saying 'Well done.' So, I thought that I was doing well." The bus continued until it reached its final destination, then Leela asked the driver if he knew where Emily Griffith School was. The driver did not know, but attempted to help him, though unsuccessfully. Leela got off the bus, lost in downtown, and he began asking people for help. It was his first experience, and, "Even if I am from different background, if I'm an immigrant, they knew that; but they not caring about who I am, what color I am, what race I am, what religion I belong to, they try to help me."

The situation for refugees like Asbi and Leela was explained by Harry Budisidharta, an Indonesian lawyer who serves as the Deputy Director of Aurora, Colorado's Asian Pacific Development Center: "They can immediately get a work permit, they can get driver's licenses, they get health care. After one year, they can apply for a green card. Then after five years they can apply to become U.S. citizens."[28] The both had work permits, so soon after arriving they were looking for work, since their allotment is limited, and they had to repay their airfare to the U.S. This need for income is especially true in expensive cities like Denver. Asbi got a job as a dishwasher in a hotel, but didn't last as he couldn't tolerate the constant standing. From that he moved on to working nights for a pickle company. Leela found a job in the Denver Public Schools as an assistant teacher.

Both Asbi and Leela were soon assisting new refugees as they arrived in the Denver metropolitan area. Asbi began as a volunteer during the day when he worked for the pickle company at night. He would drive people from the airport to their homes, then drive to deliver items donated by organization to the families. He was volunteering for the African Community Center, an organization that, in spite of its name, serves the worldwide refugee community that is settled in Denver. His volunteer job led to a regular job, and from that he progressed to an executive position in the large organization. Leela soon emerged as a full-time organizer and one of Denver's leaders in the refugee community. Among other things, he became board president of a community support organization and attended the National Immigrant Integration Conference in December 2015 in Washington, D.C. He also chaired the city's Immigrant and Refugee Task Force.

They both became U.S. citizens after five years of residency. Both also expressed considerable optimism about their many opportunities in the U.S. and their acceptance in Colorado.

There has been a dimming of their enthusiasm since the presidential campaign and election. Says Asbi, "Before the election we were having a kind of fear that we would be deported, or that we would be considered as refugees forever. We have our past experience that we fled our country, lived in other's countries as refugees, and also had to leave that country." Leela's similar sentiment is, "Refugees, they have fear in the community. We're thinking that we're going to be deported even if we're in the country legally. Our government has changed and Donald Trump, he is giving very bad speech against refugees in this nation."

# PICTURE ME HERE

*Photo by Bhawani Dahal*

It was in a refugee camp like this that Asbi, Leela and many others Lhotshampas in Nepal spent their lives growing from children to adults. Bhawani, who took this photo of the Beldangi II Refugee camp in Nepal, was resettled in 2014 after spending 22 years here. His photo was part of a creative artistic project that made their experience more available to the public. In 2012, Brigid McAuliffe, a photographer and videographer, had a meeting in Aurora, Colorado with Lauren Dorn and Erin Preston among others and they came up with an idea to explore the refugee and broader immigrant experience both artistically and through providing photography workshops. They began by meeting with a group of Bhutanese women for five months and offering workshops that fostered closer relationships.[1] This inspired them to explore an ongoing program and their group launched *Picture Me Here* in 2013.

Nearly 4000 refugees had come from Bhutan to Colorado by this time, with the most settling in the Denver Metropolitan area.[2] Having worked with Bhutanese groups and realizing they had little or no access to photography in the refugee camps, where they spent an average of twenty years, the group was inspired to go to the Beldangi refugee camp for Bhutanese refugees in Nepal where most of those resettled in Denver had once lived, find refugees approaching resettlement in Colorado, and have them record the experience. Their plan was to bring cameras to Nepal and teach refugees bound for Colorado how to use them. This would capture both camp life in Nepal, plus the adjustment to the U.S. The instructors and interpreters went to Nepal in April 2014. The United Nations Refugee Agency granted them access to camps and helped them locate people who were likely to soon resettle in Denver.

Once they were there, they provided cameras and taught two weeks of classes on photography to fourteen camp residents who would soon be resettling in Colorado. The participants were allowed to keep their cameras and continue documenting their journey and resettlement with the help of instructors from Emily Griffith Technical College in Denver.

This relationship with Nepal refugee camps carried on and the program expanded to other areas of the world. The photographs enjoyed considerable recognition and acclaim, allowing Denver, and through media and online all of Colorado, an insight into the lives of some of the area's new residents.

Boys playing at refugee camp, pictured by Bhawani.

*Photo by Bhawani Dahal*

Durga observed some of the elders at the camp.

*Photo by Durga Basnet*

Bhim's neighbor sieving rice to make the family's food, a process she goes through twice daily.

*photo by Bhim Bahadur Bhattarai*

Kalpana took this photo of a boy playing marbles in a camp. He said he played marbles and other games when he was in the camp.

*Photo by Kalpana Rai*

Child in camp.

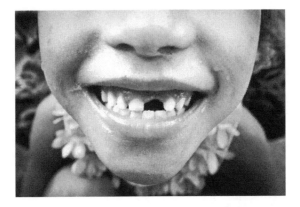

*Photo by Kalpana Rai*

The Nepalese have castes, and that was carried with them to Bhutan and the refugee camps. Mohan said of this photo that she took, "When I see this dirty girl, I took photo. She looked sad. Maybe she is from the shame caste. The King made the castes in ancient times. Brahmin is the upper caste. Next is Chhetris. Next is Vaishyas (Monger, Tamang, Rai, etc…) and Shudras (Kami, Damari, Sarki, etc…). The lower castes cannot enter into the Brahmin home. The King of the Brahmin made those rules."

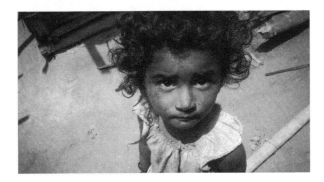

*Photo by Mohan Rai*

A refugee as he finally leaves camp, photograph by Mani.

*Photo by Mani Kumar*

Birendra had his photo taken after resettling in Denver, as he stands at the counter of the gas station where he worked on the night shift. He has since become a teacher for Emily Griffith's Picture Me Here.

*Photo by Birendra Dhakal*

Mia took this picture of her sister who, she said, wants to be like Princess Diana.

*Photo by Maria Mu*

Maria's photo of her grandmother resting was taken, she said, because of her importance to the family, including taking care of Maria's sisters and brother

*Photo by Maria Mu*

Isaiah calls this his self-portrait, since he took it when he was studying for his exam for medical interpreter training. He says it shows his personality, that he's studious, and physical appearance, because he wears glasses.

*Photo by Isaiah Gwa*

Maria photographed her sister wearing the uniform her aunt wears for work at the meat-packing factory. This is a major refugee job in the Denver area that pays high wages for unpleasant work. Maria's aunt left for work at 2 P.M. and returned at 2 A.M. but had to stop because she got sick.

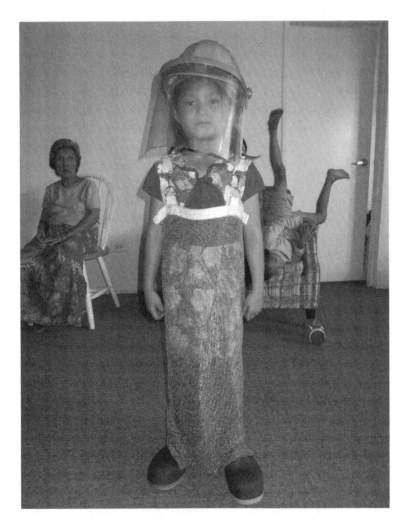

*Photo by Maria Mu*

# CHAPTER SIXTEEN: RASULO, SOMALIA

Rasulo was born in Somalia. Many people have heard about Somalia because of popular movies based on real events. *Captain Phillips* was a 2013 film starring Tom Hanks about Somali pirates who hijacked the container ship *Maersk Alabama* in 2009 and took Phillips and his crew hostage. This was not an isolated event, as The World Shipping Council noted in 2011 that over half of the 439 pirate attacks in the world and over half of the 45 merchant vessel hijackings in the world occurred in the Gulf of Aden, off the coast of Somalia, and in the nearby Indian ocean.[1] Somalia has been called the piracy capital of the world.

An earlier movie that focused on Somalia is the 2001 film *Black Hawk Down.* This is the story of 160 U.S. Army Rangers and Special Forces who were dropped in the Somalian capital, Mogadishu, by Black Hawk helicopters to capture a warlord and were met by hundreds of Somali gunmen. Two helicopters were destroyed and 18 Americans died. Images of a captured U.S. pilot and American bodies being dragged through the streets were seen worldwide.

The less publicized story behind what led to *Black Hawk Down* reveals more about Rasulo's country. Somalia was experiencing famine while the clan-based or tribe-based warfare prevented any response. There were raids on humanitarian aid and President George H. W. Bush announced that the United States would intervene as part of a United Nations peace-keeping force to assure the delivery of that relief. On December 9, 1992, U.S. naval commandos landed in Somalia. By seeing that the outside aid got to those in need, American forces saved anywhere from 100,000 to a million lives and cut the number of refugees in half.[2] Dominic Tierney reported, "Overall, 43 Americans died in Somalia, or one for every 2,500 Somali lives saved. But in the American mind, Somalia became synonymous with a single word: failure."[3]

The then not so famous Osama bin Laden wrote in August 1996, "Your most disgraceful case was in Somalia... you left the area carrying disappointment, defeat, and your dead with you."[4] Terrorism is also commonly associated with Somalia.

Somalia is a Texas-sized country shaped a bit like a seven that is on the Horn of Africa protruding into the Indian Ocean. Calling Somalia a country is almost an exaggeration, considering its condition and history since it came into existence. Rasulo comes from Kismayo, south of the major city, Mogadishu. The area that is now Somalia has been occupied by Somalis since ancient times, and ages ago Persian and Arab traders established posts there while nomadic tribes occupied the interior. In the nineteenth century, the Europeans came to the region. The British arrived in the Gulf of Aden in 1839 to develop a coaling station for ships traveling to India. The French and Italians followed later for similar purposes and took different spots on the coastline. When the scramble for Africa began in 1880, these countries were contending for power, while an African rival, its neighbor to the west, Ethiopia, joined the struggle in seeking Somalian territory. In the mid-twentieth century, it would eventually become British Somaliland and Italian Somaliland.

Rasulo's home was in what had been the Italian colony. He says, "For the first time when the Italians were in there it was not about tribe-based. It was about whoever lives in Somalia, you are Somalian."[5] At the time, it was just one Somalia, based on language. While there are different dialects, everyone spoke the same language. No single tribe or clan had power over the others.

In 1960, the British and Italian parts of Somalia gained independence. They joined together to form a country officially named the United Republic of Somalia. As a republic, it was going to be ruled by a president and Aden Abdullah Osman Daar was the first president to be elected. Somalia was a country made up of clans and tribes, and adopting Western democracy was not an easy adjustment. Since independence, Somali governments have promoted the false notion that Somalia is a homogeneous nation.[6]

Rasulo believes that introducing elections in Somalia is a case where democracy did not lead to a more inclusive government. He explains that once a president was elected, he would turn to members of his tribe to hold the important positions in the government since they were closest to him. He says, "Italians, they did not have this in mind. They say Somalia if you're going to be independent we're going to give you this, we're going to build you that, go ahead." So, the president could choose his vice president, his prime minister, his secretary of agriculture and the rest of his administration and they would all be from his tribe. "You look at it, there's only one tribe that's governing. So, then the other tribes say, wait a minute. What is going on here?"

This was to have special relevance to Rasulo, as he is a Bantu, and his tribe had very little power in Somalia. With independence came persecution that would only grow worse. Bantu-speaking peoples constitute a portion of the population of nearly all African countries south of the Sahara. Rasulo says, "Bantu tribe is majority in central Africa but when you come to Somalia it is just a little piece." There are over 300 Bantu groups, each with its own language or dialect, the best-known being the Swahili and the Zulu. In Somalia there are Bantu who are indigenous to the country and others whose ancestors were brought there as slaves from Bantu-speaking tribes in the Nineteenth Century and have integrated into society. They are a persecuted minority, viewed and treated as foreigners. Their "predominant Negroid physical features are distinct from that of the Somali nomads and give them a unique identity."[7] Rasulo puts it, "Those who are looking like me, I suppose that is the easiest way to express it."

The Bantu were able to establish themselves as farmers and were the backbone of agricultural production in southern Somalia. Rasulo notes, "They are agricultural people, they grow everything so I don't know why they don't want someone who is producing things. They just want to keep the land to themselves." The Bantu did have their land taken and they were discriminated against. They were persecuted in politics, economics, and in education. They were allowed to do primary and secondary school but they were not allowed to go to college. People from Rasulo's area of the Juba were variously referred to as *Wagosha* ("people of the forest"), *Jareer* (a term for Africans with kinky hair), while Somali Bantu in general were sometimes called *adoon* and *habash*, words that mean "slave." They were also called *ooji*, which is Italian for "today" and is a reference to Somali's idea that Bantus lacked the ability to think beyond what was happening at the present time.[8] Such stereotyping and name-calling was a part of their persecution.

The country stumbled through border wars, an assassination of its president, a coup, famine and widespread starvation as opposition plots by different clans and warlords grew to claim control of the government. A failed coup led a clan to form the Somali National Movement in the early 1980s. The Siyaad Barre regime's response was to attack cities where the resistance was located, and human rights organizations reported that more than 50,000 were killed.[9] The insurgency grew and led to a full-scale civil war in 1988. The first battle of Mogadishu started in late December 1990. Little notice was taken by the outside world as the international community was completely focused on the beginning of the Gulf War.

Washington's view at the time was that whoever emerged as the victor would have U.S. support.[10] In January 1991, Siyaad Barre's regime collapsed and there was a power struggle that reduced the country to anarchy.

This is where Rasulo's story as a refugee begins. He said, "I left Somalia when I was seven years old. I lived in a refugee camp in Kenya. It was 1992. The civil war started and it was getting very bad and my dad just tried to kind of save us." His family made its way north to Dadaab Refugee Camp in Kenya. "I was seven when I entered camp, and came to Denver when I was 24, so I pretty much grew up in the refugee camp." Dadaab camp is run by the UNHCR with partners CARE International and Doctors Without Borders. Other NGOs including UNICEF and local Kenyan organizations provided support and local police provided security with occasional backup from the Kenyan Army. The year Rasulo fled was the beginning of a Bantu exodus from Somalia and by 1994 there were 10,000 in Kenyan refugee camps.[11]

Dadaab remains extremely large and in 2016 was named the world's largest refugee camp with approximately half a million inhabitants.[12] Each refugee family in the Dadaab camp was given a canvas tent, basic cooking utensils, and a can for collecting drinkable water from taps located around the camp. Wheat, beans, salt, sugar, and oil were handed out once every two weeks, and other food could be purchased at the refugee camp market. As for toilet facilities, they would dig their own latrines. The Bantu faced discrimination in the refugee camps also and to protect themselves against nighttime bandit attacks, they constructed compounds, guarded by armed sentries. In the years when Rasulo first arrived, the Bantu suffered violent attacks. Refugee women were vulnerable to rape while collecting firewood in the bush and were reported to sometimes be asked their clan affiliation before being attacked.[13]

For Rasulo it worked out. He says, "I started my primary school in the refugee camp. I got my secondary degree in the refugee camp. I went to college in Kenya for two years. I got my associate degree back home then."

So, he had become and adult in the refugee camp and was hoping to move on to something else. "The resettlement in the United States is not as quick as you can think. It takes for my family about three and a half years just to get in the process, to get the process started." Rasulo started in 2001and they did a demographic study on him, did a background check, and took it to the United Nations. There they checked the information he had given to see if it matched with what they had, to see if it was accurate. From there his and other Bantus' information went to either their "ambassador or to the United Nations." In late 2001, the United Nations took these cases, 200,000 Somalian Bantus, to the United States and said, "We have these people, they cannot go back to Somalia because of the civil war, they're being persecuted, they've been having problems since then, how can we help them?"' The United States agreed to resettle 12,000 Somali Bantu who live in the refugee camps.

Rasulo spoke of President Clinton agreeing to settle Somali refugees in the United States but the process was frozen after 9/11. He stated that the first Somali that was settled in the USA came in 2004, the first in Denver came that year. "I was fortunate to come in July, 2004. I was one of the first to be resettled in the U.S." This is apparently a reference to Somali Bantus, as records show the first Somali to settle in Colorado arrived in 1986 and about 800 had arrived by 2003. His arrival in 2004 did begin a dramatic shift, as 275 arrived in Colorado, up from 77 and 40 the two previous years. This marked the beginning of consecutive years of three digit arrivals and by 2014 the number from Somalia had reached 3,575.[14]

Rasulo was fortunate to be early when hundreds of thousands had fled Somalia. But being early came with responsibilities as he notes: "It has been very tough. I was not only one of the first, but one of the first who speaks English, so I had a very heavy load to help them with daily survival." He became the person many of the Somali newcomers turned to for help making their way as they attempted to resettle. He continues to take on this role. It can involve anything with resettling in a new place and he helps them look for homes, look for schools, get work and see doctors, many other details. Very common is translation, which he often does, and ends up being frequently junk mail. But new arrivals don't know, as he explains, "A piece of mail come and they will come to me and say, 'What did it say?' And I say look it is just an advertisement. And all these guys they come, hey, tell me about it and it's a King Soopers ad." He says that he still remembers what it's like for the very first time with all these things, and their health, their kids' education. That is why he supports them even if it can be quite a bit of work.

Being a Muslim, Rasulo has also had to adjust to life in Denver. "Being Muslim at first it was tough," he recalls. In his early years, he didn't know many people and was very confused, still making the huge adjustment from his previous life. The Iraq War was ongoing and there were still terrorism concerns following 9/11. He found people in Denver to be very welcoming and open at the time: "They wanted to learn something from me, and I was getting some help from them, teaching me transportation and other things."

Now that he is a citizen and fully adjusted after over ten years of living in Denver, he is less satisfied, though he doesn't seem to be referring to Denver when he says, "It's just recently that things aren't so good but for that time they were very open."

Since Somalia was put on the first Executive Order of five countries with restrictions for entering the U.S., then the second of four, he feels differently: "Now one of banned countries. You're having hope then turning hope around. It's like being told there's no hope at all." In his view this is a group punishment based on individual actions while many innocent victims suffer. He says, "It's not about one individual who did something wrong. What about those thousands and thousands of children that are innocent who have hope of coming to the United States?" He believes that the ban on Somalian refugees will destroy all their hope of getting an education and having a better life. "I'm working in the United States of America and contributing in any way that I can. Those kids will be like me. They will grow up here and get a chance to contribute to the culture." While the travel ban was in a state of limbo, having been rejected in federal court, but still on appeal, he said "Absolutely it is kind of an insult." Rasulo adds, "Even those who had been in camp since 1990s and had been hoping to come a couple weeks ago, they cannot come. We say no, we are shutting our doors, so stay away from us. So, they are back in the refugee camps." He remains hopeful that the government will "work on this, tweak it around" so that refugees from Somalia will soon he allowed to arrive without suspicion or restriction.

Rasulo believes the only hope for his country is to allow children to escape and become refugees so like him, they can learn of a different life. In America we sometimes think of Millennials as obsessed with video games and overeducated, underemployed, living off their parents. While these stereotypes certainly don't reflect reality for all, they provide an interesting comparison for the argument Rasulo makes for refugees from Somalia. He says, "From 1990 to 2006 to right now, those people that were born in the civil war, they don't even know what the peace looks like. They have no idea, because they were born in a civil war, they grew up in a civil war, they got married in a civil war, they have children in a civil war. There is no regular education They just learn from what they see. The only thing they know is get a gun, and if you kill somebody, you get something. If they don't have an education, they're dead. And if they can't become refugees, they're stuck there. They know is get your AK47. It is highly available. You see somebody that is killed and you pick up that. It's your own. There are too many children, their entire life is based on that gun. Just go and kill somebody, loot something, to get something out of that."

So, there is no proper way to educate young teenagers and for them to find legitimate employment that will support them. Violence is their option unless they can flee the country and become refugees. Then there is hope, as education is provided and if they are resettled, some will go on to higher education. "Being a refugee is a hope, but now with the ban, that is less. And refugee camp that is just basic living things. It is just basic, basic, basic. So, there is not that much elevation for them there but if there is hope for them to come here from there, that is the excellent hope. So, they can be educated here."

Reports on Voice of America cited studies that showed that local militias and war lords have recruited children to be soldiers as have as the terrorist group al-Shabab and even the Transitional Federal Government, the closest thing to an actual official army. While most are between 10 and 17 years old, some are as young as seven and eight.[15]

Somali is a truly failed state, without a legitimate government since 1991, making it the longest failed state in the world.[16] It is tragic in so many ways. In the most recent listing it ranked as the world's most corrupt state.[17] It has been judged the worst country in Africa for rule of law.[18] It has also been rated the world's worst place to be a mother.[19]

Given these conditions, Rasulo sees hope only in the young people who are raised outside the country. He says that the old ways and tribal and clan rivalries that doom the country to stagnation carry over when they become immigrants and refugees. There is hope of a Somalian diaspora returning, but Rasulo doesn't think it will matter unless they have changed. He believes it is possible that some people will go back and try to make things better as Somalians rather than as their tribe. But that change is not taking place among those who spent time in refugee camps and resettled in Denver. Denver is still tribe oriented. There are some Somali stores, some Somali restaurants and people look for their tribe when they congregate. Within a restaurant, each tribe will have its own location. "So that is how it has been since they grew up. They do that no matter what the setting. I go there to the restaurant I know that is where my tribe will be, I sit there. My tribe will come they will sit with me," says Rasulo.

As with many refugee conditions, he sees the hope lies with the children. "The children doesn't have that much about it yet." The children who are born here will look around. They don't act that way so much because when they are in school, when they are other places they are more intermingled. There are many different ethnic groups in their classrooms. What encourages him is "If they can intermingle here then maybe they can intermingle back there."

Rasulo's other concern was that people have misperceptions about Muslims. He said, "Every community there's a black sheep." His argument is that in any group a person could name it would contain someone in it who does something bad, and when a Muslim does something bad it is not fair to say that Muslims are bad. "You know, every fish has different smell. So, if you see one fish bite you today and you say all fish is bad," is his metaphor, adding, "that's not how you should react." He encourages people to study Muslims and learn from Muslims, also to find the bad Muslims. What upsets him is when people make generalizations about Islam without having taken the time to learn about it. Regarding learning about Muslims and Islam, he says, "Google, Wikipedia, don't trust those sources. Maybe somebody who doesn't like Muslims put something up so don't trust them to be good sources." He recommends going to the community members, people who know the religion: "You won't become a Muslim right away." He is a regular Bible reader since he wants to be able to explain things in both his religion and Christianity.

Rasulo will not return to Somalia "unless things change considerably."

"If I go back to visit it's a 50- 50 chance. You either come back alive or you are dead. I don't want to risk that," he says. If it becomes stable and things are safe then he would return, but, "Right now, when there is a war going on and every other second things are exploding, I don't want to risk that." He still believes there is hope, though it is likely to take a long time. That hope is the younger people, if they can escape the influences and get an education, learn to live without tribe or clan prejudices then return as the new, capable generation to revitalize and modernize his failed state.

# CHAPTER SEVENTEEN, REFUGEES, REQUIREMENTS, RULES

Refugees constitute a special category of immigrant. The lawful definition of a refugee in the U.S. was taken directly from a meeting of 26 UN states in Geneva. This followed a UN resolution to draft and sign a convention relating to the Status of Refugees, and a Protocol relating to the Status of Stateless Persons.[1] They specified "events before January 1, 1951," relating to World War II refugees, but their definition of what made a person a refugee was: "Owing to a well-founded fear of being persecuted for reasons of race, religion, nationality, membership of a particular social group or political opinion, is outside the country of his nationality and is unable or, owing to such fear, is unwilling to avail himself of the protection of that country; or who, not having a nationality and being outside the country of his former habitual residence as a result of such events, is unable or, owing to such fear, is unwilling to return to it."[2]

The process begins when people are in a United Nations refugee camp, or occasionally at an embassy, or when a specially trained nongovernmental organization refers an applicant to the UN for resettlement. Applicants first apply for refugee status resettlement with the UN High Commission on Refugees. They determine whether they can return to their home country, settle in the country they are in, or be resettled in a third country. Resettlement is the final option for displaced people, and less than one percent of refugees have ended up resettled in new countries.[3]

For those being resettled in the U.S. it is a lengthy process that involves layers of checking into their background.

Initial documentation and biographic information is collected which is transferred to a State Department-funded Resettlement Support Center. The Department of State and Homeland Security oversee the vetting with the help of other departments. With the information collected, the center conducts a detailed interview with the applicant, then enters the documentation into a State Department system. It cross-references and verifies data, and sends the information needed for a background check to other U.S. agencies. From there, five units, the National Counterterrorism Center, FBI, Department of Homeland Security, Defense Department, and the State Department screen the applicant using data from the centers. The screening process includes checks for security threats, such as connections to suspected terrorists or criminals, and past crimes or immigration violations.[4] While calls are currently being made for "extreme vetting" it has been at least very thorough up to this point.

Medical screening also takes place for contagious diseases and there is a cultural orientation class as the change in coming to the U.S. as a refugee is extreme. While this class is helpful, it can't begin to prepare refugees for the total change they are about to encounter.

When it is time to resettle, this is a cooperative effort arranged between the U.N. and one of nine nongovernment voluntary agencies, six of which are faith-based.[5] Especially active in the Denver area is Lutheran Immigration and Refugee Services. When one of these agencies receives a case of an individual or family that is to be resettled, travel plans to the area where they operate are coordinated by the International Organization for Migration. What might come as a surprise to some is that while the plane ticket is paid for at that time, the refugee is required to repay the entire cost of the ticket to the agency that sponsored him or her.

These agencies represent an important aspect about the shared responsibility nature of the program as it was set up. Lawrence Bartlett, Director of Refugee Admissions in the

U.S. Department of State, said, "The way the program was designed in 1980 when Congress set it up is that it would really be this public-private partnership. There would be federal money from tax payers that would supply partial support. But it would only meant be partial and it was meant to be complimented with public funding. And the public funding is less specific. At the moment, we have nine agencies that are partners on the U.S. side and the nine agencies have 350 sites around the United States. They're in about 180 different towns but some of them have more than one site. What most of them do is private fundraising."[6] These volunteer agencies are critical in the refugee experience. Along with the nine that greet newcomers at the airport, there are many more that get them settled in a place to live, assist with finding places to learn or improve English, help with finding medical care, shopping, and understanding transportation systems as well as help in the search for employment.

This can be a shocking adjustment to take in, considering that most arrive from war-torn underdeveloped countries. They are carrying their few possessions in a plastic bag and are plopped down in a major metropolitan area where they don't speak or understand the language or have any real idea about how anything works.

Perhaps looking it from the reverse point of view would make it easier to sympathize with the problem they face. Assume the reader is from Los Angeles, Denver, Philadelphia, or any U.S. city of considerable size and has never seen much else. Then you're dropped in the Congo or in rural Burma or Somalia with only a change of clothes and some personal mementos in a plastic bag, and a greeter welcomes you, then he departs and leaves you on your own. You're an outsider in an environment you haven't the slightest idea of how to navigate. There are just dirt paths, no ATMs, no street signs, just dense jungle all around. You need to go to the bathroom but there aren't any. No chance you will find a real hotel here, so where will you sleep? What will you eat? There are these barefoot people passing by that can't even speak English; yet, they are clearly content and have everything solved. They seem happy and well fed. What comes next? You have no influence, you're confused and can't find your way around or even know what to look for. You can't ask, since they don't understand you. What's that strange food they're eating? What was that sound?

Now think of someone from a developing country where famine and starvation were killing many or ethnic cleansing took his or her friends and family and he or she managed to survive. After a subsistence life in a refugee camp, that person from half a world away in both latitude and longitude is dropped in a U.S. city and is expected to get started, to begin a new life. While it's a better option, it's a very difficult challenge, and those who take it on and struggle to make the adjustments are an inspiration that shows how in spite of adversity and inhumanity, the human spirit can prevail.

Refugees are the one category of immigrant that has special status. They can immediately get a work permit and are eligible for driver's licenses. They also receive some initial benefits for the transition of beginning to get adjusted to the U.S. Refugees receive a three month grant of money, plus medical assistance. Those that qualify can a get TANF (Temporary Assistance for Needy Families), and if their income is low enough they are eligible for SNAP (Supplemental Nutrition Assistance Program), formerly called Food Stamps. The low income who are elderly, blind, or disabled might receive SSI (Supplemental Security Income). After one year, they can apply for a green card, but most are challenged and limited by their English ability, so many take classes and the aid they receive is minimal. They are quick to take whatever job is available.

Housing is often difficult, as refugees are relocated in areas where housing costs are not low. This can lead to many relatives sharing small quarters in some cases, but in time many are earning adequate incomes and living in nicer housing, driving newer cars. When they arrive, the agency that resettled them has usually found them housing of some sort, and in many cases, they have been placed near relatives. Agencies also often supply used furniture that is in place for the nation's newcomer.

Greeters are typically very helpful and often accompanied by members of the community or even relatives when refugees arrive, making them feel as welcome as possible. Then all the strangeness set in. There is the initial help to allow newcomers to settle in to a residence and find health care if it is needed while receiving three months of government assistance, but refugees need work to make ends meet and they have proved to be eager workers.

Their eagerness to work has led to claims by some, including Donald Trump, that they are taking "American" jobs.[7] This claim was echoed by the anti-refugee website *Refugee Watch* that stated refugees are just a source of cheap labor, and industry is interested in cheap labor. Colorado Integration Partnership Coordinator Joe Wismann-Horther countered that in his view, "I think this is not a tenable explanation of what happens."[8] He explained that refugees took jobs in meat packing plants, the largest single refugee employer in the Denver area, because the pay is $13-15 per hour and no other entry level job can compete with those wages. He also notes that historically the meat packing industry has relied on an immigrant work force. He added that it's not refugees who suffer from exploitation in the workplace so much as undocumented workers. Employers are aware of that, they use that to either not pay the undocumented wages or pay them really low wages with the threat of them not complaining or they will turn them in. Refugees are documented and not vulnerable to these threats.

Another point Wismann-Horther makes is that many area senior homes depend on immigrants as well as refugees as employees for caregiving, cleaning, and food service. He observed, "Refugees tend to work harder than your16-year-old high school kid. That's who they're competing with for some of their jobs."[9] Adult refugees compete for high school jobs. What studies show is that refugees and immigrants on the same level, those without high school education, do not compete for the same work with native counterparts. The top occupations with the largest number of immigrants without high school diploma are maids and house cleaners. For native born workers without high school degrees, the occupations with the largest number of workers are cashiers and truck drivers.[10]

Along with finding work, the refugee has two dates hanging over his or her head. Whilst they immediately get a work permit, after one year they can apply for a green card. Then they are really residents and can come and go as they please. The big step is that after five years, if they have avoided committing a crime, they can apply to become a United States citizen. This requires passing a test on English proficiency as well as a test on U.S. history and government. For many people who come to America later in life this is a daunting task. Older refugees often find it more comfortable to locate in communities made up mainly of people from their home country, where they can continue to converse in their native tongue and celebrate traditional culture.

Though they often attend English language classes, it does not come easily at all and is a source of considerable anxiety and frustration. This comment from a Denver refugee over 55 years of age illustrates that: "We want to get citizenship, but because we have no language, we won't be able to get citizenship...Without English, it is difficult to get citizenship, so it would be very helpful if someone who knows can tell someone to help us get the citizenship."[11]

The test is in two parts, civics and English. The civics section is a short multiple choice quiz of ten randomly selected questions on U.S. history and government. There were over five million immigrants and refugees who took this test between October 1, 2009, and September 30, 2016 and the pass rate was 91%.[12] A study was done on natural-born voting age U.S. citizens, where a very large number of people of varying ages from both red and blue states were chosen randomly and given the civics test required for naturalization. A third of the voters failed (the pass rate was 65%).[13] On a survey accompanying this test 77% agreed that all Americans should be able to pass.[14]

For refugees, if a person fails one section, the test can be retaken again in a short time. If the test is failed again, then the applicant has to reapply and start the process over. There are some refugees, especially the elderly with age-related memory loss, who are not capable of passing the exam, as they never manage to learn English to a point of proficiency. Provisions can be made if a doctor agrees. Then there are also people like Asbi (Asbi and Leela), who has made it part of his job to see that people achieve citizenship. While his main job is explaining the local school system to new refugees, he wears many hats. For those in need of help with the naturalization test, he makes sure they are going to English classes and doing well before they apply. For the elderly who have no chance of passing the test, he checks to see if they are receiving medical treatment. This can provide a loophole if an applicant suffers from dementia, forgetfulness, or some traumatic event that affects the person's ability to learn English a doctor can write a note, and there is a form to be filled out. If they have the form Asbi accompanies them to their interview, where they present it. When this form is received, the English test and the history test are generally waived. Says Asbi, "They simply ask where are you from and where are you now? And how old they are. That's it."[15]

# CHAPTER EIGHTEEN:
# ROY, AFGHANISTAN

Roy left Afghanistan in 2002 during the time the country was under attack by the U.S. and Britain. This is now being widely described in the media as America's longest war[1] though that is a difficult claim to specify, when undeclared wars such as the American Indian Wars, the Vietnam War, and the Korean War have vague and conflicting dates applied to them, and as in Afghanistan, were never technically declared as wars. To Afghans such as Roy, its history of war is a much longer one than the U.S. involvement there.

Afghanistan had been at war for a fair share of Roy's life by the time he made his exit and became a refugee. In 1979, the Soviet Union had invaded to "restore order" after a coup brought Marxist-Leninists to power and that inspired a nationwide rebellion by Islamist fighters. These fighters, called the *mujahedeen*, were backed by Pakistan, Saudi Arabia, and the United States, and carried on a ten-year war that eventually led the Soviets to withdraw.

Following that, the successful mujahedeen then fought for power amongst themselves. In 1996, the Taliban took control of Kabul, Roy's home town, and instituted Sharia law, an Islamic law code systemized during the 8th and 9th centuries that among other things, forbade female education and prescribed severing of hands or even execution as punishment for petty crimes.[2] In Roy's view, "The Taliban took over because we already been fighting for twenty years of war. There was not a lot of things to stand up for."[3]

That same year Osama bin Laden, the leader of al-Qaeda, was welcomed to Afghanistan after being expelled from Sudan. With al-Qaeda's support, the Taliban gained control over most of the Afghan territory while a small share remained under the Northern Alliance.

Then came September 11, 2001. The plot to hijack and crash four U.S. airliners brought immediate attention to Afghanistan. As Roy notes, "In 2001 nineteen of those hijackers were from Saudi Arabia. How many were from Afghanistan?" But some of them had trained in Afghanistan and President George W. Bush's administration soon settled on a strategy of removing the Taliban from power in Afghanistan and demolishing al-Qaeda. In his speech to the nation immediately following the attack, Bush did not condemn Islam but spoke of terrorists as people who were distorting the religion for their own purposes. He said, "The terrorists practice a fringe form of Islamic extremism that has been rejected by Muslim scholars and the vast majority of Muslim clerics...Its teachings are good and peaceful, and those who commit evil in the name of Allah blaspheme the name of Allah."[4] This is certainly the view that is shared by Roy. It is why some of Trump's comments, like the call during the campaign for a total ban on Muslims, have him concerned.

Bush announced that Afghanistan had to turn over Bin Laden and expel al-Qaeda. After some exchange of offers and rejections, the U.S. initiated military actions in early October, initially striking Kabul and several other locations with air strikes. Soon the war was on to replace the Taliban. Roy recalls, "The structures, you know the schools, they are blown down. The churches are gone. There used to be churches over there, and Christians, and synagogues. It's all blown down." He said the infrastructure was destroyed, the transportation system ruined, and the electricity was out. "Basically, it was wild. There was no authority, no government."

Roy managed to get away during the first year of the war, and, "When I left everything was destroyed, especially Kabul." He became a refugee, but he says, "I see a lot of bad things over there, bad experiences. I did see not only Muslim against Muslim, I see against Christian and Jews." He had a positive comment about Afghanistan that he thought was an important similarity between its history and that of the U.S. His description was, "We love freedom. In Afghanistan people fight a long time. That's one thing we have in common – always want to be free."

The UN placed him in Denver, "So we ended here and we stayed here." He found people helpful as he resettled, noting, "I got treated well when I got here by social services and they helped us along. Church helped us a lot." He said you have to just settle down and do your job, the same as everybody else. His English wasn't very advanced, and he took English as a Second Language classes for six months in Denver libraries.

His grammar and pronunciation improved, but Roy says that though his knowledge of English is not perfect, he can "manage to communicate with people and, you know, solve problems." Once his language skills were better, he began to look for employment, and took whatever work was available. Like most refugees, he began with entry level jobs, first working as a dish washer, then in hotels. Following that he became a driver for both Uber and Lyft. During this time, he acquired a green card, then after five years, applied to be a U.S. citizen. He didn't find it challenging like many refugees do, as he was well informed and was interested in history, so his knowledge is broad. His description of the citizenship test was, "You have to know some things about history, about cultural stuff."

Roy's major concerns since coming to the U.S. seem to be about religion. He's a Muslim and doesn't feel that he is persecuted personally or suffers because of it. When one sees Roy, there is nothing apparent about his appearance that draws attention to his religion or hardly anything suggests that he is foreign. But he is proud of who he is and says, "I'm Muslim. So far nobody has come by to say 'you Muslim, get out of here.' " He adds that if that ever happened, his response would be, "You need to get out of here." He added, "Oh yes, maybe a few people, they get surprised when I say I'm Muslim."

His optimistic view of why people might find it surprising that he is a Muslim is there are not very many Muslims in the area. He says, "Maybe if there were more Muslims, then more people would take me as normal." He contradicted himself a bit with "I didn't get any bad treatment because I being Muslim, because there's not a lot of Muslims here, that's why."

Roy accepts that living in America means he must tolerate hearing vitriolic rhetoric aimed at Muslims that associates their religion with violence, since, "It's a free country. When you're living in a free society, I mean, people speak their mind. You have to take it." He believes that Muslims might have a difficult time in Denver, but thinks Christians are also having a hard time here as well. He is referring to the poverty he sees that affects all races and religions. A big change from Afghanistan that he really appreciates is that the law requires the separation of church and state. "I mean keeping religion out of politics is a good thing," he says.

Roy believes there is a great deal of misunderstanding of Islam in the Denver area. Lack of awareness contributes to mistaken ideas, is a point he makes. What people don't understand, he says, is that, "Muslims, they're not bad people, they're just like me, just a regular guy, working." Roy states that there have been Muslims in the U.S. for a long time, though the number hasn't been large, and people don't notice that they might be their gardener, the cook in their restaurant, the janitor who is cleaning up after them, their local police officer, their doctor. Or they could be their driver like he is.

His views on religion are informed and ecumenical. He observed that people who say there is something "wrong" with the Muslim religion, "They're wrong, they need to restudy their beliefs." He was referring to religious history and what are often called the Abrahamic religions, those that trace their origin to Abraham and are monotheistic. As he explains it, "Muslim beliefs are just the same thing as Christianity. So, if there's something wrong with Muslims, there's something wrong with Christianity, too. And with the Jews. Christians, Jews, and Muslims are cultural cousins."[5] Roy is willing to accept religions beyond the Abrahamic tradition, taking the broad-minded view, "You can see God in different ways. I believe Jews, Christians, Buddhists, Hindus, Muslims, we all have the right belief. But it is different ways to approach God."

While his approach to God is as a Muslim, Roy is disappointed in what he's hearing from the president. He said, "There's a problem with what Trump is saying, with how he sees Muslims. Not all Muslims are bad. Just certain Muslims in certain countries. So maybe Trump will find some solution to not call all Muslims crazy, extremists."

Roy is well aware of the dangers of Muslim extremism, and has no sympathy for it. He has very strong opinions on its cause, and why there are so many problems in the Middle East and in Muslim countries. For him there is no doubt where the real problem lies. He contends that the issue is "one or two countries that are projecting extremists." This is, he asserts, "just like Hitler in Germany and Nazis." While that seems to be a common comparison to make for people or ideas someone dislikes, he explains, "It's just like fascism. They have this backward, twisted ideology. They want to spread this out to all around to all the Muslim countries, make them extremist."

What Roy was speaking about is Wahhabism, and his view is shared by many with knowledge of the Middle East and the spread of terrorism.[6] The Wahhabi movement was founded in the 18th century and early on formed an alliance with the House of Saud. Sunni madrassas were spread across the Arabian Peninsula teaching the idea of a supposed return to the austere practices of the earliest

Muslims of the Seventh Century. Jihad was initiated against Muslims who refused to adopt Wahhabi practices. Though the Ottoman Empire controlled the area for a time, when Saudi Arabia emerged as a country in 1932 under the House of Saud, its ties to Wahhabism were intact. With Saudi oil money, these ideas and practices were exported widely.[7]

To Roy this is all clear. He says, "Wahhabism. That's the whole point. I wish politicians they would understand this word." That is the form of Islam that Osama bin Laden brought with him to Afghanistan.

Roy thinks there will be peace between Israel and Palestine because "Palestine used to be a wasteland." But he believes because of this twisted view of Saudi Arabia, Arab states have been convinced they are supposed to "go fight the Jews because they took all your land," when it was really just a small piece of land. Roy gets enthusiastic as he asserts, "Politicians are missing it. It's affecting everything, everyone in the world." His solution for Middle East problems is "going after the actual snake's head. Where is the snake sitting? The snake is in Saudi Arabia." He isn't advocating attacking the country, just being open and confronting them. He wants the U.S. to tell them, "Hey, you have to stop this. It's all Muslims you're killing." It really upsets him that he sees a Muslim country responsible for "killing more Muslims than anyone else." Ron has no interest in returning to live in Afghanistan. The country's continuous wars have away taken too much. "I make my peace with that country. It hurts really bad inside." He's now an American, emphasizing, "I feel in this country, it's home. This is home now."

In spite of this, he is optimistic about Afghanistan. He says he doesn't think the Taliban will regain control. They were able to gain control because there had already been war for over twenty years. What's changed since he left, he notes is, "The new generation is growing, going to school. They see what happened and aren't going to let it happen again." Once more, the prospect of a better future lies with an educated younger generation. For Ron, "I wish one day that become a peaceful country and I can go back just to visit, to see." Hopefully he will be able to make that visit to a better place than the one he left.

# CHAPTER NINETEEN: MAHN, VIETNAM

The largest number of refugees to come to the U.S. following the post-World War II boom has been the Vietnamese who began arriving after the fall of Saigon in 1975. By 2014 there were 1.3 million Vietnamese immigrants residing in the United States.[1] 10,788 were living in Colorado at that time.[2] Mahn was one of those who fled what had been South Vietnam after the communist victory and became a Denver resident. His escape didn't come easy, but he was persistent and he finally successfully managed it on his twenty-second attempt.

The U.S relationship with Vietnam has been long and goes back to imperialist times. Following World War II when the Japanese had conquered the area, the French returned and attempted to assert their authority over their colony of Indochina that included Vietnam and several of its neighbors, while Ho Chi Minh was leading the fight for independence. The United States provided the French with financial assistance and the first U.S. military advisors were sent to Vietnam when Harry Truman was president in 1950.[3] After the French suffered a disastrous defeat in 1954 at Dien Bien Phu, Indochina was divided into Laos, Cambodia, and Vietnam.

It was clear by mid-1954 that the French had lost and a conference was held in Geneva, Switzerland to determine Vietnam's future. The conference announced that Vietnam was to become an independent country and national elections would be held in July 1956 to choose a government. In the time before the elections the country would be divided along the seventeenth parallel with a government to administer each half. All Viet Mihn soldiers, those who had fought against the French, were to go to the North and all soldiers who had fought for the French were to go to the South. The United States and the South Vietnamese refused to guarantee they would abide by the Geneva Accords, as the Accords recognized a communist government in the North. This was the time when Mahn's father was sent to Pleiku, a town in the Central Highlands, located in the far north of South Vietnam. He was there to begin a school as the first elementary teacher.

The 1956 elections were not held as the South refused to participate. The leader of the North was the independence hero, Ho Chi Minh, while the U.S. supported the unpopular leader of the South, Ngo Dinh Diem. In 1957 there were communist uprisings in the South and two years later the first Americans were killed. Kennedy became president in 1960 and his advisors recommended an increase in the number of American troops involved, which had been gradually going up; in 1962 that number passed 10,000, and was beyond 500,000 in 1969, as the U.S. began seeking exit strategies as casualties and dissatisfaction with the war increased. The U.S. was directly involved in a war where its participation over 25 years would involve escalation from advisors to combatants and massive bombing both in Vietnam and in neighboring Cambodia. The result would be increasing success by the North and the U.S. withdrew combat units in 1973.

Mahn's family fled when the communists were approaching his home of Pleiku. He was a child at the time and they headed to the coast. There they stayed with the South Vietnamese military and they were ambushed. He says the location was a strategic point that opened the way for the conquest of the South.

From his life as a young boy he remembers the carnage well, commenting, "I saw awfulness. I saw people die everywhere. Cut off their hand, their leg, everything. I saw the tank, big truck cross over peoples' bodies."[4]

They survived and soon headed back to Pleiku but the town had been burned when the communists invaded. His father's school had also been ransacked and looted with everything left in total disarray. Mahn's father placed great value on education, something he passed on to his son. What his father did next, Mahn did not appreciate at the time, but he says, "I'm impressed, now I'm impressed." He went through the chaos and cleaned up everything, arranged it all, and put every file for every student in order. It would end up being his final act as a teacher, but he had been devoted to his work.

Another thing his father and mother had done is anticipate that things were going bad, that their government might not survive, so they bought a small plot of land. They were going to farm their land if they were driven from their home and livelihood. Mahn said his father's job was gone because the teachers in the South were replaced by people from North Vietnam.

Mahn was ten at the time of the fall of Saigon marked final victory for the North in 1975. The number of Vietnamese civilians who died in the war is estimated at about two million, while 1.1 million North Vietnamese fighters and Viet Cong were killed along with an estimated 200,000 to 250,000 South Vietnamese soldiers.[5] There were 58,220 U.S. casualties.[6]

With the new communist government, there were many from what had been South Vietnam attempting to get away. The rush to leave had begun as the fall of Saigon was taking place. There were 140,000 South Vietnamese, mainly political leaders and army officers, and also some professionals, who escaped the communist takeover.[7] Mahn's parents had lost contact for some time with his older sister and brother who lived in Saigon and were college students. His parents found encouragement when they learned that their older children had escaped before the government's fall. Mahn's uncle was a high-ranking officer in the South Vietnam Air Force and he had taken them with him when army officers were allowed out.

While some escaped, Americans were soon expressing concern for the "Amerasians," children born in Vietnam to Vietnamese women and American fathers during the war years. Because they were of "mixed blood," the Vietnamese government regarded them as "bui doi," or "the dust of life," and only after Congress passed legislation establishing them as immigrants, would they begin being admitted to the U.S.[8]

Soon many Vietnamese were attempting to escape persecution as over a million were forced into re-education camps and agricultural collectives,[9] and the U.S. put a trade embargo on Vietnam.

Mahn and his family made their first attempt at escaping from the country when he was 13, as they tried to take advantage of the relations between China and Vietnam, which were very strained. It was 1978 and though China had provided economic and technical assistance to Vietnam, there was fighting on the border between the two countries. China had supported the government in Kampuchea (Cambodia) that Vietnam had overthrown, China resented Vietnam relying more on Soviet assistance and there was a mass exodus of refugees. This included 170,000 Vietnamese of Chinese origin who fled to China that year.[10] Mahn says the government was in on this as they collected a fee from Chinese who wanted to leave "and then they go die on the South China Sea." The Vietnamese government was charging the Chinese the equivalent of $2,000 to $3,000 per person to depart,[11] and ridding the country of what it considered undesirables and gaining hard currency, though many were successful business owners and professionals who added to the economy.

But it was a chance and Mahn and his family were desperate. They took a Chinese name in hopes of becoming a part of the program. They were unsuccessful as an international conference announced other countries would accept refugees from Vietnam and the Chinese halted the welcoming of immigrants from its southern neighbor. By this time "boat people" were arriving in neighboring countries at a rate of nearly 12,500 per month, but none were willing to accept them.[12]

That had been just the beginning. Mahn said many of his failures to escape had been because his family was a victim of tricks or scams by people who were taking advantage of desperate people like him. He recalled several of his earlier attempts: in 1981 when he was 16, he and one of his sisters were making their way to the South China Sea, and they were arrested in Phước Thái village and taken to Biên Hòa on the edge of Saigon, where they were jailed for over a month and a half. The time he was released remains clear to him, because much celebration was going on. It was April 30, Liberation Day, that marked the fall of Saigon and the reunification of the country. The next day was May 1, International Labor Day, a public holiday in the country.

The next year he was one of the "boat people." These are the most famous refugees who left Vietnam. It was a very dangerous undertaking. People left in all sizes of boats that varied in seaworthiness. Once at sea there were hazards of weather, lack of food and water, and piracy attacks, plus, if they were lucky enough to reach land, they were unlikely to be welcomed. Many were towed back out to sea, rather than allowed to land. In 1981, the year before they left, there were 14 documented mass murders of Vietnamese boat people in Thai waters by Thai pirates. In the first months of 1982, there were 484 murders and 583 rapes, and officials recovered 199 girls from Thai houses of prostitution who had been abducted from the boats leaving Vietnam. While the UN proposed a $3.6 million fund to help Thailand patrol the waters, the Thais requested more. The U.S. response was to offer a contribution of $600,000.[13]

In 1982 Mahn and his sister tried to leave on board a 12.5-meter (40 foot) boat that had over hundred people on board. Their boat stalled and they floated in the South China Sea for several days and nights. Fortunately, they were rescued by a State-owned iron ship. The unfortunate part is they were towed to Vũng Tàu where he managed to get away but his sister was imprisoned for over a year. He continued making attempts to get out from various points in the south of Vietnam. He also went to the north near the border and attempted to get a boat to Hong Kong. His efforts to flee continued both on foot and by water.

While Mahn was obviously anxious to escape the communist regime, he next had a bright spot where he "spent several years living on boats as boat keeper. I enjoyed that life in rivers around Saigon waterways." He did much traveling around Vietnam in the next few years both in the south and the north. He says that after having that job he felt frustrated, had no work, his spirit was very down and he considered suicide. Then came 1987, which Mahn describes as "the turning point of my life, where I found true faith." He was raised as a Buddhist, but converted to Christianity, and it has become the guiding force in his life since that time. He headed to Cambodia in December of that year in his 21st attempt to escape from Vietnam but again it was a failure.

January 1988 was when success finally came. Vietnam had invaded Cambodia in 1978 to remove Pol Pot, the leader of the Khmer Rouge who was responsible for the death of two million Cambodians in his four-year rule. Vietnamese troops occupied the country and were still there when Mahn left Vietnam. He says the final phase of his escape was by small boat and it came at the

Vietnam-Cambodia border. The area was occupied by the Vietnamese Peoples' Army. "You know, the Vietnamese Peoples' Army, that's my generation," he recalls.

This was his way out: "You could bribe them. It was their last year in Cambodia. They were happy to get some money. They were about to get back to Vietnam and they would do anything to get compensation."

In January of 1988 in Cambodia Prime Minister Hun Sen was meeting with the King, Norodom Sihanouk. Security was everywhere from the capital, Phnom Penh, to the border with Thailand. Mahn had to wear a Vietnamese Army uniform, "You can get uniform anywhere, flea market. Russian-made cloth uniform." That was good for hiding his identity in Cambodia but it was dangerous with the Vietnamese Army: "They know so well, they can see you wear the clothes. They can check you out for I.D. card, it's easy. I pray I get through." He paid someone in the army and they arranged the way for him to get out from Phnom Penh. He had positive feelings about life there, mentioning, "If I couldn't have left Cambodia I would have stayed in Phnom Penh."

Mahn arrived at the border of Thailand at midnight, transported in a small boat to land. He had to get out of his army clothes because they were not popular in Thailand as they were having a border conflict at the time. But he had made it. "I was so happy."

He was soon in a refugee camp, that he described as complex, because it was very large and included Vietnamese, Cambodian, Chinese, Laotian, Hmong, mixed with a lot of political exiles. He appreciated the kindness of the country in hosting them and said with its potential conflicts the Thai military controlled the situation very well: "The life there, many people they don't like it. But for me, it's wonderful. In my country, I have no future. I could not go to school." He was so happy to have finally escaped that this was a terrific improvement. He added,

"So refugee camp for many people, that's awful, for me that's wonderful."

Things were about to improve for Mahn. In August 1989 he came to Denver. His sister sponsored him because she had come in 1975 and he thinks his relocation was easier than it was for some others because of her already being here and letting him know what life was like. She made him feel welcome when he arrived and asked what he wanted to do. He said it was his wish to go to college, which he thought was unrealistic, since he hadn't finished high school. His sister was a graduate of the University of Colorado at Boulder and said, "This is the land of opportunity. You can do college if you want."

Mahn found a night job stocking shelves at King Soopers for $4.35 an hour and began to pursue his dream. He was 24 and couldn't attend high school so he bought a study guide for the GED that he studied during the day several weeks, while he worked nights. He had some background in English, having taken night classes in Saigon, ESL class in the refugee camp and studied it on his own. He soon had his high school qualification and enrolled in Metro College in Denver.

In 1994, he met a woman who had fled from Vietnam by boat after she finished high school. She made it to the Philippines and eventually to the U.S., where she resettled in Arizona and studied computers and information systems in college. Mahn says, "She's better than me because she graduated from high school." Her job brought her to Denver, and they eventually married and had a family. They now have three children.

He found college a challenge since he had dropped out in tenth grade and hadn't attended school for ten years. With all he was doing, he managed to graduate after six years and he found work at a CPA firm, where he has continued to be very happily employed.

As for life in Denver, Mahn says, "I've been treated well here. I have no issue at all, none at all. I love the life here." He tries to teach his children about the value of freedom, but not about all of his past and things they cannot yet understand. He is very happy to be here and displays an American flag proudly while openly professing his love for this country.

# CHAPTER TWENTY: ABIRA, SYRIA

Abira is an immigrant, not a refugee, and she is the leading authority on Syrians in Denver. Early on she mentions, "Last week we have new baby, a girl so she is number 225,"[1] noting that the local community had just increased. She knows them all. Abira arrived in Denver before the great refugee crisis began. She grew up in the nation's capital, Damascus, where she attended private school and was taught by French nuns. In her youth she learned French and eventually earned a bachelor's degree in French Literature. It had been her dream to work as an international translator or interpreter; she had Christian friends in Syria and, despite the ongoing conflicts in the country, they have remained friends on Facebook to the present. They didn't divide along religious lines, instead, "We accept each other, we respect each other."

It seemed she had settled into what would be her life, but that would be changed by a man far away who was born in Palestine, and lived in the U.S. since he was a teenager. He had spent decades in America but was single and, she says, some friends of his asked if he wanted to get married. They had mutual contacts with both and said, "There's this girl in Syria." An introduction was arranged that went well, and eventually, Abira had a fiancée. It wasn't a popular idea with her friends. She recalls, "Everyone used to say, are you crazy, are you going to go to America? They're going to kill you for one dollar. How you going to go there? This was the image in Syria, she explained, because they saw all the Hollywood movies with people killing each other or as divorced or homeless.[2]

Abira was ready for a new life as a U.S. citizen. In 2002 she immigrated to the U.S. It was not an easy time, shortly after 9/11, the battle with Saddam Hussein beginning, and her dressed in her hajib. "We married, we continued our life here as Muslim American people," And she worked at a church and taught Arabic lessons. After having three boys who started attending school, she says she realized that not every American is divorced or homeless. Her introduction to being Muslim in the U.S. came soon. While she had been volunteering at a church, she met with a teacher there, who said to her, "You as Muslim, you don't know about Jesus." This is a common mistake Christians make about Islam. The *Oxford Dictionary of Islam* states that Jesus is mentioned 25 times in the Quran as the Spirit of God and the Messiah.[3] She said to him, "Who told you that? If I don't believe in Jesus, that means I'm not a Muslim." She was shocked, advised him that he had to do some studying first and then he might know who she was.

She and her husband hoped to save their culture and wanted the next generation to know what was good about it. It was their plan to blend the best of both cultures as she said, "Because, you know, here in the United States, we have the good and bad. There too, we have the good and bad. So, we raise our kids that we can have the good from here and the good from there and we combine them."

Life was carrying on, then in 2015 Abira's husband died of a heart attack. She was suddenly a widow with three children under age 10: "People helped me after I became a widow and my kids became orphans. I see it as my role now to help others." A woman heard her speaking Arabic with a Syrian accent and came up to her and asked 'Are you Syrian?' Abira told her that she was and asked the woman if she needed help. That was a new beginning, as she found she could be very useful to new arrivals in the community. That was 2016 and there were ten Syrian families in Denver: "I start to ask them how can I help you, what do you need, do you need anything? And they would say how do I do this, where do I find this." She and some of her friends began collecting things, used clothes, furniture, whatever might be helpful.

Before long she had a real organization and with many volunteers, showing Denver at its best, as there were 50 Syrian families in 2017. Volunteers showed up "from everywhere. Muslim, Christian, Jewish, nonreligious people, anyone. Just when they heard I help these families, they say, how can we help, and please let us know." Early on, one became her "partner" - a young man who made a much greater opportunity from what she was doing. He told her, "I can help, volunteering for nothing. I have a truck. I don't need any money, I don't want anything. I can help you, moving these couches, moving this furniture." With that, they collected all sorts of things and Abira's role came to be the dispatcher. She says, "I'm the person who used to organize it because I'm the person who likes all this paper and writing, organizing everything." People would call and tell her that they had something, such as two chairs, a loveseat, dressers, and a table, and she knew what the families needed and would arrange where everything would go. Her man with the truck would pick everything up and distribute what was appropriate to each family selected. Some Syrian families suspected Abira of favoritism, and thought she preferred certain families because she gave one a couch or something that was in good condition, when another received a similar item that was battered and used. She was just processing, as she notes, "But for me, it's like, this is what I have today. Today I have the poor condition couch, yesterday I had the good condition couch. So, every day I see the needs of these families and I give it to them."

She expanded by getting aid from Islamic Help of North America. Her local group's requests for used clothes had not been adequate to meet the needs when the weather turned cold and Abira sought their help. She told them, "We need 50 jackets, X Large, 24 long jackets for the ladies, seven small size." Though she had been grieving for her husband, she had found a way to move on. She has continued with that work, though it has modified, since that time: "People helped me after I became a widow and my kids became orphans. I see it as my role now to help others."

Abira soon learned that poverty existed in Denver and there were others who needed help. Syrian refugees often found housing in the least expensive places available and Denver's property market has been booming, making this a challenge. In her years in Denver she hadn't visited Colfax Avenue, which the *New York Times* said "is often described as one of America's wickedest streets,"[4] though this only describes some of its many miles. She said upon seeing it, "When I go there because all these families resettle there, I start to see all these poor people. They need a lot of help." If they needed help, someone had to do it and she had found that her work should be expanded.

Her group started to send what was being donated to others not just Syrians. They sent seven full bags to an Algerian family and told them to just take whatever seemed useful. They also distributed shampoo and detergent. She had several Syrian refugee women who would sort through the donated clothes, because, "A lot of used ones, it's not good, it's for trash." They put the useless clothes in a big black trash bag and set it out for trash pickup. Abira has a vivid memory of what happened next: "It doesn't take ten minutes. We see there is a lady, she tried to see the clothes, she took the bag and she disappeared. I cannot explain my feeling at that moment." They immediately decided to put clothes that were in good condition out, so the woman could come and take them, since what she took wasn't worth using for dusting. "So, every time we put one bag, it's good clothes. It's like just take it and go. And the next day you can see the kids, they wear what I trashed," she said.

Her focus remained on the Syrians who she said didn't feel their agencies were doing enough to make them feel welcome. While they received assistance with papers, vaccines, registration at the schools, "They need your love. When you look at their face they want to feel this respect, acceptance. Because they don't leave their homes just to come here and take your opportunity of work." When Abira mentions refugees coming and taking work, that is just one among the frequent misconceptions she feels are prevalent about Syrian refugees. She adds, "The ideas that they came here as terrorists, as believers in Sharia, it's like a lot of mix up of stuff and it's not the main reason. They came here because they bombed their home. They lost everything. They just go run away from any bombardment there."

Once they arrive in Denver and get settled, especially around the Colfax area, they're surrounded by people they can't speak with so they just use sign language. They sit with each other and have just the "feeling language." The hospitality of the Syrian culture is "Whatever I have, I should let you test it. And we here as American Muslim Syrian people, we continue this hospitality. This is how our parents raise up us to be, provide everything good for anyone, regardless white, black, Muslim, Christian, Jewish." Syrians' religion has made finding work a greater challenge when they arrive. Meatpacking is the major refugee employer and pays the highest wages, but they won't work there because it is handling meat, and that is not allowed. They also have problems with jobs in restaurants because of the liquor involved, which they cannot deal with; but after 90 days they have to take almost anything else. Making their way around the city is another immediate concern. Those who aren't English-speaking often use Arabic GPS on their phones, but some still get lost. Abira gets contacted and they give her Arabic GPS so she can guide them. She worries about what will happen if they get lost and their battery runs out of power. They could ask a policeman but what policeman is going to be able to help if he doesn't speak Arabic? She also gets call from clinics for translations of doctors' questions and their patient's responses.

Abira has also seen a darker side of Denver that Syrian arrivals have brought out. She says, "There is a lot of bad experience here for them. I need to convince them that we are here, good. Some of them have been treated badly for sure." She spoke of what had happened to a refugee a month earlier. The woman, who was pregnant, took her children to the bus stop for school in her neighborhood every day to drop them off. She had to cross the street than wait on the corner until the bus arrived. Every day, one of her neighbors would be there and shout at her, insulting her. She did not understand all he was saying, and contacted Abira. She said he was using these words she didn't know and Abira recalls the encounter, "And for me, I know this is a bad word here, s-word, f-word. And I told her really? Are you sure? And she told me yeah, this is what I heard." Shortly after that the man came out with his dog, which was usually on a leash. This time he it wasn't. He commanded the dog to attack the woman and it ran after her. She was very frightened and ran, "and now, more than 20 days, she lost her baby." Abira told her at the time that she needed to report this, but the woman wouldn't. Abira considered filing a report but chose not to interfere, because, "They're scared to report it to the police. Who knows what these people are going to do to them." So, the woman lost her baby after a Denver man ordered his dog to attack her, because she feared that contacting the police would lead repercussions from her neighbor, rather than protection.

Abira had her own personal unpleasant encounter in the parking lot where she was waiting for one of her sons. Her other two were with her and the lot was very crowded, but she was trying to maneuver, going left and right, to make progress. A man shouted at her, "Come on, move your car, you dumb Muslim." She was nervous and had her kids, who had recently lost their dad, and they were waiting for their older brother. She had been doing everything she could to move her car and driving the same as everyone else. She was worried that her kids felt that their mom was weak. They started to cry. She told them to just look at the license plate and write down the number, "then let's go to the principal's office." The school's administration told her that it was her choice about whether they reported it to the police. She chose not to, as she didn't want this parent to feel shame in front of his daughter, and with her son and his daughter at the same school, there would be many future activities where they would encounter each other. She added generously, "One day he's going to know that I'm a good mom and I want him to stay a good dad."

That was typical of Abira's guiding belief that, "Every human being has good things in his heart."

# CHAPTER TWENTY-ONE: ADJUSTMENT AND ASSIMILATION

Whether people favor the admission of refugees or oppose it, it is a concern as to whether these new residents will fit into American society. There are dire predictions of disaster,[1] such as Representative Steve King's "We can't restore our civilization with somebody else's babies,"[2] while the President's detractors and those who sympathize with refugee resettlement were energized to protest his initial executive order that put a temporary ban on entry into the U.S. for most people from seven predominantly Muslim countries. The Gallup Poll immediately following that order found the public disapproved of it by double digits (42% Approve, 55% Disapprove),[3] and it inspired widespread protests and gatherings in support of refuges and other immigrants.

While passions about whether refugees adapt to the U.S. have run high for years, the State of Colorado did a very constructive thing. They employed a group of scholars from Quality Evaluation Designs to devise and conduct a long-term study to see the degree to which refugees integrate into local society and tried to isolate areas where there were problems that might be better addressed. This study was given the title *The Refugee Integration Survey and Evaluation*, with the acronym *RISE*,[4] and was carried out over a five-year period. The first year was devoted to planning and designing surveys. The following four provided really meaningful information, and in the fifth they wrote their final report.

A cohort of "nearly all adult Burmese, Bhutanese, Somali, and Iraqi adult refugees who arrived from January

2011 through March 2012" were interviewed and measured on highly academic surveys in different categories that had been identified as being related to integration in mainstream society. The first interviews of these refugees took place in the year of their arrival which was labeled "Baseline." A year later the group went through a second interview session, called "Baseline + 1," or "B+1". These interviews continued for four continuous years through B+3, so changes could be measured. There were 467 participants who were followed all the way through the process.[5]

The report opened with the statement, "For refugees, the American Dream remains not only an ideal, but a goal. Those supported to rebuild their lives in the United States in order to escape persecution and the ravages of war have experienced misery, death and living conditions impossible for most of us born in the United States to imagine."[6] The committee identified ten "pathways" that lead to social integration: Employment and Economic Sufficiency, Education and Training, Children's Education, Health and Physical Well-Being, Housing, Social Bonding, Social Bridging, Language and Cultural Knowledge, Safety and Stability, and Civic Engagement.[7] Of these factors, cluster analysis showed high scores in three were especially critical indicators of successful integration, and the report paid more attention to these categories. These were Employment and Economic Sufficiency, Social Bridging, Language and Cultural Knowledge. Low scores on Housing and Social Bonding could be signs of integration distress.[8]

Through their assessments of the first three years, the evaluators identified and categorized three distinct groups by degree of integration: high, medium, and low.[9] Within the low integration groups that were having difficulties adapting to life in America, there were three distinct subpopulations: stay-at-home mothers, women 55 years or older without work, and men 55 years or older with or without work.[10]

Many of the people among those who are low integrators had significant disabilities.

Stay-at-home mothers were particularly challenged when they needed to have child care in order to work, and could not afford it because they were not working or had no relatives locally available. This often made them somewhat shut-ins, fearful of others and going out, and unable to advance, since attending school for English classes was difficult, though some provide child care. Since they gravitated to the least expensive housing the areas they were living in were sometimes unpleasant. Said one, "They fight and yell at each other. It bothers me. The apartments are sometimes good but sometimes not, it's bad. There's some people who knock on people door and they sleep in the building. They knock on other people's who live there...I never call the police. I've never called before. I don't know how. Since I've got here I have never called the police. Both of us [she and her husband] don't really know. [And] I don't really know anybody [in the building.]"[11] Inability of refugees to speak English related directly to the "Language & Cultural" pathway, which survey analyses revealed as critical for successful integration. Elderly participants (defined as those over 55) expressed the most concern about how the inability to speak English well would impede their ability to gain citizenship, since passing a test administered in English is part of the process. These elders, who relied exclusively on others to manage their way in U.S. culture, struggled to find help in this area and many rarely leave home unless accompanied by someone with whom they felt safe. Even then, it was normally to go to work, for medical appointments, adult daycare, to visit a family member or neighbor's home, or to go to church. They would feel safe in the confines of their apartment, but less so when they entered any unfamiliar surroundings.

Early in the report was a "Findings" statement that "Elderlies evidencing low integration experienced significant barriers along their individual integration pathways, yet contribute significantly to their family's integration."[12] This was followed by a series of quotes from "elderlies" which included the following:

Woman: "Sometimes I do feel scared when I see [people outside the ethnic community] in the road, or when I see some other people coming to the apartment. I don't understand the language, so I don't know what kind of people they are, what they are thinking. Usually when I come out of the apartment and then if I see any Nepali I would stay there and talk, if not ...If I see other people, then I come back to my room."

Elderly man's son: "He doesn't really know how to get places, since he cannot read the name on the street, or the sign. It's a problem, a challenge."

Woman: "I do not know anything; I cannot go on my own. This will make me unhappy."

Man: "We cannot go by ourselves though. If we go, we will get lost. If someone comes to take us, then we will go."

Woman: "I haven't met [people outside of the apartment] because I do not go out of my apartment. Some friends [of my children's] do visit the house sometimes but not very often because they all go to work."[13]

Regardless of this sense of isolation and constraint, the elderly participants in the project expressed contentment and appreciation for their resettlement in the U.S. While many were concerned about citizenship, which is required in order to continue receiving monthly Supplemental Security Income [SSI] checks, and the expressed frustration with their inability to speak English, they reported that the quality of their lives was generally good. It was certainly an improvement over where they had come from. An important factor contributing to this comforting feeling was the awareness that their children would have good lives. The report states, "This knowledge seemed to make the challenges they face bearable."[14] Again there was a series of quotes from interviews with elderly refugees that supported the conclusion:

Man: "First of all, my goal and my dream is for my children to come to this country to learn and to get education."

Woman: "My goal and dream is for my children to get education, to finish school, and then to help our people and then to go back there and help people. To help the current people back home. There are a lot of needs back home, like teaching, like other stuff, a lot of stuff there, so if they can go back and help [in the camp and Burma]."

Part of the way the elders helped their children involved contributing to household finances and taking on responsibilities so those who were able to could work.

Woman: "I just help by cook for them in the morning, send them to school in the morning, and then clean the house and then take care of them...I also take care of the seven - month old grandkid five days a week."

Son of Elderly Man: "He [father] is helping a lot financially, because he has SSI. With the help of his finance, we are able to pay the home rent, and pay for the bills." Woman, "I have a little granddaughter. I take care of the granddaughter and I will also make food for them." [children and grandchild]

Man: "We have a disabled child, a daughter, so she [his wife] takes care of everybody [disabled daughter and three grandkids] ...Whenever she's doing something in the apartment like cleaning or cooking food, I look after the grandkids until she's done."[15]

Those refugees placed in the low integration category frequently spoke of experiences of isolation and most felt safe at home, but resisted venturing outside where the world felt unsafe and unfamiliar. They were dependent on caregivers and were unable to initiate actions or overcome barriers through their environment. Whether this was a cause or result of low integration was uncertain.[16]

The report then turned to economic security, one of the prominent pathways identified in successful integration. As for the refugees being a drain on society, it was found that they steadily increased in work participation and reached very near full employment among those capable of working. The report stated, "The percentage or refugees employed for 30 hours or more increase from 60% at Baseline to 92% at B+3."[17] Since Baseline is the arrival year in report, B+3 meant this had been achieved after four years as Denver residents. This statistic received considerable media attention,[18] though the reporting in this section is a bit difficult to read clearly[19] as many refugees are ineligible for inclusion in the workforce due to age or disability. All is completely presented in the report.[20]

Chris is from Burma and by *RISE* definitions an elder. He offered comments beyond the scope covered in the report. His experience has been that economic success has come with discrimination. He said, "American freedom is you work hard. Those people that were born here, they have more. They have more freedom because they already have almost everything that they need. But those people that come here with nothing, they don't have much freedom, because they are attached to their work. Because we have a language barrier, we can't go anywhere. We aren't educated. That mean even at work, there are many discriminations that we have to face."[21] Chris worked at OraLabs, assembling lipstick packages for retail sales. In his view, the jobs were divided along racial, or ethnic lines with refugees placed at the bottom. He also says that they were not rewarded in accordance with their productivity, commenting, "If we finish, 200 of quantity, that the people above us that are educated can maybe do only about a hundred. Those people who work in the lowest level they will work to produce the lipstick. They produce more and are good workers."[22] His point is that refugees take low paying jobs or double up on jobs to make ends meet so they are less free since subsistence is often their goal, while people in better paying work are free to enjoy life in more ways: "So, you have freedom, then freedom in each level. You have freedom, but if you don't work hard you don't have freedom. So, that mean you cannot just be lazy and don't do nothing. But those people who hold a high position, they have more freedom."[23] While some complain that refugees are taking jobs, there is a question of whether they are sometimes being exploited since they are such hard workers and legal, but resettled in locations where they must take any available employment, and they come from pasts that make them fearful of complaining to authority.

The average family monthly income for the refugees in the study was $700-$999 during their first year. By their fourth year it was $1,300-$1,599 with a number of families reporting incomes beyond $2,500.[24] Overall, the group continued to relate to its own culture and ethnic group over the four years, but also began to interact more, indicating progress on the "social bridging" pathway. When asked "Do you spend time with people of a culture, ethnic group, language, or religion different from your own?" 48% of the group originally responded "yes," while three years later that was up to 65%.[25] Similarly, as far as adjusting to American life, the study said "We observed a notable increase in the percentage of respondents who could correctly identify the location of the White House and Congress. A similar increase was seen in the proportion of respondents who reported celebrating an American holiday."[26]

The report noted that differences in age are "highly, highly significant" when predicting integration level.[27] This is supported by people who work closely with the refugees. Patima Saptoka is a receptionist at the Asian Pacific Development Center, a facility in Aurora, Colorado that offers many services to Denver metropolitan area refugees. She speaks five languages and knows the people who come to the Center well. She said, "The younger generation gets more chance to do things, to get involved. The old are like, we're done. It's our life now. We'll do whatever we want to do. They don't even bother to learn English. That's the more complicated age"[28]

Patima's colleague, Chris Halligan, who came to the Denver area from Dublin, commented, "One of the things is this whole generational gap. The younger generation, they can assimilate better, they are taking care of their parents. I saw a lot of children snapping at their parents. I'm Irish Catholic – you don't snap at your mom and dad. They had this power over them because they're so much more assimilated."[29] In its final conclusion, the reports said that "integration among the overall cohort steadily increased" and "Our quantitative and qualitative data suggest that no one is more concerned about successful integration than refugees themselves. As they describe the challenges they face overcoming obstacles along several pathways, they also expressed hope and gratitude"[30] for the opportunity to make new lives in this strange country.

The *RISE Report* was a very careful study of how refugees adapted over four years of first living in America, and it showed that they made considerable progress in learning English, worked hard, and made good lives for themselves, kept their cultures alive, but also adapted to their new culture and its traditions and were anxious to be U.S. citizens. While this has not been everyone's view of refugees, it was what actual research showed to be the case. The *Huffington Post*'s evaluation was, "The Colorado study showcases integration progress from refugees as they spend more time in the United States."[31]

# CHAPTER TWENTY-TWO: FRIGHTENED CHILDREN

The reactions of adults are one thing. The fears of refugees and immigrants that have been politicized by people in public office and media opportunists, and the rhetoric used that has labeled them as outsiders also affects their children. They are more fragile targets.

As comments continually show, and the *RISE Report* confirmed, their children's future is refugees' greatest hope for coming to America. Some also see possibilities for improvement in the prospect that their children might bring the American tradition of the melting pot back to their home countries. This latter group believes that if their diaspora returns home, they will not assume life must be bound by the tribal or ethnic divisions that led to the strife that their parents were forced to flee. In the U.S., while there are certainly problems, their families have found that their children are more likely to mix with other diverse groups, and don't share ethnic or tribal distinctions from their home countries in the way that the older generation may continue to harbor after coming to the United States.

Young children can be affected by political rhetoric and feel it personally. This has been particularly true of comments made by Donald Trump as a candidate and President. The children of refugees often end up attending schools where other refugees and minorities are also students, due to the cost of housing, and the practice of placing refugees in areas where they can find others who can help them adjust and navigate their relocation. Their views aren't necessarily reflections of what they hear at home, but they presented them as what they hear in discussions with their schoolmates of various backgrounds.

Korena is an eight-year-old Burmese girl, who was born in a refugee camp in Thailand. She said, "I'm really concerned about what the President is going to do in the future. He's treating other people not the way you would want them to treat you."[1] This was echoed by Jarry, a 12-year- old Burmese, who was also born in a refugee camp in Thailand. Her comment was, "About the President, we don't hate him. But, we don't like his attitude, the way he acting to everybody. One thing that concerns me is what I hear, the things he's doing to women." She added, "I don't feel good that he's doing that to women. That's one of my concerns. The people who want to come to the United States, they'll have to wait a long time to come over here, so I'm really concerned about their siblings they have over here. Like, if they'll be able to make it to come over here."[2]

Hser, who is 10 years old, and was also born in a refugee camp in Thailand, said, "We don't hate Donald Trump. It's just his behavior that he acts to people. And we don't feel safe and comfortable with him around."[3]

11-year-old Rowin, also Burmese and born in a refugee camp in Thailand, made the statement, "A few things I feel about the President is I feel very uncomfortable, because he makes me feel unsafe and not want to live here. And refugees, I feel very bad because I have aunts, uncles over there and sometimes they feel like they can't come and visit, with him as the president."[4]

The final word belongs to KuKu, who, is only six years old. She was born in United States to refugee parents from Burma, so a U.S. citizen by birth. While she didn't articulate specific complaints, she thinks Santa won't bring Donald Trump presents because he hasn't been nice.[5]

# CHAPTER TWENTY-THREE:
## INSIDERS' VIEWS

The fate of refugees is dependent on decisions and actions of others. This is evident in the *Refugee Act of 1980* and the executive orders on travel bans barring entry for refugees into the country. A look at the views of some of those, other than the president, whose views can impact the lives of Denver refugees and others in Colorado helps round out how they will be received, given many states were refusing Syrian refugees, the controversy over sanctuary cities and states, and the varying recent attitudes on refugees.

Colorado's Governor, John Hickenlooper, has been a big supporter of refugees in Colorado. He commented, "Refugees have a valued place in the fabric of our communities. They enrich our culture and inspire many of us as we recognize the hardships so many have faced simply to call Colorado home."[1]

Colorado Senator, Michael Bennet, offered a similar sentiment, "The President's revised refugee executive order remains a significant departure from our nation's proud history of welcoming people in need of protection." He added that they are the most thoroughly vetted group that enters the United States, and that an order preventing these people fleeing violence and extremism "harms-not enhances-our national security. Targeting certain groups will undermine our counterterrorism efforts by stoking anti-West sentiment among ISIS followers and other extremists." It's Bennet's view that the president needs to work on a plan that will not only make us safer, "but is also consistent with our values."[2]

Bennet's Colorado Senate partner, Cory Gardner, had a more nuanced response. He began by praising the nation's heritage of welcoming immigrants and being a beacon of hope, and later stated, "I firmly believe that any reforms should not penalize or disrespect those who achieved residency or citizenship legally, nor adversely affect those who have pending applications for visas or citizenship."[3] This sounds encouraging for refugees and immigrants, who arrive as legal residents. Since he mentions "pending applications," that raises questions about those who had been previously approved, but found their status in question by the executive orders on travel bans. Gardner seems much more concerned with undocumented workers entering the country, and speaks of the need for border security, coupled with still finding a way to have sufficient labor available. He writes, "I remain a strong supporter of a workable E-Verify system that gives employers the assurance they are hiring workers legally residing in our country. I also believe that a guest-worker program should be a part of any border security proposal. Without a functioning guest-worker program, border security programs will fail."[4]

Lawrence Bartlett, who speaks with special authority on refugee matters, began his direct contact with other cultures when he was a Peace Corps volunteer in Yemen in the 1970s and continued through the present. In 1999, he came to the U.S. State Department, and for the past 18 years has been the Director of Refugee Admissions for the United States. He has overseen the handling of refugee admissions from the Clinton administration through two terms of both George W. Bush and Barack Obama and remains in his position for President Donald Trump.

Breitbart News called Bartlett "an Obama holdover," overlooking Bush and Clinton, and said he was one of ten bureaucrats Trump could fire immediately.[5] He is likely the foremost refugee spokesman and has a somewhat optimistic view. His thoughts were expressed several months before the presidential election and six months before the executive ordered travel bans; however, the rhetoric of the campaign had been very much a factor by this time. He said, "So, as we see rhetoric against migrants or against immigrants or against people of different faiths, we are concerned. What I think has been heartening and affirming is we hear time and time again is that the refugees are well received, that the people who are working with them, the citizens of these communities, are really receptive to having these refugees in their midst."[6]

The relationship between federal and state was pointed out by Kit Taintor, Colorado State Refugee Coordinator. She wrote, "While refugee resettlement is a federal program, with primary decision making on how many refugees arrive and where they come from under the provenance of the President and the Department of State, refugee resettlement ultimately plays out at the local level."[7]

Bartlett noted that things are not all great. "It's not a hundred percent, because there are people who aren't tolerant of others, but I have to say the vast majority in these communities have a real understanding of the difficulties these refugees have faced, and are very welcoming." He said that some states that have questions about the program and about whether the security vetting component that refugees undergo is sufficient. He continued, "They've also had concerns about Syrians, but that's again about security and their lack of knowledge about the security requirements that people have to pass." At that time, 31 governors had said they would not accept Syrian refugees.[8]

Even though there have been two executive orders banning Syrians from entering the country, public opinion has changed since then. The month after 31 governors said they would not accept Syrians, only 43% of Americans supported accepting such refugees. On April 20, 2017, 57% supported accepting Syrian refugees, while only 38% were opposed.[9]

One place that has been very welcoming in Colorado is Aurora. Aurora is a city of 350,000 that is part of the Denver metropolitan area and home to a large number of the refugees who settle in the area. Variety is the word that best describes Aurora, the 54th largest city in the country, where whites are slightly in the minority. It ranks as having the country's ninth most diverse neighborhoods, and as the tenth most integrated city.[10] The mayor of this city is Steve Hogan, and he takes pride in the culture of Aurora. Mr. Hogan wrote, "Aurora is a city that strives to be welcoming, and a city of both caring and inclusion. We do not view immigrants and refugees as a challenge, we view what they bring as an opportunity. All who live here have had a hand in making Aurora successful. That obviously includes the many immigrants and refugees who have settled here. Whether it is participation in small businesses, or in delicious new restaurants, or in our educational sector, this city would not be what it is without the 20% of our population that was born in a country other than the United State of America."[11]

Kevin Mohatt, the Community Outreach Coordinator at Emily Griffith in Denver, said in June, 2016, "After the terrorist attack in Belgium and after California we fielded a lot of fear and antipathy in the community."[12] His observation was that he thought that some of the community that was fearful had an agenda, while there was a groundswell in the community who wanted to volunteer and help support resettlement.

Bartlett pointed out a recurring theme: "I think there is just a lack of understanding of other cultures and I think Muslims have been vilified because of other conflicts in the world, and a number of the conflicts are in Muslim areas." This was a comment echoed by a number of people. He added that refugees are perceived as someone who is different by American citizens, people who haven't had contact with non-Americans. "But the great part of that is, is that when people come into contact with refugees they realize they're just people."

He said the State Department doesn't consider taking in refugees as the primary response to a crisis. The primary response is providing assistance to people who are nearby. So, the United States had provided 5.6 billion dollars for international support since the beginning of the Syrian crisis. It was usually only after four or five years that the resettlement process began, because it was clear in some situations that people weren't going to go home, which was the first choice.

Bartlett also commented on challenges many refugees face, bringing up language as so many mention. He said, "We're taking refugees out of places where sometimes people might not even be literate in their own language." The countries vary. People from Syria and Iraq are highly literate, not always highly educated, while those from places like Congo are not. He says that the tragedy for refugees is the longer they've been out of their countries, the less education they've been able to acquire, and the less opportunities for growth. He still remains optimistic, saying, "We don't believe there's anybody who can't make it. But certainly, there are groups where it is harder." Many of the older generation Bhutanese and Burmese who spent decades in camps and came to Colorado would be in this category.

For the person who has observed this from the broadest perspective for the longest time, Bartlett remains enthusiastic. He believes in the idea that since the beginning of this country this has been a nation of immigrants, and immigration hasn't stopped. He has confidence in refugees, saying, "They've known hardship, but they're resilient. Frankly, they become great Americans." And on the reverse side, he adds, "I think it changes the lives of people who come in contact with them as much as it changes the refugees." Kim Taintor added, "The actual arrival to the US is just the beginning of a long journey towards integration for refugees, and it is the local community in which they resettle that offers them the environment to find that which they have been seeking: safety, stability and opportunity."

In Colorado, a refugee expert with extensive experience is Joe Wismann-Horther. Joe is another Peace Corps volunteer. He first began working with refugees in 1999 at Ft. Dix, where refugees from Kosovo were being resettled. He recalls, "It was my first experience watching people get off a plane with a plastic bag that said IOM (International Organization for Migration) with all of their belongings."[13] Following years of nonprofit work, his current job title is Integration Partnerships Coordinator, where he focuses on long-term integration of Colorado refugees. Joe uses the Vietnamese as the example of successful refugee integration when he speaks in Denver. They are the "first generation refugees" and he says, "Their narrative is just tremendous. Just the nail polishing industry is a couple billion dollars." He notes that it has been a changing scene for refugees over the years. Ten years ago, the state was in the midst of the Tom Tancredo era,[14] the anti- immigrant era. He said refugees had a different existence in Colorado then because they were kind of "under the radar." The focus was on undocumented workers, so refugees didn't receive much media attention. In his opinion Colorado had a good record on reaching out to support refugees until the beginning of the presidential campaign, and with the Syrian crisis and events overseas. Now, "They're being kind of put into a category of risk in the U.S. The racism that's cropped up in this election has affected refugees as well." Joe's view of the local critics is and those who resist refugee resettlement "are a small but vocal group," while overall, he is convinced that "Colorado is a fairly welcoming." Kim adds to this that in Colorado, "Local neighbors, employers, teachers, volunteers, nurses, bus drivers and grocery clerks all play vital roles in the refugee resettlement process; they may not be formal roles, but they are perhaps the most vital to integration success."

Joe stresses that welcoming refugees is an American tradition: "When I do presentations now I show slides of refugees from World War II, from Vietnam, from Bosnia," to make that connection between then and now, because it's a different looking population. But it's still a population that's been dislocated, that's been persecuted, and he contends the U.S. has a leading role to provide sanctuary and security.

Lawrence Bartlett mentioned that they base arrival placement less on the state than the community. He explained that they looked at the local community and its capability to provide jobs, as well as the housing situation in the community, because refugees need to have safe, but affordable housing. He noted that while the Denver area provided a very welcoming environment for refugees, there was a growing concern about whether continued resettlement could be sustained because the cost of housing had been increasing so rapidly that it might not be a workable solution.

Kevin Mohatt commented on this current challenge. He describes refugee resettlement as a "village enterprise," because it involves the whole community. He thinks resettlement hasn't really been good about educating the community or cultivating the community, building public will. It existed after World War II when there were enough communities of faith and others who thought it was a good thing to do, and when the Vietnamese refugees came, there was 32-month support for new arrivals. He says there has been a 41% dip in funding for refugee resettlement and there's and support was down eight with the housing crisis.

Joe shared this sentiment, saying that his biggest concern when they resettle refugees is whether they provide an adequate platform for them to get their feet on the ground so they can work towards economic stability and some upward mobility: "I think the terrain from 1980 to today is entirely different. So, you look at housing costs and the amount of budget that goes to each refugee and we are reaching a point where I'm not sure that it's making sense." He had recently visited a family of four, one who was paralyzed from waist down, and their apartment cost $1700 a month, while their benefit was $900. He wondered how long they would last.

He's becoming pessimistic about Denver's future as a refuge destination, "So, it's not about our community, about whether people will welcome them, whether there's employment. But the cost of childcare, the cost of housing, limited transportation, make it really hard for refugees. I'm really beginning to wonder about it."

Joe's hope from dealing so closely with the refugee community in the Denver metropolitan area is the same as theirs, the children. In his words, "One part of this narrative that allows me to sleep at night is that most refugees are here because they're banking that their kids are going to have a better life. I think it's their kids and their kid's kids that show that progression."

# CHAPTER TWENTY-FOUR: CONCLUSION

The refugee situation in Denver reflects what is taking place in the rest of the U.S. As the stories of these current Denver residents reveal, their lives have greatly improved after fleeing horrific situations. They are now settled in their new home, where there is opportunity for a new start, and they are successful. Some are helping their community members who have followed them and are making the dramatic adjustment to living in the United States, while others are still involved in the transition. Unfortunately, there is a chill in the entire community that is not of their making, for they feel uncertainty and insecurity.

When vague language lumps refugees, immigrants, illegal immigrants together in talk of securing the border and making the country safe, many are caught up in irrational fears. While there have been terrorist attacks in Europe since masses of refugees who had not been vetted poured in, it has been Europeans who went to join the ISIS self-proclaimed caliphate, or other extremist groups, who were associated with those attacks. There have also been the terrorist attacks in recent years on U.S. soil, but again those were committed by radicalized U.S. citizens, not refugees. The politically motivated fearmongering following this is not based on evidence, only on "what if" and "it could happen" suggestions designed to find scapegoats for uncertainty in a changing world.

How great of a danger are the refugees and foreign-born terrorists? Of the roughly 768,000 total murders committed in the United States from 1975 to the end of 2015, 3,024 (or 0.39 percent) were committed by foreign-born terrorists in an attack, 98.6 percent of whom were killed on September 11, 2001.[1] When we look at refugees, the number gets smaller. Of the 3,252,493 refugees admitted from 1975 to the end of 2015, twenty ended up being terrorists, which amounted to 0.00062 percent of the total. As for the threat they have represented, the last time refugees were involved in political terror was when a trio of Cuban refugees carried out the three fatal attacks in the 1970s.[2] What comparable miniscule realistic threat has ever been exaggerated into demands to make America safe with executive orders, banned countries? Three murders forty years ago are the reality, not the rhetoric.

Interviewing refugees and hearing what they have overcome arouses both sympathy and admiration. The various hardships these people have endured will always haunt them, but they have begun new lives and work hard in what is a difficult process of starting new lives in a foreign land. The transition is most difficult for older people who are the most embedded in their cultures, and find learning English especially challenging. They are often joined with family, and their hope is for the younger children. That is the recurring theme when meeting refugees and those who work with them regularly. The younger ones who were born in camps then resettled, or the children of refugees who were born after their parents resettled in the United States may keep their culture alive. But they find adaptation easy and speak English so they can receive educations, and advance and mingle in society here. They are the hopes their families are struggling for, and have suffered much in hopes for their success.

While some have had incidents of persecution or insult and others are familiar with it, most feel that Denver is a welcoming community. They resent the attitudes being expressed about refugees, and though that is especially true of Muslims, it is echoed by those of other faiths. They have all felt there are voices expressing anti-foreign rhetoric that labeled them as unwelcome.

The refugees are people who are contributing to the Denver community. Many are employed below the level of their qualifications, though several are community leaders. Not only are their contributions economic, as they are eager workers, but they add diversity and broaden the cultural horizon to help make this a more cosmopolitan urban area. They are happy to be here and Denver is a better place because of their presence.

We as a country have long celebrated accepting those fleeing violence and oppression with pride. It has now been 114 years since Emma Lazarus' words were mounted in the Statue of Liberty

*Give me your tired, your poor,*
*Your huddled masses yearning to breathe free,*
*The wretched refuse of your teeming shore.*
*Send these, the homeless, tempest-tost to me,*
*I lift my lamp beside the golden door!*

The lamp has been lifted and Denver has welcomed these, whose stories are told, and many more. That is the tradition that has made America the beacon of hope for the downtrodden of the world. All of us who are not Native Americans have ancestors who came to the American melting pot from somewhere. We have celebrated the American Dream of our forefathers starting over with the opportunity to achieve a better life. These refugees now keep that that proud heritage alive.

# EPILOGUE

Since this book was written there have been a number of events that have occurred that are related to topics discussed and worth mention.

The Supreme Court agreed in June 2017 to hear argument on a case decided at the Circuit Court level that had temporarily stopped President Trump's revised travel ban. That ban barring citizens of six majority Muslim countries from entering the U.S. has prevented 24,000 refugees from entering the country. The Supreme Court said the ban could continue for the time being except for those with a "bona fide" relationship with organizations or persons in the United States, or "close" family ties with someone in this country. Arguments in the final Court decision on the constitutionality of the travel ban were scheduled for October 10, 2017. The addition of Neil Gorsuch to the Court in April is not a cause for optimism for those who hope to see the ban declared unconstitutional. This Court date was cancelled when the travel ban was modified to include non-Muslim countries, which temporarily appeared as though it might allow the ban to be reinstated. A federal court judge blocked the ban on October 17, hours before it was to take effect. The Supreme Court announced on December 4 that it would allow a revised version of the travel ban, which included North Korea and Venezuela along with majority Muslim countries, to be fully enforced while legal challenges continued in lower courts.

The continuing belief many hold that this is a nation for whites was dramatically exposed in August. When local officials in Charlotte, Virginia, voted to take down a statue of Confederate General Robert E. Lee, white nationalists organized a "Unite the Right" rally in response. They described the purpose of the rally as to "take America back," and it attracted white supremacy advocates including neo-Nazis, skinheads, Ku Klux Klan from near and far. Former KKK leader David Duke was among those who attended, saying the rally was a "turning point" in the effort to help people like him "fulfill the promises of Donald Trump."

They descended on Charlotte and marched on the University of Virginia campus on the evening of Friday, August 11. Many were heavily armed, some were giving the Nazi salute, while chants of "Jews will not replace us" and "white lives matter" were heard. There were Confederate flags, swastikas, anti-Semitic and anti-Muslim banners in the eerie torch-lit procession. The next day counter-protesters turned out to object to their presence. Clashes broke out and an "alt-right" white nationalist drove his car into a crowd of counter-protesters, killing one and injuring 19. That day there was a bill signing ceremony and President Trump ignored a question about white nationalists expressing support for him. He said, "We condemn in the strongest possible terms this egregious display of hatred, bigotry and violence, on many sides." The white supremacist *Daily Stormer* said "Trump comments good...Really, really good." President Trump's statement of apparent equivalency between the counter-protesters with the white supremacists, Neo-Nazis, Ku Klux Klan was severely criticized not only by Democrats but also by many leading Republicans.

June 20, 2017 was World Refugee Day. It was reported there were nearly 66 million displaced people in the world, and the number who were refugees was approaching 23 million.

In a blow to those abroad who saw pictures of the Statue of Liberty and heard the hopeful words of "The New Colossus" it appears that President Trump plans to reduce the number of refugees admitted to the United States over the next year. When he took office, he reduced the number to 50,000 as part of his original executive order banning travel from seven predominantly Muslim countries. In the previous year, President Obama had allowed 110,000. The President is required by the Refugee Act of 1980 to consult with Congress and submit the refugee limit by October. There are indications President Trump will go for less than 50,000 and his senior advisor for policy, Stephen Miller, has been said to have advocated for reducing the number to as low as 15,000.

A second shock to noncitizens came on September 5 when Attorney General Jeff Sessions announced that the Trump Administration had decided to end the Deferred Action for Childhood Arrivals program, known as DACA, established by President Obama that shields 800,000 immigrants from deportation. The people protected are the Dreamers, who arrived in the U.S. as children and know no other home and Trump had promised to end the program when he was a candidate. A six month phase out of the program was included in Sessions' statement to allow Congress time to come up with some solution in immigration reform that would address the fate of Dreamers. Polling at the time of the announcement showed that majorities of Democrats, Independents and Republicans favor allowing Dreamers to remain in the country and only 15% wish to see them deported. The same holds for self-identified Trump voters, where two-thirds think the Dreamers should stay and only 26% want to see them deported. In Congress, there is support in both parties for letting people who came to America as children remain in the country. At a mid-September meeting between the President and Democratic leadership it appeared there might be a possibility that a deal was possible for DACA to be saved and the Dreamers would not face deportation, but nothing concrete has yet emerged at this time.

Locally, the Denver City Council unanimously passed a bill on August 28 to show that it supported its refugee and immigrant communities. According to the new law, city employees, including law officers, will not collect information on immigration status. The city will not detain anyone on behalf of ICE beyond that person's sentence. The city will not share anyone's citizenship information for the purpose of immigration enforcement. The city also will not allow ICE agents into a jail without a warrant. Denver had formalized its status as a sanctuary city.

The world of refugees and Burma was back in the news when its government alleged there had been attacks by Rohingya militants on government border posts in the Rakhine state. The government's response was attacks on the Rohingya that were described by the UN human rights chief as a "textbook example of ethnic cleansing." Out of a population of about one million in the country, over 600,000 Rohingya have fled to Bangladesh since August 25, 2017 and over 800,000 are now surviving as refugees in places not equipped to handle them. UN Ambassador Nikki Haley expressed gratitude to Bangladesh for taking in the influx of refugees and both the U.S. and the UN have called on Burma to halt its activities that are destabilizing the region.

Aung San Suu Kyi, Burma's de facto leader, has come under considerable criticism for her failure to speak out or respond to the crisis. She continues to adopt the military junta's position that the Rohingya crisis is a "huge iceberg of misinformation" distributed to benefit "terrorists." Among those who have criticized her recently are Nobel Peace Prize winners Malala, Archbishop Desmond Tutu, Shirin Ebadi and there is an online petition with over 400,000 signatures demanding she return her Nobel Prize. She cancelled her visit to the UN as the Security Council called for "immediate steps to end the violence, de-escalate the situation, re-establish law, and ensure the protection of civilians." U.S. Secretary of State Rex Tillerson and British Prime Minister

Teresa May both labeled the Burmese actions against the Rohingya as "ethnic cleansing."

Much more will unfold in the near future that will impact the lives of refugees.

# NOTES

## CH.1, INTRODUCTION

1. Barack Obama, "Statement by the President on World Refugee Day." The White House, https://obamawhitehouse. archives.gov/the-press-office/2014/06/20/statement-president-world-refugee- day, June 20, 2014.

2. Jonathan Swan, "Trump: Refugees could be Trojan Horse," *The Hill*,http://thehill.com/blogs/ballot-box/presidential-races/260370-trump-refugees-could-be-trojan-horse-for-isis, Nov 16, 2015.

3. Emily Schulyheis, "Donald Trump warns refugees could be "Trojan horse" for U.S.," *CBS News*, http:// www.cbsnews.com/news/donald-trump-warns-refugees-could-be-trojan-horse-for-u-s/ June 13, 2016.

4. John A. Goodwin, *The Pilgrim Republic: An Historical Prospective of the Colony of New Plymouth*, (Boston: Ticknor, 1888)

5. Sam Lucerne, *Theocracies* (New York City: Essential Library, 2011) 12, "For more than four decades the Massachusetts Bay Colony remained a theocratic colony functioning in the new world."

6. Walter Herbert Burgess, *John Robinson, Pastor of the Pilgrim Fathers: A Study of His Life and Times* (London: Williams & Norgate, 1920), 333.

7. See entire *Refugee Act of 1980*, "Public Law 96-212 – Mar.17, 1980," https://www.gpo.gov/fdsys/pkg/STATUTE-94/pdf/STATUTE-94-Pg102.pdf.

8. "History of the U.S. Refugee Resettlement Program," *Refugee Council USA*. Audrey Singer and Jill H. Wilson, "From 'There' to 'Here': Refugee Resettlement in Metropolitan America," *The Brookings Institute, Living Census Series*, Sep 2006.

9. Adrian Edwards, "Global Forced Displacement Hits Record High," *The UN Refugee Agency*, http://www.unher.org//en-us/news/latest/2016/6/5763b65a4/global-forced-displacement-hits-record- high.html, Jun 20, 2016.

10. Ibid.

11. *Refugee Act of 1980*, Public Law 96-212, Sec. 207, a1.

12. "History of the U.S. Refugee Resettlement Program."

13. Philip Connor and Jens M. Krogstad, "Key Facts About the World's Refugees," *Pew Research Center*, http://www.pewresearch.org/fact-tank/2017/01/27/key-facts-about-refugees-to-the- u-s/, Oct 5, 2016.

14. Don Barnett, "A New era of Refugee Resettlement," *Center for Immigration Studies*, http://cis.org/RefugeeResettlement, Dec 2006.Connor and Krogstad, "Key Facts About the World's Refugees".

15. Jie Zong and Jeanne Batalova, "Refugees and Asylees in the United States," *Migration Policy Institute*, http://www.migrationpolicy.org/article/refugees-and-asylees-united- states#Refugee%20 Countries%20of%20Origin, Oct 28, 2015.

16. Radhika Sanghani, "Angela Merkel: The Most Powerful Quotes from TIME's Person of the Year," *The Telegraph*, Dec 10, 2015.

17. Phillip Connor, "U.S. Admits Record Number of Muslim Refugees in 2016," *Pew Research Center*, Oct 5, 2016.

18. Joey Bunch and Mark Mathews, "Colorado Will Accept Syrian Refugees, Hickenlooper Says," *Denver Post* Apr 19, 2016.

19. *Colorado Office of Economic Security: Division of Refugee Services*, https://sites.google.com/a/state.co.us/cdhs-re.

20. David Elwell, Sarah Junker, Stefan Sillau, Eva Aagaard, "Refugees in Denver and Their Perceptions of Their Health and Health Care, *Journal of Health Care for the Poor and Underserved,* Vol. 25, 2014, 128.

21. "Refugees-Asylees-Secondaries in Colorado FY 1980-2014.pdf," *Colorado Office of Economic Security: Division of Refugee Services,* https://drive.google.com/file/d/0B- 9dBwl5XFYdWHZRU1RIai13Y3c/view.

22. Ibid

23. Ibid.

24. Alex Noweasteh, "Terrorism and Immigration: A Risk Analysis," *CATO Institute, Policy Analysis No.798,* https:// Sept 13, 20

## CH.2, GEORGETTE, CONGO

1. Anneke Van Woudenberg, "Democratic Republic of Congo: On the Brink," *Humans Rights Watch* online, https://www.hrw.org/news/2006/08/01/democratic-republic-congo-brink, Aug 1, 2006

2. Ibid.

3. See Chapter 3.

4. Jeremy Hein and Tarique Niazi, "A Well-Founded Fear: The Social Ecology of 21st Century Refugees," *Harvard International Review,* Vol. 31, No. 3, Fall 2009, 40.

5. "The Heart of the Hutu-Tutsi Conflict," *PBS Newshour,* http://www.pbs.org/newshour/updates/africa-july-dec99-rwanda_10-08/, Oct 8, 1999.

6. Susanne Buckley-Zistel, Dividing and Uniting: The Use of Citizenship Discourses in Conflict and Reconciliation in Rwanda, *Global Society,* Vol. 20, No. 1, January, 2006.

7. Helen M Hintjens, "When Identity Becomes a Knife: Reflecting on the Genocide in Rwanda," *Ethnicities*, Vol.1, Iss.1, Mar 1, 2001, 26-28.

8. John Prendergast and David Smock, "Post-Genocidal Reconciliation: Building Peace in Rwanda and Burundi," *United States Institute of Peace,* http://www.usip.org/publications/post-genocidal-reconstruction-building-peace-in- rwanda-and-burundi, Sept 1, 1999. Hein and Niazi, "A Well-Founded Fear: The Social Ecology of 21st Century Refugees."

9. Editorial Board, "After Rwanda's Genocide," *The New York Times*, Apr 9, 2014, A22.

10. Ola Olsson and Heather Congdon Furs, "Congo: The Prize of Predation," *Journal of Peace Research*, Vol. 41, No. 3, May 2004, 325.

11. Filip Reyntjens, "The Second Congo War: More than a Remake," *African Affairs*, Vol. 98, No. 391, Apr 1999, 250.

12. This and all quotes by Georgette in chapter are from Georgette, interview with Robert Dodge, Denver, December 20, 2016.

13. Reyntjens, "The Second Congo War: More than a Remake,"250.

14. bid., 241

15. "About the Great Lakes Region," *U.S. Department of State*, https://www.state.gov/s/greatlakes_drc/191417.htm.

16. Van Woodener, "Democratic Republic of Congo: On the Brink".

17. See Gerard Punier, *Africa's World War: Congo, the Rwandan Genocide, and the Making of a Continental Catastrophe* (New York: Oxford University Press, 2008)137-141.

18. Thomas M. Calzaghe, "Review: Life and Death in the Congo: Understanding a Nation's Collapse," *Foreign Affairs,* Vol. 80, No. 5, Sept- Oct., 2001, 143.

19. John Mecum Baku, *Corruption in Africa: Causes Consequences, and Cleanups* (Lanham, MD: Lexington Books, 2010), 54.

20. See Guy J. Golan, "Where in the World Is Africa?: Predicting Coverage of Africa by US Television Networks," *International Communication Gazette,* Feb 1, 2008, Vol. 70, No. 41, 2008. Susan D. Moeller, "'Regarding the Pain of Others': Media, Bias and the Coverage of International Disasters," Journal *of International Affairs*, Vol. 59, No. 2, Spring/Summer, 2006. Jacoba Urist, "Which Deaths Matter? How the Media Covers the People Behind Today's Grim Statistics," The *Atlantic*, http://www.theatlantic.com/international/archive/2014/09/which-deaths-matter-media-statistics/380898/, Sept 29, 2014. Historian Gerard Prunier noted that significant African events of this time that received some notice, such as the Rwanda genocide, the end of apartheid in South Africa, as well as war in the Congo "semi-forgotten in the wake of September 11, Gerard Prunier, *Africa's World War: Congo, the Rwandan Genocide, and the Making of a Continental Catastrophe* (New York: Oxford University Press, 2008), XXXVIII.

21. Vava Tampa, "Why the World is Ignoring Congo War," *CNN*, http://www.cnn.com/2012/11/27/opinion/congo- war-ignored-vava-tampa/, Nov 27, 2012.

## CH.3, FROM COLONIALISM TO REFUGEES

1. Patricia S. Daniels, Stephen G. Hyssop, *National Geographic Almanac of World History*, 3rd Edition (Washington, D.C., National Geographic, 2014) 316.

2. Kipling, Rudyard, "The White Man's Burden," originally published in McClure's Magazine, Feb 1899 to encourage the U.S. to annex its recently conquered Philippines. *Rudyard Kipling's Verse: Definitive Edition* (Garden City, NY: Doubleday, 1929).

3. Mike van der Linden, "To Whom Belongs the Land? Territory, Sovereignty, and Imperialism in the History of

International Law," *European Society of International Law: Conference Paper Series*, No. 15/2015, May 2015.

4. David Renton. David Seddon, Leo Zeelie, *The Congo: Plunder and Resistance* (New York: Zed Books, 2007), 2.

5. Ibid., 27.

6. Laurent Licata and Oliver Klein, "Holocaust or Benevolent Paternalism? Intergenerational Comparisons on Collective Memories and Emotions about Belgium's Colonial Past," *International Journal of Conflict and Violence*, Vol.4, No.1, 201047.

7. Robert Harms, "The End of Red Rubber: A Reassessment," *The Journal of African History*, Vol. 16, No. 1, 1965, 79.

8. Tony Ward, "State Crime in the Heart of Darkness," *The British Journal of Criminology*, Vol. 45, No. 4, July 2005, 440.

9. Renton. Seddon, Zeilig, *The Congo: Plunder and Resistance,* 31.

10. Brantlinger, Patrick. "'Heart of Darkness': 'Anti-Imperialism, Racism, or Impressionism?'" *Criticism*, Vol. 27, No.4, Fall, 1985, 365.

11. Arthur C. Doyle, *The Crime of the Congo* (New York: Doubleday, Page & Company,1909).

12. Mark Twain, *King Leopold's Soliloquy: A Defense of His Congo Rule* ((Boston: P.R. Warren, 1905).

13. Joseph Conrad, *Heart of Darkness*, originally a novella in *Youth: A Narrative; and Two Other Stories* (London: J. M. Dent & Sons, Ltd., 1902).

14. Conrad, *Heart of Darkness* (New York: Bantam Classics, 2004), 105.

15. Brantlinger, Patrick. "'Heart of Darkness': 'Anti-Imperialism, Racism, or Impressionism?'" *Criticism*, Vol. 27, No.4, Fall, 1985, 365.

16. "Leopold II King of Belgium," *Encyclopaedia Britannica*, https://www.britannica.com/biography/Leopold-II-king-of-Belgium. Mark Dummett, "King Leopold's Legacy of DR Congo Violence," BBC News, http://news.bbc.co.uk/2/hi/africa/3516965.stm, Feb 24, 2004.

17. Tarek Osman, "Why Border Lines Drawn with a Ruler in WWI Still Rock the Middle East," *BBC News*, http://www.bbc.com/news/world-middle-east-25299553, Dec 14, 2013.

18. Ibid.

19. Gabriel Scheinmann, "The Map that Ruined the Middle East," *The Tower*, http://www.thetower.org/article/the-map-that-ruined-the-middle-east/, No. 4, July 2013.

20. See Michael Gunter, "Iraq, Syria, ISIS and the Kurds: Geostrategic Concerns for the U.S. and Turkey," *Middle East Policy Council*, Vol. XXII, No. 1, Spring 2015. Andrew Phillips, "The Islamic State's Challenge to International Order," Australian Journal of International Affairs, Vol. 68. Iss. 5, Aug 2014. Edward P. Fitzgerald, "France's Middle Eastern Ambitions, the Sykes-Picot Negotiations, and the Oil Fields of Mosul, 1915-1918," *The Journal of Modern History*, Vol. 66, No. 4, Dec 1994.

21. Pierre Englebert, Stacy Tarango, and Matthew Carter, "Dismemberment and Suffocation: A Contribution to the Debate on African Boundaries," *Comparative Political Studies*, Vol. 35, No. 10, Dec 1, 2002, 1096

22. Ibid, 1113.

23. C. I. Eugene Kim and Chester Hunt, "Education and Political Development: A Comparison of Korea and the Philippines," *Journal of Developing Areas*, Apr 1968, 411.

24. "The Russian Refugees: Hebrews in Brooklyn Taking Measures for Their Relief," *New York Times*, March 6, 1882, 8.

25. Ibid.

26. "The Statue of Liberty Facts - The Statue of Liberty & Ellis Island," http://www.libertyellisfoundation.org/statue-facts.

27. Roberto Suro, "The Statue of Liberty's Real Stand," *Washington Post*, July 5, 2009.

28. David E. Nye, *American Technological Sublime* (Cambridge, MA: MIT Press, 1996) 271. Yasmin Sabina Khan, *Enlightening the World: The Creation of the Statue of Liberty* (Ithaca, NY: Cornell University Press, 2010) 105-106.

29. History.com staff, "Ellis Island," *History*, http://www.history.com/topics/ellis-island, 2009.

30. John Bodnar, "Symbols and Servants: Immigrant America and the Limits of Public History," *The Journal of American History*, Vol. 73, No. 1, June, 1986, 141.

31. Suro, "The Statue of Liberty's Real Stand."

32. See Gad Nahshon, "Emma Lazarus, The New Colossus' 125th Anniversary of the Statue of Liberty," *Jewishpost*, http://www.jewishpost.com/culture/emma-lazarus-the-new-colossus.html, "the New Colossus is a national Jewish sonata. Why? Lazarus was influenced then by the terrible Russian Czarist genocide of Jews in Russia and East-Europe. The 1880's were the era of the pogroms: 'Kill the Jews in order to save Russia.' The 'golden door's' target was to save these Jews, these refugees."

33. "The New Colossus," *The Poems of Emma Lazarus* (Boston: Houghton, Mifflin, 1888), 202.

34. "Emma Lazarus," *National Park Service*, https://www.nps.gov/stli/learn/historyculture/emma-lazarus.htm.

35. Susan Welch et. al., *Understanding American Government* (Belmont, CA: Wadsworth Publishing, 2011), 21.

36. "Emma Lazarus," *National Park Service*.

37. Philipp Frank, *Einstein: His Life and Times* (Boston: Da Capo Press, 2002), 277.

38. Welch et. al., *Understanding American Government,* 21.

39. Suro, "The Statue of Liberty's Real Stand."

40. Pamela Engel, "Trump on Syrian Refugees: 'Lock Your Doors, Folks,'" *Business Insider,* http://www.businessinsider.com/trump-syrian-refugees-isis-2016-4, Apr 25, 2016.

41. Julie H Davis, "Trump Orders Mexican Border Wall to Be Built and Plans to Block Syrian Refugees," *The New York Times*, Jan 26, 2017, A1.

42. Gary Lichtenstein et.al., *The Refugee Integration Survey and Evaluation (RISE) Year Five: Final Report: A Study of Refugee Integration in Colorado*; known as *RISE Report* (Denver: Colorado Office of Economic Opportunity, 2016), 2.

43. Setu Nepal, interview with Robert Dodge, Aurora, CO, May 6, 2016.

## CH.4, MOHAMMED, SYRIA

1. "The World Factbook," *Central Intelligence Agency*, https://www.cia.gov/library/publications/the- world- factbook/geos/sy.html.

2. Louisa Loveluck and Zakaria Zakaria, "Despite U.S. Missile Barrage, Syria, Continues Airstrikes against Rebels," *Washington Post,* Apr 8, 2017.

3. Jamey Katen and Sarah El Deeb, "UNHCR: Number of Syrian Refugees Tops 5 Million Mark," *Associated* Press, https://apnews.com/9a16fa6594994aa0a8e2fc84cfdbef62, Mar 30, 2017.

4. "Civil War in Syria," *Council on Foreign Relations*, http://www.cfr.org/global/global-conflict- tracker/p32137#!/conflict/civil-war-in-syria, May 5, 2017.

5. This and all other quotes from Mohammed, Mohammed, interview with Robert Dodge, interpreter, Abira, May 3, 2017.

6.   Zamira Rahim, "Syria's Assad Brushes Off Amnesty Report on Prison Executions as 'Fake News'," *Time*, http://time.com/4666806/assad_syria-amnesty-international/, Feb 10, 2017.

7.   "Saydnaya Prison Is Where the Syrian State Quietly Slaughters Its Own People," *Amnesty International*, https://www.amnesty.org/en/latest/campaigns/2016/08/syria-torture-prisons/, Feb 7, 2017.

8.   See "Syrian Refugees Build City in Jordan Desert," *Deutsche Welle,* http://www.dw.com/en/syrian-refugees-build-a-city-in-jordan-desert/a-19385363#, Jul 7, 2016.

## CH.5, BURMA IN TURMOIL

1.   "Reryfugees-Asylabees in Colorado FY 1980-2014," 1.

2.   The ruling military junta changed the name of the country from Burma to Myanmar in 1989, a change that many countries accepted, but not the US or the UK. For more information, see *"Who, What, Why: Should It Be Burma or Myanmar?"* Dec 2, 2011, *BBC News*, http://www.bbc.com/news/magazine-16000467.

3.   The earliest claim appears to be that archeological digs indicate the Pyū people began converting as early as the First and second century A.D. following overland and maritime trade and emigration of monks from southern India, William J. Topich, Keith A. Leitich, Westport, *The History of Myanmar* (CT: ABC-CLIO/Greenwood, 2013), 16. More common is the fifth century, as seen in Helmut Köllner, Axel Bruns, *Myanmar (Burma),* (Palm Beach, FL: Hunter Publishing, 1998), 22. "Fifth or sixth century" is as close as Joseph Kitagawa comes to naming a date in *The Religious Traditions of Asia: Religion, History, and Culture* (New York: Routledge, 2013), 121. According to Barbara O'Brien, "it is most likely that Theravada Buddhism was first adopted by the Pyu people of what is now southern Burma during the 4th century," "Buddhism in Burma, Part I, Overview and

History," *About History*, http://buddhism.about.com/od/
throughasiaandbeyond/a/Buddhism-In-Burma-Part-1.htm.

4. Michael Jerryson, ed,, *The Oxford Handbook
of Contemporary Buddhism* (New York:
Oxford University Press, 2016), 214.

5. See Shelby Tucker, Burma: *The Curse of
Independence* (London: Pluto Press, 2001), 27-30.

6. Ibid., 30.

7. David I. Steinberg, "The Problem of Democracy in the
Republic of the Union of Myanmar: Neither Nation-State
Nor State-Nation?," Southeast Asian Affairs, 2012, 222.

8. Jean-Pierre Cabestan and Aleksandar Pavković,
eds. *Secessionism and Separatism in Europe and
Asia: To Have a State of One's Own (Politics
in Asia)* (London: Routledge, 2013), 180.

9. Ibid.

10. "Ethnic Nationalities of Burma," *Oxford Burma Alliance*,
http://www.oxfordburmaalliance.org/ethnic-groups.html.

11. Ibid.

12. Robert H. Taylor, "Perceptions of Ethnicity in
the Politics of Burma," *Southeast Asian Journal
of Social Science,* Vol. 10, No. 1, 1982, 8.

13. Alan Axelrod, Jack A. Kingston, *Encyclopedia of World
War II, Volume 1*(New York: Facts on File, 2007)135.

14. Ibid.

15. Ibid.

16. David Maybury-Lewis, Ch. 3, "Genocide against
Indigenous Peoples," Alexander Laban Hinton, ed.,
*Annihilating Difference: The Anthropology of Genocide*
(Berkeley: University of California Press, 2002), 50.

17. Steinberg, "The Problem of Democracy in the
Republic of the Union of Myanmar," 235, n.11.

18. Ashley South, "Burma's Longest War: Anatomy of the Karen Conflict," *Transnational Institute Burma Center Netherlands*, March 2011, 6. Steinberg, "The Problem of Democracy in the Republic of the Union of Myanmar," 221.

19. Steinberg, "The Problem of Democracy in the Republic of the Union of Myanmar," 223.

20. Taylor, "Perceptions of Ethnicity in the Politics of Burma," 9.

21. Konsam Shakila Devi, "Myanmar Under the Military Rule 1962-1988," *International Research Journal of Social Science*, Vol. 3, No.10, Oct 2014, 46-47.

22. Steinberg, "The Problem of Democracy in the Republic of the Union of Myanmar," 224.

23. "List of Least Developed Countries (as of May 2016)," *United Nations Committee for Development Policy*, http://www.un.org/en/development/desa/policy/cdp/ldc/ldc_list.pdf.

24. Devi, "Myanmar Under the Military Rule 1962-1988," 48.

25. "Burma Sanctions Program," Office of Foreign Assets Control, Department of the Treasury, https://www.treasury.gov/resource-center/sanctions/Programs/Documents/burma.pdf, Sept 9, 2015.

26. Aung San Suu Kyi, "Speech at Shwedagon Pagoda," *Aung San Suu Kyi, Freedom from Fear* (London: Penguin Books, 1991), 200.

27. R.H. Taylor, "Myanmar 1990: New Era or Old?," *Southeast Asian Affairs*, 1991, 201.

28. Ibid.

29. David Steinberg, "Globalization, Dissent, and Orthodoxy: Burma/Myanmar and the Saffron Revolution," *Georgetown Journal of International Affairs*, Vol.9, N0.2, Summer/Fall, 2008, 53.

30. Kate McGeown, "Burma: The Revolution That Didn't Happen," *BBC News*, Sept. 26, 2008, http://news.bbc.co.uk/go/pr/fr/-/2/hi/asia-pacific/7635419.stm.

31. Daniel Pepper, "Aftermath of a Revolt: Myanmar's Lost Year," *New York Times*, WK5, Oct. 4, 2008.

32. "Factbox-Key facts about Cyclone Nargis," *United Nations,* http://www.reuters.com/article/idUSSP420097, Apr, 2009.

33. "Comparing Hurricanes - Nargis and Katrina," *Coolgeography*, http://www.coolgeography.co.uk/9/Risky_Earth/Comparing%20Hurricanes/Comparing_hurricanes.htm.

34. Ibid.

35. Matias Thomsen, "The Obligation Not to Arbitrarily Refuse International Disaster Relief: A Question of Sovereignty," *Melbourne Journal of International Law*, Vol. 16, No. 2, 2015. Nick Schifrin, Jonathan Karl, "Myanmar's Leaders Play Politics with Disaster," *ABC News*, http://abcnews.go.com/International/Weather/story?id=4818210, May 9, 2008.

36. "Why Burma's Rohingya Muslims are among the world's most persecuted people," CBC News, http://www.cbc.ca/news/world/why-burma-s-rohingya-muslims-are-among-the-world-s-most-persecuted-people-1.3086261, May 25, 2015.

37. Ibid.

38. "Historical Background," *Human Rights Watch*, https://www.hrw.org/reports/2000/burma/burm005-01.htm.

39. Ibid.

40. "Why Burma's Rohingya Muslims are among the world's most persecuted people".

41. Karin Roberts, "Rohingya Refugees from Myanmar Have Been Persecuted for Decades," *New York Times,* May 12, 2015.

42. Jane Perlez, "Myanmar Policy's Message to Muslims: Get Out," *New York Times,* Nov 6, 2014.

43. "Myanmar wants ethnic cleansing of Rohingya - UN official," *BBC*, http://www.bbc.com/news/world-asia-38091816, Nov 24 2016.

44. Jonah Fisher, "Where is Aung San Suu Kyi?," *BBC*, Nov 24, 2016.

45. "Rohingya Myanmar: Nobel Winners Urge Action Over 'Ethnic Cleansing,'" *BBC News,* Dec 30, 2016.

## CH.6, DRUCIE, BURMA, KAREN

1. This and all quotes from Drucie, unless otherwise noted, come from Drucie Bathing interview with Robert Dodge, Aurora CO, Jan 16, 2017.

2. Cgeditor, "KNU Chairman Passed Away," *Chinland Gruardian.co* http://www.chinlandguardian.com/index.php/multimedia/item/1640-knu-chairman-passed-away, Sept 18, 2009.

3. From "Summer 1969," unpublished poem by Drucie Bathin.

4. Melanie Asmar, "A World Away: Without Drucie Bathin, Thousands of Refugees from Burma Would Be Lost in Denver," *Westworld*, Vol. 35, No. 20, Jan12-18, 2012, 12.

5. Ibid.

6. South, "Burma's Longest War," 8.

7. In Asmar, "A World Away," 14.

8. On Burmese Buddhists violence against Christians, see Hannah Beech, "When Buddhists Go Bad," *Time*, July 1, 2013, 60.

9. Asmar, "A World Away," 14.

10. Ibid.

## CH. 7, GRANDMA ESTER, BURMA

1. This and all quotes from Ester, Ester interviewed by Robert Dodge, interpreter, Drucie Bathing, Denver, Feb 19, 2017.

2. Michael W. Charney, *A History of Modern Burma* (London: Cambridge University Press, 2009),

3. Suffocation with plastic bags has been one of the frequent torture methods employed by the Burma Army according to a recent report on ethnic violence called "Trained to Torture."

## CH. 8, RHETORIC

1. Donald Trump, Tweet, June 16, 2015.

2. Aubrey Allegretti, "Refugee Crisis: Donald Trump Says He'd Send Syrians Fleeing War-Torn Country Back Home," *The Huffington Post*, http://www. huffingtonpost.co.uk/2015/10/01/donald-trump-refugees-syrian_n_8225856.html Oct 1, 2015.

3. Donald Trump, Tweet, Dec 7, 2015.

4. Donald Trump, Jr., Tweet, Sep 19, 2016.

5. "Executive Order: Protecting the Nation from Foreign Terrorist Entry into the United States," *The White House*, https://www.whitehouse.gov/the-press office/2017/01/27/executive-order-protecting-nation-foreign-terrorist- entry- united-states, Jan 27, 2017.

6. "Executive Order Protecting the Nation from Foreign Terrorist Entry into the United States," The White House, https://www.whitehouse.gov/the-press-office/2017/03/06/executive-order-protecting-nation-foreign-terrorist-entry- united-states, Mar 6, 2017.

7. Philip Hone, Mayor of NY City, *The Diary of Philip Hone, 1828-1851*(New York: Dodd, Mead, 1889), Sept 20, 1833 entry.

8. Woodrow Wilson, speech, Washington, D.C., May 16, 1914.

9. Joseph G. Cannon, Speaker of the House, (R, IL), address, General Convention of the International Order of B'nai B'rith, Washington, D.C., Apr 6, 1910.

10. *Bugajewitz v. Adams*, 228 U.S. 585, 590.

11. Grover Cleveland, speech 1897.

12. Noweasteh, "Terrorism and Immigration: A Risk Analysis."

13. Politico Staff, "Full Text: Donald Trump Immigration Speech in Arizona," *Politico*, Aug 31, 2016.

14. "The Latest: Trump: Trump Says Immigrants Taking Minorities' Jobs," *AP: The Big Story*, http://bigstory.ap.org/article/09215cf7f37f4c6ea05f92f8c83e6125/latest-fbi-expected-release-clinton- documents- soon, Aug 30, 2016.

15. "Donald J. Trump: Address on Immigration," *Trump Pence Make America Great Again*, https://www.donaldjtrump.com/press-releases/donald-j.-trump-address-on-immigration, Aug 31, 2016.

16. See Katelyn Fossett, "The Trouble with Trump's Immigrant Crimes List," *Politico Magazine,* http://www.politico.com/magazine/story/2017/03/donald-trump-immigrant-crimes-list-214878, Mar 17, 2017; Rafael Bernal, "Reports Find That Immigrants Commit Less Crime Than US-Born Citizens," *The Hill*, http://thehill.com/latino/324607-reports-find-that-immigrants-commit-less-crime-than-us-born-citizens, Mar 19, 2017; Nazgol Ghandnoosh and Josh Rovner, "Immigration and Public Safety," The Sentencing Project, http://www.sentencingproject.org/wp-content/uploads/2017/03/Immigration-and-Public-Safety.pdf; Criminal Immigrants: Their Numbers, Demographics, and Countries of Origin, *Cato Institute*, No 1, Mar 15, 2017.

17. Alex Nowrasteh, "Illegal Immigrant Crime Wave? Evidence Is Hard to Find," *Fox News*, http://www.

foxnews.com/opinion/2017/07/12/illegal-immigrant-crime-wave-evidence-is-hard-to-find.html, Jul 12, 2017.

18. See "Immigration: Myths and Facts," https://www.uschamber.com/report/immigration-myths-and-facts, Oct 24, 2013.

19. Francine D. Blau and Christopher Mackie, Eds., *The Economic and Fiscal Consequences of Immigration* (Washington, D.C.: National Academies Press, 2016).

20. See Josh Hampson, "We Risk More in Not Accepting Refugees into the US," *The Hill*, into- the-us refugees-into-the-us, Oct 29, 2015; Krostad and Radford, "Key Facts About Refugees to the U.S."; Ronald Balley, "Hey GOP Fearmongers: Not One Terrorist Act by Refugees in U.S. *Reason*, http://reason.com/blog/2015/11/16/hey-gop- fearmongers-not-one-terrorist-ac, Nov 16, 2015; Chris Nichols, "America's Refugee Vetting Robust, Not 'Haphazard' as Calif. Congressman Claims," *Politifact*, http://www.politifact.com/california/statements/2017/feb/03/tom-mcclintock/americas-refugee-vetting-already- robust-not-haphaz/, Jan 31, 2017.

21. Kaitlin Mulhere, "The Immigration Crackdown's Surprising Victim: Your Tuition Bill," *Time*, http://time.com/money/4700953/applications-international-students-us- universities/, Mar 14, 2017.

22. Elizabeth Redden, "Will International Students Stay Away? Four in 10 Colleges Are Seeing Drops in Applications from International Students Amid Pervasive Concerts That the Political Climate Might Keep Them Away," *Inside Higher Ed*, https://www.insidehighered.com/news/2017/03/13/nearly-4-10-universities-report- drops-international-student-applications, Mar 13, 2017; Mulhere, "The Immigration Crackdown's Surprising Victim".

## CH.9, HLIANG MOE, BURMA, BAMAR

1. "Myanmar's Government Last in World for Freedom of Expression." *AsiaNews.it.*, http://www.asianews.it/news-

en/Myanmar's-government-last-in-world-ranking-for-freedom-of-expression- 10308.html, September 15, 2007.

2. "1988 Uprising and 1990 Election," Oxford Burma Alliance, http://www.oxfordburmaalliance.org/1988-uprising--1990-elections.html.

3. This and all other quotes from Hliang Moe come from Hliang Moe Than interviewed by Robert Dodge, Aurora, CO, Jan 11, 2017.

4. "1988 Uprising and 1990 Election."

5. "Reviewing U.S. Commitment to Refugee Protection," *Human Rights First*, March, 2010, 20.

6. "Refugees-Asylees-Secondaries in Colorado FY 1980-2014.pdf."

7. "Rohingya Myanmar: Nobel Winners Urge Action Over 'Ethnic Cleansing'," *BBC*, http://www.bbc.com/news/world-asia-38470232, Dec 30, 2016.

## CH.10, WHO IS AN AMERICAN?

1. "Declaration of Independence, A Transcription," *National Archives*: America's Founding Documents, https://www.archives.gov/founding-docs/declaration-transcript. For an in-depth discussion, see John R. Wunder, "'Merciless Indian Savages' and the Declaration of Independence: Native Americans Translate the Ecunnaunuxulgee Document." *American Indian Law Review*, Vol. 25, No. 1, 2000.\William Cohen,

2. "Thomas Jefferson and the Problem of Slavery," *The Journal of American History*, Vol. 56, No. 3, Dec 1969, 503, 506.

3. "The Constitution of the United States: A Transcription," Article I, Section 2, Clause 3, National Archives: America's Founding Documents, https://www.archives.gov/founding-docs/declaration-transcript.

4. Hiroshi Motomura, "Whose Alien Nation?: Two Models of Constitutional Immigration Law," *Michigan Law Review*, Vol. 94, No. 6, May 1996, 1929.

5. For a discussion see Neal Katal and Paul Clement, "On the Meaning of 'Natural Born Citizen'," *Harvard Law Review*, Vol. 128, No. 16, Mar 11, 2015.

6. Peter Brimelow, rev, "Alien Nation: Common Sense About America's Immigration Disaster," *Population and Development Review*," Vol. 21, No. 3, Sep 1995, 663.

7. Samuel Morse, *Imminent Dangers to the Free Institutions of the United States Through Foreign Immigration, and the Present State of the Naturalization Laws* (New York: [s.n.], 1835).

8. "Donald J. Trump Statement on Preventing Muslim Immigration," *Trump Pence: Make America Great Again!*, https://www.donaldjtrump.com/press-releases/donald-j.-trump-statement-on-preventing-muslim-immigration, Dec 7, 2015.

9. Ray A. Billington, "Anti-Catholic Propaganda and the Home Missionary Movement, 1800-1860." *The Mississippi Valley Historical Review*, Vol. 22, No. 3, Dec 1935, 365.

10. Maria Monk, *The Awful Disclosures of Maria Monk, of the Hidden Secrets of Nun's Life in a Convent Exposed* (Manchester: Milner, 1836).

11. Lorraine Boisoneault, "How the 19thCentury Know Nothing Party Reshaped American Politics, *Smithsonian.com*, http://www.smithsonianmag.com/history/immigrants-conspiracies-and-secret-society-launched-american-nativism-180961915/, Jan 26, 2017. Edward T. O'Donnell, "Bring Us Your Tired, Your Poor. Or Don't," *New York Times,* May 7, 2006, CY4.

12. Joyce Vialet, "A Brief History of U.S. Immigration Policy," *Congressional Research Service: The Library of Congress*, Report No. 80-223 EPW, Dec 22, 1980, 9.

13. Lorraine Boisoneault, "How the 19thCentury Know Nothing Party Reshaped American Politics".

14. Ibid.

15. Raymond J. DeMallie, "The Lakota Ghost Dance: An Ethnohistorical Account," *Pacific Historical Review*, Nov. 1982, 396.

16. "Chinese Exclusion Act," https://www.ourdocuments. gov/doc.php?flash=false&doc=47.

17. *Chae Chan Ping v. United States*, 130 U.S. 581, 1889.

18. "U.S. Immigration Before 1965," *History*, http://www. history.com/topics/u-s-immigration-before-1965.

19. David M. Kennedy, "Overview: The Progressive Era," *The Historian*, Vol.37, No.3, May,1975, 468.

20. "The Night President Teddy Roosevelt Invited Booker T. Washington to Dinner," 24.

21. Hiroshi Motomura, "Whose Alien Nation?: Two Models of Constitutional Immigration Law," *Michigan Law Review*, Vol.94, No.6, May 1996, 1930.

22. Thomas C. Leonard, "Retrospectives: Eugenics and Economics in the Progressive Era," *The Journal of Economic Perspectives*, Vol. 19, No. 4, Autumn 2005, 216.

23. James S. Pula, "American Immigration Policy and the Dillingham Commission," *Polish American Studies*, Vol. 37, No. 1, Spring 1980,16.

24. Arleen Marcia Tuchman, "Diabetes and Race, a Historical Perspective," *American Journal of Public Health*, Vol. 101, No.1, Jan 2011, 11.

25. "The Immigration Act of 1924 (The Jonson-Reed Act)," U.S. Department of State, *Office of the Historian,* http:// history.state.gov/milestones/19211936/ImmigrationAct.

26. Mae M. Ngai, "The Architecture of Race in American Immigration Law: A Reexamination of the Immigration Act of 1924," *The Journal of American History*, Vol. 86, No. 1, Jun 1999, 73.

27. "The Immigration Act of 1924 (The Jonson-Reed Act)," *U.S. Department of State Office of the Historian*, http://history.state.gov/milestones/19211936/ImmigrationAct.

28. Ngai, "The Architecture of Race in American Immigration Law," 70.

29. Adam Serwer, "Jeff Sessions's unqualified Praise for a 1924 Immigration Law," *The Atlantic*, Jan 10, 2017.

30. "Refugees," United States Holocaust Memorial Museum, https://www.ushmm.org/wlc/en/article.php?ModuleId=10005139.

31. Allida Black et. al. eds., *Eleanor Roosevelt, John Kennedy, and the Election of 1960: A Project of the Eleanor Roosevelt Papers* (Columbia, S.C.: Model Editions Partnership, 2003).

32. Public Law 96-212-Mar.17, 1980, https://www.gpo.gov/fdsys/pkg/STATUTE-94/pdf/STATUTE-94-Pg102.pdf.

## CH. 11, NURULAMIN, BURMA, ROHINGYA

1. "Myanmar wants ethnic cleansing of Rohingya - UN official," *BBC*, http://www.bbc.com/news/world-asia-38091816, Nov 24 2016

2. Maung Zarnii and Alice Cowley, "The Slow-Burning Genocide of Myanmar's Rohingya," *Pacific Rim Law & Policy Journal*, Vol. 23, No. 3, 2014. 703.

3. Martin Smith, "The Muslim Rohingyas of Burma." *Rohingya Reader II, Burma Centrum Nederland, Amsterdam*, October,1996,10.

4. Zarnii and Cowley, "The Slow-Burning Genocide of Myanmar's Rohingya," 697. Smith, "The Muslim Rohingyas of Burma."

5. This and all quotes from Nurulamin, Interview, Nurulamin with Robert Dodge, interpreter, Drucie Bathin, Denver, CO, March 26, 2017.

6. | Smith, "The Muslim Rohingyas of Burma."

7. | Wai Moe, "Naypyidaw Orders New 'First Cuts'," *Irrawaddy*, Mar 4, 2011.

8. | Samuel Cheung, "Migration Control and the Solutions Impasse in South and Southeast Asia: Implications from the Rohingya Experience," *Journal of Refugee Studies*, Vol. 25, No.1, Dec. 15, 2011, 3.

9. | Greg Constantine, "Between Burma and Bangladesh: Rohingya, a Stateless People," *Pulitzer Center*,http://pulitzercenter.org/reporting/between-burma-and-bangladesh-rohingya-stateless-people, Apr 18, 2012.

10. | Brown, "Why Burma's Rohingya Muslims are among the world's most persecuted people."

11. | Constantine, "Between Burma and Bangladesh."

12. | Joe Wismann-Horther, interview with Robert Dodge, Denver Aug 3, 2016.

13. | "Malaysia Finds 'Migrant' Mass Graves Near Thai Border," *BBC*, http://www.bbc.com/news/world-asia-32863514, May 25, 2015.

14. | Pope Issues Stinging Criticism of Myanmar's Treatment of Rohingya." *Reuters,* http://www.reuters.com/article/myanmar-rohingya-pope-int-idUSKBN15N120, Feb 8, 2017.

15. | "Who Will Help Burma's Rohingya?" *BBC*, http://www.bbc.com/news/world-asia-38168917. Jan 10, 2017.

16. | Richard C. Paddock, "Aung San Suu Kyi Asks U.S. Not to Refer to Rohingya," *New York Times*, May 7, 2016, A6.

17. | "Aung San Suu Kyi calls for 'Space' as Kerry Pushes Her on Myanmar's Rohingya," Straits *Times* (Singapore), May 22, 1916.

18. | "Interviews with Rohingya Fleeing from Myanmar Since 9 October 2016," *Flash Report*, (New York: United Nations Commission of the High Commissioner), 2017.

19. Ibid., 40-42.

## CH. 12, DISTINCTIONS

1. See Peggy Pascoe, *What Comes Naturally: Miscegenation Law and the Making of Race in America* (New York: Oxford University Press, 2010). Pascoe was a recognized scholar on race and capitalized White to mark what she said had often been an unmarked group and identify it as a group when it has been commonly taken as the norm in society.

2. S.358 – Immigration Act of 1990, Public Law No: 101-649, https://www.congress.gov/bill/101st-congress/senate-bill/358, Nov 29, 1990.

3. Warren R. Leiden and David L. Neal, "Highlights of the U.S. Immigration Act of 1990, *Fordham International Law Journal*, Vol. 14, Iss. 1, 1990, 329.

4. Ibid., 330-331.

5. Ibid., 336.

6. Jeffrey S. Passel and D'Vera Cohn, "Overall Numbers of U.S. Unauthorized Immigrants Holds Steady Since 2009," Pew Research Center, http://www.pewhispanic.org/2016/09/20/overall-number-of-u-s-unauthorized-immigrants-holds-steady-since-2009/, Sept 20, 2016, 1.

7. Ibid.

8. "Executive Order: Enhancing Public Safety in the Interior of the United States," *The White House*, Jan 25, 2017.

9. Amanda Hoover, "Attorney General Sessions Escalates Threats Against Sanctuary Cities," *Christian Science Monitor*, http://www.csmonitor.com/USA/Politics/2017/0328/Attorney-General-Sessions-escalates-threats-against- sanctuary-cities, March 28, 2017.

10. Sheda M. Aboii, "Undocumented Immigrants and the Inclusive Health Policies of Sanctuaries," Vol. 7, http://

harvardpublichealthreview.org/undocumented-immigrants-and-the-inclusive-health-policies-of-sanctuary- cities/, 2016.

11. Reena Flores, "Donald Trump: 'Anchor Babies' Aren't American Citizens," CBS News, http://www.cbsnews.com/news/donald-trump-anchor-babies-arent-american-citizens/, Aug 19, 2015.

12. Heather Fathali, "The American Dream: DACA, DREAMers, and Comprehensive Immigration Reform," *Seattle University Law Review*, Vol. 37, No. 221, 238.

13. Laura E. Enriquez and Abigail C. Saguy, "Coming Out of the Shadows: Harnessing a Cultural Schema to Advance the Undocumented Immigrant Youth Movement," *ResearchGate*, Jun 2015, 108.

14. Van Le, "Snapshot of Polling and Public Opinion on Immigration Executive Action & Larger Debate," America's Voice, http://americasvoice.org/blog/snapshot-polling-public-opinion-immigration-executive-action-larger- debate/, Jan 20, 2015.

15. Teresa Wiltz, "Unaccompanied Children from Central America," *The Huffington Post*, http://www.huffingtonpost.com/entry/unaccompanied-children-from-central-america-one-year- later_us_55db88b4e4b04ae497041d10, updated 13, 2017.

16. Ibid.

17. Annie Hylton and Sarah Salvadore, "'They Said We Would Pay with Our Lives'," *Slate*, http://www.slate.com/articles/news_and_politics/gender_and_migration/2016/08/as_central_american_gangs_targetyounger_kids_more_minors_are_fleeing_to.html, Aug 31, 2016.

18. Ibid.

19. Geneva Declaration Secretariat, "Lethal Violence Against Women and Girls," *Global Burden of Armed Violence*, 2011, 94.

20. Johnathan T. Hiskey et.al., "Understanding the Central American Refugee Crisis: Why They Are Fleeing

and How U.S. Policies Are Failing to Deter Them," *American Immigration Council*, Feb 1, 2016

21. Katherine M. Donato and Blake Sisk, "Children's Migration to the United States from Mexico and Central America: Evidence from the Mexican and Latin American Migration Project," *Journal on Migration and Human Security*, Vol. 3, No. 1, 2015, 63.

22. Katherine M. Donato and Blake Sisk, "Children's Migration to the United States from Mexico and Central America."

23. Joe Wismann-Horther interview with Robert Dodge, Denver, Aug 3, 2016.

24. Ibid.

25. See Tal Koplan, "10 Big Asylum Cases in the U.S.," *Politico*, http://www.politico.com/story/2013/08/10-big-asylum-cases-in-the-us-095047, Aug 1, 2013.

26. This and all quotes from Alexander, Alexander, interview with Robert Dodge, Denver, Feb 2, 2017.

27. "How Does a Felony Affect Immigration Status?," *FindLaw*, http://immigration.findlaw.com/deportation-removal/felony-convictions-and-immigration-status.html.

## CH. 13, MIMI, BURMA, KAREN

1. This and all quotes from Mimi, Mimi Salto, interview with Robert Dodge, Aurora, CO, Oct 14, 2016.

2. "Refugee Camps," *Burmalink*, http://www.burmalink.org/background/thailand-burma-border/displaced-in-thailand/refugee-camps/.

3. Sirinya Siriyanun, "The Political Problem of Karen Refugees: Thai and International Perspectives,"http://www.worldresearchlibrary.org/up_proc/pdf/117-144870470182-86.pdf, Nov 29, 2015, 4.

4. "Mae La," The Borer Consortium, http://www.theborderconsortium.org/where-we-work/camps-in-thailand/mae-la/.

5. "The Political Problem of Karen Refugees," 83.

6. "The Political Dr. Cynthia Maung," Mae Teo Clinic, http://maetaoclinic.org/about-us/dr-cynthia-maung/.

## CH. 14, KAHASSAI, ETHIOPIA

1. Sarah Erdman, "Embracing the Ancient in Ethiopia," *National Geographic Expeditions*, http://intelligenttravel.nationalgeographic.com/2014/04/03/embracing-the-ancient-in-ethiopia/, Apr 3, 2014.

2. See Brian Villmoare et. al, "Early Homo at 2.8 Ma from Ledi-Geraru, Afar, Ethiopia," *Science*, Vol.347, Iss. 6228, Mar 20, 2015; Pallab Ghosh," 'First human' discovered in Ethiopia," *BBC News*, http://www.bbc.com/news/science- environment-31718336, Mar 4, 2015.

3. "Ethiopia, History, Language and Culture," *World Travel Guide*, http://www.worldtravelguide.net/ethiopia/history-language-culture.

4. "Ethiopia, a Brief History," Ethiopian Embassy, U.K., http://www.ethioembassy.org.uk/fact%20file/a-z/history.htm.

5. Graham Hancock, *Sign and the Seal: The Quest for the Lost Ark of the Covenant*, (New York: Simon & Schuster, 1993).

6. Getnet Tamene, "Features of the Ethiopian Orthodox Church and the Clergy," *Asian and African Studies*, Vol. 7, No. 1, 1998, 90.

7. Lars Berge and Irma Taddia, *Themes in Modern African History and Culture* (Padova, Italy: LibreriaUniversitaria, 2013), 177.

8. Edward L. Ayers et. al, *American Passages: A History of the United States, Volume 2* (Belmont, CA: Wadsworth Publishing, 2011), 555.

9. This and all following quotes from Kahassai in chapter are from: Kahassai, interview with Robert Dodge, Denver, Apr 1, 2017.

10. Girmachew Alemu Aneme, "Apology and Trials: The Case of the Red Terror Trials in Ethiopia," *African Human Rights Law Journal*, Vol. 6, Iss. 1, Jan 2006, 65.

11. Ibid., 66.

12. Firew Kebede Tiba, "The Mengistu Genocide Trial in Ethiopia," *Journal of International Criminal Justice*, Vol.5, No.2., May 2007, 518.

## CH. 15, ASBI AND LEELA FROM BHUTAN

1. David Van Praagh, *The Greater Game: India's Race with Destiny and China* (Montreal: McGill-Queens University Press, 2003), 328.

2. John S. Bowman, ed., *Columbia Chronologies of Asian History and Culture*, (New York: Columbia University Press, 2002) 384-388.

3. Joseph C. Mathew, "Bhutan: 'Democracy" From Above," *Economic and Political Weekly*, Vol. 43, No. 19, May 10-16, 2008, 29-30.

4. John Bray, "Bhutan: The Dilemmas of a Small State," *The World Today*, Vol. 49, No.11, Nov. 1993, 213.

5. Zubia Ikram, "Bhutanese Refugees in Nepal: An Analysis," *Pakistan Horizon,* Vol. 58, No. 3, Jul 2005, 103-104.

6. Van Praagh, *India's Race with Destiny and China*, 328.

7. John S. Bowman, ed., *Columbia Chronologies of Asian History and Culture*, (New York: Columbia University Press, 2002) 384-388.

8. Ramesh Chandra Misra, Bhutan: Society and Polity (Delhi: Indus Publishing, 1996), 84.

9. This and all quotes from Leela come from Leela Timsina, interview with Robert Dodge, Aurora, CO., Dec 16, 2016, unless noted. Noted quotes from Leela are from his unpublished manuscript.

10. Gary Leech, "Happiness and Human Rights in Shangri-La," *Critical Legal Thinking*, http://criticallegalthinking.com/2013/03/25/happiness-and-human-rights-in-shangri-la/, March 25, 2013.

11. Ferdinand deVarennes, "Constitutionalising Discrimination in Bhutan: The Emasculation of Human Rights in the Land of the Dragon," *Asia-Pacific Journal on Human Rights and the Law,* Vol. 2, 2008, 71.

12. Bray, "Bhutan: The Dilemmas of a Small State,"215.

13. This and all quotes from Absi come from Asbi Mizer, interviewed by Robert Dodge, Denver, Dec 20, 2016.

14. Leela Timsina, "A Leap from Destituteness to Prosperity," unpublished manuscript.

15. "Bhutan: Human Rights Violations Against the Nepali-Speaking Populations in the South," *Amnesty International*, https://www.amnesty.org/en/documents/asa14/004/1992/en/, Dec 1, 1992.

16. Ikram, "Bhutanese Refugees in Nepal: An Analysis,"

17. Robert Muggah, "Distinguishing Means and Ends: The Counterintuitive Effects of UNHRC's Community Development Approach in Nepal," *Journal of Refugee Studies*, Vol. 18, No. 2, 155.

18. Timsina, "A Leap from Destituteness to Prosperity."

19. Muggah, "Distinguishing Means and Ends," 155.

20. Carlos Illescas, "Aurora Reaching Out to Refugee Community," *Denver Post*, Dec 21, 2013.

21. Mark Van Ommeren, Joop de Jong, Bhogendra Sharma, "Psychiatric Disorders Among Tortured Bhutanese Refugees in Nepal," *General Psychiatry*, Vol. 58, No.5., May, 2001.

22. Setu Nepal, interview.

23. See "Suicide and Suicidal Ideation Among Bhutanese Refugees - United States, 2009–2012." *Morbidity and Mortality Weekly Report*, Vol. 62, No. 26, 2013.

24. Indian Court Frees Bhutanese Refugees, Rules Their Detention Illegal," *OCA News.com*, http://www.ucanews.com, March 4, 1996.

25. Timsina, "A Leap from Destituteness to Prosperity".

26. Michael Hutt, "The Bhutanese Refugees: Between Verification, Repatriation and Royal Realpolitik," *Peace and Democracy in Southeast Asia*, Vol.1, No.1, Jan, 2005, 49-52.

27. "90,000th Bhutanese Refugee Flying to US from Nepal for Resettlement," *The Himalayan Times*, Sept 20, 2016.

28. Harry Budisidharta, interview with Robert Dodge, Aurora, CO, May 10, 2016.

## PICTURE ME HERE

1. Brigid McAuliffe, E-mail to Robert Dodge, May 14, 2017.

2. "Refugees-Asylees-Secondaries in Colorado FY 1980-2014.pdf," *Colorado Office of Economic Security: Division of Refugee Services*, https://drive.google.com/file/d/0B-9dBwl5XFYdWHZRU1RIai13Y3c/view.

## CH. 16, RASULO, SOMALIA

1. "Piracy," *World Shipping Council*, http://www.worldshipping.org/industry-issues/security/piracy.

2. Dominic Tierney, "Black Hawk Up: The Forgotten American Success Story in Somalia," *The Atlantic*, https://www.theatlantic.com/international/

archive/2010/12/black-hawk-up-the-forgotten- american-success-story- in- somalia/67305/, Dec 2, 2010.

3. Ibid.

4. Barry Rubin, Barry M. Rubin, Judith Colp Rubin, Anti-American Terrorism and the Middle East: A Documentary Reader (New York: Oxford University Press, 2004), 137.

5. This and all quotes from Rasulo, come from Rasulo, interview with Robert Dodge, Denver, March 17, 2017.

6. Dan Van Lehman and Omar Ono, ""The Somali Bantu: Their History and Culture," *Culture Profile,* No.16, Feb 2003, 4.

7. Ibid.

8. Ibid.

9. Ibid., 11.

10. Roland Marchal, "Warlordism and Terrorism: How to Obscure an Already Confusing Crisis? The Case of Somalia," *International Affairs,* Vol.83, No.6, Nov 2007, 1992.

11. Van Lehman and Omar Ono, ""The Somali Bantu," 10-11.

12. Laura Hammond, "Somalia Rising: Things Are Starting to Change for the World's Longest Failed State," *Journal of East African Studies,* Vol. 7, No.1, Jan 2016, 190.

13. Ibid., 11-12.

14. "Country of Origin of Colorado Refugee and Asylee Arrivals Between FY 1980-2014," "Refugees-Asylees- Secondaries in Colorado FY1980-2014. pdf." *Colorado Office of Economic Security: Division of Refugee Services.* https://drive.google.com/file/d/0B-9dBwl5XFYdWHZRU1RIai13Y3c/view.

15. See "Somali Militias Recruiting Child Soldiers, New Report Says," Voice of America, http://www.voanews.com/a/amnesty-international-report-says-somali-militias-recruiting-child-soldiers-125890388/142505.html, July

19, 1911. Mohamed Olad, "Number of Child Soldiers in Somalia May Top 5,000, UN Reports," *Voice of America*, http://www.voanews.com/a/five-thousand-child-soldiers-somalia-united-nations- report/3379769.html, Jun16, 2016.

16. Hammond, "Somalia Rising," 183.

17. Peter Leftie and Charles Omondi, "Somalia Tops Global Corruption List, *African Review*, http://www.africareview.com/special-reports/Somalia-tops-global-corruption-list/979182-3786252-comew4/, Jan 25, 2017.

18. Astrid Zweynert, "Somalia Ranks Worst in African Rule of Law Index," *Reuters,* http://af.reuters.com/article/investingNews/idAFKCN0HO0R820140929, Sep 29, 2014

19. "Somalia Ranked Worst Place to be a Mother, Australia Among Best Places," *Australian Broadcasting Company*, May 5, 2014.

## CH. 17, REFUGEES, REQUIREMENTS, RULES

1. "Final Act: of the United Nations Conference of Plenipotentiaries on the Status of Refugees and Stateless Persons," UNHCR: *The UN Refugee Agency*, http://www.unhcr.org/en-us/3b66c2aa10, 6.

2. Ibid., 14.

3. "Refugee Admissions," *U.S. Department of State,* https://www.state.gov/j/prm/ra/.

4. "U.S. Refugee Admissions Program,*" U.S. Department of State,* https://www.state.gov/j/prm/ra/admissions/index.htm; Rebecca Shabad, "Inside the U.S. Vetting System Trump Wants to Replace," CBS, http://www.cbsnews.com/news/inside-u-s-vetting-for-visas-refugees-and-improvements- that-could-be-made/, Feb 27, 2017.

5. The nine volunteer resettlement agencies are Church World Service (CWS); Ethiopian Community Development Council (ECDC); Episcopal Migration Ministries

(EMM); International Rescue Committee (IRC); US Committee for Refugees and Immigrants (USCRI); Lutheran Immigration and Refugee Services (LIRS); United States Conference of Catholic Bishops (USCCB); World Relief Corporation (WR). Teresa Walsh, "8 Facts About the U.S. Program to Resettle Syrian Refugees," *U.S. News & World Report*, https://www.usnews. com/news/articles/2015/11/20/8-facts-about-the-us-program-to-resettle-syrian-refugees, Nov 20, 2015.

6. Lawrence Bartlett, interviewed by Robert Dodge, Washington, D.C., Aug 26, 2016.

7. "The Latest: Trump: Trump Says Immigrants Taking Minorities' Jobs," *AP: The Big Story*, http://bigstory.ap.org/article/09215cf7f37f4c6ea05f92f8c83e6125/latest-fbi-expected-release-clinton-documents- soon, Aug 30, 2016.

8. Joseph Wismann-Horther interview.

9. Ibid.

10. Maria E. Enchautegui, "Immigrant and Native Low Skill Workers Compete for Different Low-Skilled Jobs," *Urban Institute*, http://www.urban.org/urban-wire/immigrant-and-native-workers-compete-different-low-skilled- jobs, Oct 14, 2015.

11. *RISE Report*, 19.

12. "Applicant Performance on Naturalization Test," *U.S. Citizenship and Immigration Services*, https://www.uscis.gov/us-citizenship/naturalization-test/applicant-performance-naturalization-test, Sep 2016.

13. "One in Three Americans Fail Immigrant Naturalization Civics Test," *Xavier University*, http://www.xavier.edu/campusuite25/modules/news.cfm?seo_file=One-in-Three-Americans-Fail-Immigrant-Naturalization-Civics-Test&grp_id=319#.WWp4jzOZOT8, Arp 27, 2012.

14. Ibid.

15. Asbi interview.

1. See Rod Nordland, "Eyewitness to America's Longest War, After Others Have Gone, " *New York Times*, Mar 1, 2017; Doug Bandow, "End America's Longest War: Bring the Troops Home from Afghanistan," *Huffington Post*, Mar 31, 2017; Gayle Tzemach Lemmon, " 'Mother of All Bombs' Reminds us that America Is Still at War in Afghanistan," *Fox News*, Apr 14, 2017; Peter Bergen, "Opium Fuels the Stalemate in America's Longest War," *CNN,* Oct 25, 2016.

2. Noel J Coulson, "Shariah: Islamic Law,"*Encyclopaedia Britannica*, https://www.britannica.com/topic/ Shariah, updated March 30, 2012.

3. This and all quotes from Roy from Roy, interview with Robert Dodge, Denver, March 8, 2017.

4. President George W. Bush, "Address to a Joint Session of Congress and the American People, September 20, 2001," *Harvard Journal of Law & Public Policy*, Vol. 25., No.2, IVX-XVI, 5

5. For a discussion of the accuracy of this observation see Reuven Firestone, "Muslim-Jewish Relations," *Religion: Oxford Research Encyclopedias,* http://religion.oxfordre. com/view/10.1093/acrefore/9780199340378.001.0001/ acrefore-9780199340378-e-17.

6. See Ambassador Curtin Winson, "Saudi Arabia, Wahhabism and the Spread of Sunni Theofascism," *Mideast Monitor*, Vol.2, No. 1, http://www.mideastmonitor. org/issues/0705/0705_2.htm, Jun/Jul, 2007. Karen Armstrong, "Wahhabism to ISIS: How Saudi Arabia Exported the Main Source of Global Terrorism,'" *NewStatesman*, Nov 27, 2014. Carol E. B. Choksy and Jamseed K. Choksy, "The Saudi Connection: Wahhabism and Global Jihad," *World Affairs*, May/Jun, 2015.

7. Ibid.

1. Jie Zong and Jeanne Batalova, "Vietnamese Immigrants in the United States, *Migration Policy Institute*," http://www.migrationpolicy.org/article/vietnamese-immigrants-united-states, Apr 2016.

2. "Country of Origin of Colorado Refugees," 1.

3. William C. Gibbons, *The U.S. Government and the Vietnam War: Executive and Legislative Roles and Relationships, Part I: 1945-1960,* (Princeton, NJ: Princeton University Press, 2014), 61.

4. This and all other quotes from Mahn, Mahn, interview with Robert Dodge, Denver, May 1, 2017.

5. Ronald H. Spector, "Vietnam War:1954 - 1975," *Encyclopaedia Britannica*, https://www.britannica.com/event/Vietnam-War.

6. "Statistical Information about Casualties of the Vietnam War," *National Archives*, https://www.archives.gov/research/military/vietnam-war/casualty-statistics.html.

7. "The Vietnam War and Its Impact - Refugees and 'boat people," *Encyclopedia of the New American Nation*, http://www.americanforeignrelations.com/O-W/The-Vietnam-War-and-Its-Impact-Refugees-and-boat-people.html.

8. "History of Southeast Asian Refugees," *Center for Empowering Refugees & Immigrants*, http://www.cerieastbay.org/web1/SOUTHEAST%20ASIAN%20RE FUGEES.html/.

9. Christopher Parsons and Pierre-Louise Vézina, "Migrant Networks and Trade: The Vietnamese Boat People as a Natural Experiment," *IZA Discussion Papers*, No. 10112, 2016, 6.

10. Marjorie Niehaus, "Vietnam 1978: The Elusive Peace," *Asian Survey*, Vol. 19, No. 1, A Survey of Asia in 1978: Part I, Jan 1979, 92.

11. Tang Thi Thanh Le and Michael J. Esser, "The Vietnamese Refugee and U.S. Law," *Notre Dame Law Scholarly Works*, Paper 906659, Vol. 1, No. 1, 1981, 658.

12. Ibid.

13. Barbara Crossette, "Thai Pirates Continuing Brutal Attacks on Vietnamese Boat People," *New York Times*, Jan 11, 1982.

## CH. 20, ABIRA, SYRIA

1. This and all quotes from Abira, Abira, interview with Robert Dodge, Denver, Apr12, 2017.

2. On the prevalence of this, see Michael Medved, "That's Entertainment? Hollywood's Contribution to Anti-Americanism Abroad," *The National Interest,* No. 68, Summer 2002.

3. John L. Esposito, *Oxford Dictionary of Islam* (New York: Oxford University Press, 2004)159.

4. Dan Frosch, "A Notorious Main Drag, in Line for Big Changes," *New York Times*, Nov 26, 2007, A15.

## CH. 21, ADJUSTMENT AND ASSIMILATION

1. See Peter Hitchens, "We won't Save Refugees by Destroying Our Own Country," *Darkmoon,*https://www.darkmoon.me/2015/we-wont-save-refugees-by-destroying-our-own-country/, Sep 8, 2015, or Refugee Resettlement Watch, https://refugeeresettlementwatch.wordpress.com.

2. Andrew Rafferty, "Rep. Steve King Defends 'Somebody Else's Babies' Remarks," *NBC News*, http://www.nbcnews.com/politics/politics-news/steve-king-defends-somebody-else-s-babies-remarks-n732741, Mar 13, 2017.

3. Frank Newport, "About Half of Americans Say Trump Moving Too Fast," *Gallup*, Feb 2, 2017.

4. Gary Lichententenstein et.al, *The Refugee Integration Survey and Evaluation (RISE) Report; A Study of Refugee Integration in Colorado* (Denver: Colorado Office of Economic Security), 2016.

5. Ibid., 6.

6. Ibid., 2.

7. Ibid., 17.

8. Ibid., 1V.

9. Ibid., 16.

10. Ibid., 17.

11. Ibid., 26,

12. Ibid., 18.

13. Ibid., 18-22.

14. Ibid., 23.

15. Ibid., 23-25.

16. Ibid., 31.

17. Ibid., 34.

18. Mark Taylor, "Study Finds Refugees in Denver Are Integrating to a Better Life," *CBS Denver*,http://denver.cbslocal.com/2016/03/15/study-refugees-denver-integration/,Mar 15, 2016; Mathew LaCorte, "Refugees Continue to Contribute to America," *The Huffington Post*, http://www.huffingtonpost.com/matthew-la- corte/refugees-continue-to-contribute_b_9951652.html, May 5, 2016.

19. Clarification by Gary Lichententenstein, E-mail to Robert Dodge, March 14, 2017.

20. *RISE Report*, 34-36.

21. Chris, interviewed by Robert Dodge, interpreter, Drucie Bathing, Aurora, CO., March 19, 2017

22. Ibid.

23. Ibid.

24. *RISE Report*, 37.

25. Ibid., 43.

26. Ibid., 44.

27. Ibid., 54.

28. Patima Saptoka, interview with Robert Dodge, Aurora, CO, May 10, 2016.

29. Chris Hannigan, interview with Robert Dodge, Aurora, CO, May 6, 2016.

30. *RISE Report*, 63.

31. LaCorte, "Refugees Continue to Contribute to America."

## CH. 22, FRIGHTENED CHILDREN

1. Korena, interview with Robert Dodge, Denver, Feb 19, 2017.

2. Jarry, interview with Robert Dodge, Denver, Feb 19, 2017.

3. Hser, interview with Robert Dodge, Denver, Feb 19, 2017.

4. Rowin, interview with Robert Dodge, Denver, Feb 19, 2017.

5. KuKu, interview with Robert Dodge, Denver, Feb 19, 2017.

## CH. 23, INSIDERS' VIEWS

1. Governor John Hickenlooper, E-mail from press secretary Jacque Montgomery to Robert Dodge, April 5, 2017.

2. Senator Michael Bennet, E-mail to Robert Dodge, Mar 21, 2017.

3. Senator Cory Gardner, E-mail to Robert Dodge, March 30, 2017.

4. Ibid.

5. Michael P. Leahy, "Top 10 Holdover Obama Bureaucrats President Trump Can Fire or Remove Today," *Breitbart*, http://www.breitbart.com/big-government/2017/02/18/top-ten-holdover-obama-bureaucrats-president-trump-can- fire-today/, Feb 18, 2017.

6. This and all quotes from Lawrence Bartlett, Lawrence Bartlett interviewed Robert Dodge, Washington, D.C., Aug 26, 2016.

7. This and other comments from Kit Taintor, Kit Taintor, Colorado State Refugee Coordinator, E-mail to Robert Dodge, May 11, 2017.

8. Ashley Frantz and Ben Brumfield, "More the Half the Nation's Governors Say Syrian Refugees Not Welcome," *CNN*, http://www.cnn.com/2015/11/16/world/paris-attacks-syrian-refugees-backlash/, Nov 19, 2015.

9. Steven Shepard, "Poll: 33: Voters Support Allowing Syrian Refugees," *Politico*, http://www.politico.com/story/2017/04/20/poll-syrian-refugees-united-states-237406, Apr 20, 2017.

10. *Who Is Aurora? 2016 Demographic Report: Current Census Data, Key Areas, and Comparisons* (Aurora: Aurora Gov.). https://www.auroragov.org/UserFiles/Servers/Server_1881137/Image/City%20Hall/About%20Aurora/Date%20&% 20Demographics/Who%20is%20Aurora%202016%20FINAL%2040MB.pdf, 9.

11. Steve Hogan, Mayor, City of Aurora, E-mail to Robert Dodge, May 9, 2017.

12. This and all comments from Kevin Mohatt, Kevin Mohatt, interview with Robert Dodge, Denver, June 28, 2016.

13. This and all other comments from Joe Wismann-Horther, Joe Wismann-Horther, interviewed by Robert Dodge. Denver, Aug 3, 2016.

14. See Thomas Tancredo, "A New Strategy for the Control of Illegal Immigrants," *The Heritage Foundation*, http://www.heritage.org/immigration/report/new-strategy-control-illegal immigration, Oct 26, 2006.

## CH. 24, CONCLUSION

1. Noweasteh, "Terrorism and Immigration: A Risk Analysis," *CATO Institute, Policy Analysis.*

2. Chris Nichols, "'Mostly True.' Odds of Fatal Terror Attack in U.S. by a Refugee? 3.6 Billion to 1," *Politifact*, http://www.politifact.com/california/statements/2017/feb/01/ted-lieu/odds-youll-be-killed-terror-attack-america-refugee/, Feb 1, 2017.

# INDEX

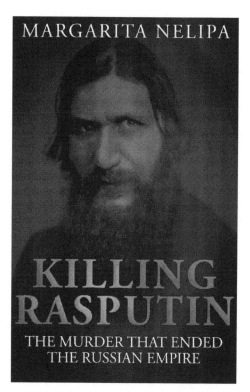

## More True Crime You'll Love From WildBlue Press

**RAW DEAL** by Gil Valle

RAW DEAL: The Untold Story of the NYPD's "Cannibal Cop" is the memoir of Gil Valle, written with co-author Brian Whitney. It is part the controversial saga of a man who was imprisoned for "thought crimes," and a look into an online world of dark sexuality and violence that most people don't know exists, except maybe in their nightmares.

### wbp.bz/rawdeal

**BETRAYAL IN BLUE** by Burl Barer & Frank C. Girardot Jr.

Adapted from Ken Eurell's shocking personal memoir, plus hundreds of hours of exclusive interviews with the major players, including former international drug lord, Adam Diaz, and Dori Eurell, revealing the truth behind what you won't see in the hit documentary THE SEVEN FIVE.

### wbp.bz/bib

**THE POLITICS OF MURDER** by Margo Nash

*"A chilling story about corruption, political power and a stacked judicial system in Massachusetts."*–John Ferak, bestselling author of FAILURE OF JUSTICE.

### wbp.bz/pom

**FAILURE OF JUSTICE** by John Ferak

If the dubious efforts of law enforcement that led to the case behind MAKING A MURDERER made you cringe, your skin will crawl at the injustice portrayed in FAILURE OF JUSTICE: A Brutal Murder, An Obsessed Cop, Six Wrongful Convictions. Award-winning journalist and bestselling author John Ferak pursued the story of the Beatrice 6 who were wrongfully accused of the brutal, ritualistic rape and murder of an elderly widow in Beatrice, Nebraska, and then railroaded by law enforcement into prison for a crime they did not commit.

### wbp.bz/foj